AAT

AF902759

Level 4

Diploma for Professional Accounting Technicians

Principles of Taxation

Course Book

For assessments from 25th January 2027 to 30th January 2028

BPP
LYCEUM EDUCATION GROUP

First edition 2026

ISBN 9781 0355 4450 9

ISBN (for internal use only) 9781 0355 4070 9

eISBN 9781 0355 4471 4

British Library Cataloguing-in-Publication Data

A catalogue record for this book is available from the British Library

Published by

BPP Learning Media Ltd
BPP House, Aldine Place
142–144 Uxbridge Road
London W12 8AA

learningmedia.bpp.com

Your learning materials are printed on paper obtained from traceable sustainable sources.

Contents

Introduction to the course

Syllabus overview

This unit introduces students to taxation for taxpayers in the United Kingdom (UK).

It introduces students to the different types of income that a UK taxpayer may have, including income from employment, self-employment, property and investments. Students will be able to calculate each type of income. Students will also be able to identify appropriate use of losses. Deductions and reliefs that apply to Income Tax are covered so that students can compute the Income Tax liability for a UK taxpayer. Students will also be able to calculate National Insurance contributions on relevant types of income. The unit also introduces students to Capital Gains Tax where they will be able to calculate chargeable gains and losses, use losses and the annual exempt amount efficiently and calculate Capital Gains Tax liabilities. Students will also be able to apply the badges of trade and to understand factors that determine whether an individual is employed or self-employed.

Students will calculate Corporation Tax for companies including income from trading, property and interest as well as chargeable gains for companies. They will be able to consider the appropriate use of losses. They will understand the treatment of qualifying charitable donations.

Students will understand the administrative requirements of UK tax law, including the implications of errors in tax returns, late filing of returns, late payment of tax and not retaining records for the required period.

Students will understand the ethical issues facing UK taxpayers and the responsibilities that an agent has in giving advice on tax issues to business clients. Students will also be able to identify tax planning opportunities, while understanding the importance of maintaining ethical standards.

Test specification for this unit assessment

Assessment method	Marking type	Duration of assessment
Computer based assessment	Wholly computer marked	2 hours

Learning outcomes	Weighting
1 Understand the United Kingdom (UK) tax system and ethical behaviour	5%
2 Calculate Income Tax and National Insurance contributions	50%
3 Identify types of income	5%
4 Calculate Capital Gains Tax payable by UK taxpayers	10%
5 Prepare tax computations for trading companies	10%
6 Understand administrative requirements of the UK's tax regime	10%
7 Understand tax planning opportunities	10%

Assessment structure

2 hours duration

To achieve the qualification and to be awarded a grade, students must pass all mandatory assessments.

Students will be awarded a grade based on performance across the qualification. Unit assessments are not individually graded. These assessments are given a mark that is used in calculating the overall grade.

The raw marks of each assessment will be converted into a percentage mark and rounded up or down to the nearest whole number. This percentage mark is then weighted according to the weighting of the unit assessment within the qualification. The resulting weighted assessment percentages are combined to arrive at a percentage mark for the whole qualification.

Assessment	Contribution of assessment to qualification grade
Financial Accounting	25%
Management Accounting	25%
Audit and Internal Controls	15%
Principles of Taxation	15%
Advanced Business Awareness	20%

Tax reference material is provided to you in the assessment. This is reproduced in this book in the Reference material section.

The guidance available about the assessment structure is based on the two sample assessments available on the AAT website. These two assessments both follow the same structure (outlined in the table below), and under previous syllabi the live assessment always followed the same structure as the relevant AAT sample assessment for that syllabus.

*Note that this is only a guideline as to what might come up. The format and content of each task may vary from what we have listed below.

The sample assessments both consisted of 9 tasks.

Task	Content	Max marks	Chapter ref	Study complete
1	**UK tax system, ethical behaviour and types of income** Multiple choice questions on: • Objectives and functions of taxation • Tax planning, tax avoidance, tax evasion and money laundering • Badges of trade • Employed v self-employed	12	1. The UK tax system and ethical behaviour 4. Employment income 5. Trading income	
2	**Trading income of sole traders, partnerships and limited companies** Multiple choice and numeric gap fill questions on: • Calculating trading income for sole traders and partners • Calculating trading income for companies	12	5. Trading income 6. Capital allowances 12. Corporation tax	
3	**Income and National Insurance contributions from employment** Multiple choice and numeric gap fill questions on: • Calculating income from employment • Calculating National Insurance contributions (NICs) payable	14	4. Employment income 10. National Insurance contributions	

Task	Content	Max marks	Chapter ref	Study complete
4	**Income from property, allocating partnership profits and class 4 National Insurance.** Multiple choice and numeric gap fill questions on: • Calculating income from property • Allocating profits between partners • Class 4 NICs	8	3. Property income 8. Partnerships 10. National Insurance contributions	
5	**Calculation of income tax** Multiple choice and numeric gap fill questions on: • Calculating taxable income • Calculating income tax payable	14	2. Calculation of income tax	
6	**Capital gains tax** Multiple choice and numeric gap fill questions on: • Calculating chargeable gains and allowable losses • Calculating capital gains tax payable	10	11. Chargeable gains	
7	**Tax computations for companies** Multiple choice and numeric gap fill questions on: • Calculating taxable total profits • Calculating corporation tax payable	8	12. Corporation tax	
8	**Administration of the UK tax system** Multiple choice questions on: • The administrative requirements of UK tax law • Penalties for non-compliance	12	13. Administration	
9	**Tax planning and trading losses** Multiple choice and numeric gap fill questions on: • Personal tax planning opportunities • Business tax planning opportunities • Trading losses for companies • Options available to sole traders and partners to relieve trading losses • How to select the relief that gives the maximum tax benefit for losses	10	14. Tax planning 9. Unincorporated trader losses 12. Corporation tax	

Skills bank

Our experience of preparing students for this type of assessment suggests that to obtain competency, you will need to develop a number of key skills.

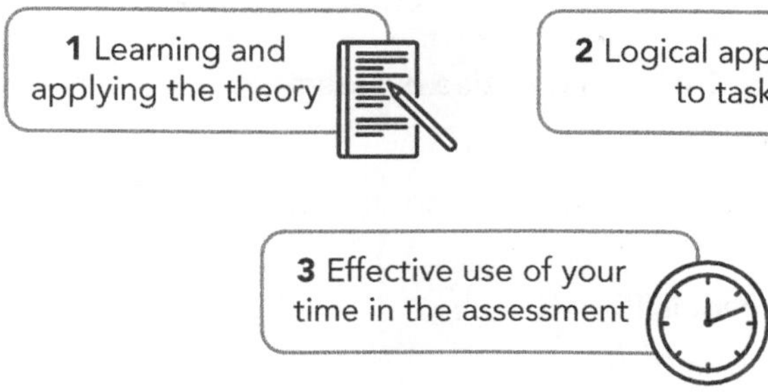

Assumed knowledge

No prior knowledge of tax is expected but if you have worked in tax then you will have an immediate advantage.

Assessment style

In the assessment you will complete tasks by:

(a) Entering narrative by selecting from drop down menus of narrative options known as **picklists**

(b) Using **drag and drop** menus to enter narrative

(c) Typing in numbers, known as **gapfill** entry

(d) Entering **ticks**

(e) Entering **dates** by selecting from a calendar

You must familiarise yourself with the style of the online questions and the AAT software before taking the assessment. As part of your revision, login to the **AAT website** and attempt their **online practice assessments**.

Introduction to the assessment

The question practice you do will prepare you for the format of tasks you will see in the *Principles of Taxation Assessment*. It is also useful to familiarise yourself with the introductory information you **may** be given at the start of the assessment.

You have **2 hours** to complete this **Principles of Taxation practice assessment.**

Information:

- The assessment contains 9 tasks. Each task is independent and you will not need to refer to your answers to previous tasks.
- The total number of marks for this assessment is 100.
- The marks for each task are shown in brackets ().

Instructions:

- Answer all tasks.
- Read each task carefully before you complete your answers.
- Where the date is relevant, it is given in the task data.
- Both minus signs and brackets can be used to indicate negative numbers unless the task instructions state otherwise.
- You must use a full stop to indicate a decimal point. For example, write 100.57 NOT 100,57 or 10057.
- You may use a comma to indicate a number in the thousands, but you don't have to. For example, 10000 and 10,000 are both acceptable.
- You will need to double click to enter values into a numerical entry gapfill or cell within a table.
- Use all available time. When you're finished answering all tasks, review your answers.
- This assessment uses reference material based on Finance Act 2026.

Once you have clicked 'Continue' you will not be able to return to this page. You will be able to view the 'Assessment information' in the references section at each task position.

(a) As you revise, use the **BPP Passcards** to consolidate your knowledge. They are a pocket-sized revision tool, perfect for packing in that last-minute revision.

(b) Attempt as many tasks as possible in the **Exam Practice Kit**. There are plenty of assessment-style tasks which are excellent preparation for the real assessment.

(c) Always **check** through your own answers as you will in the real assessment, before looking at the solutions in the back of the Exam Practice Kit.

Key to icons

Key term

A key definition which is important to be aware of for the assessment.

Formula to learn

A formula you will need to learn as it will not be provided in the assessment.

Formula provided

A formula which is provided within the assessment and generally available as a pop-up on screen.

Activity

An example which allows you to apply your knowledge to the technique covered in the Course Book. The solution is provided at the end of the chapter.

Illustration

A worked example which can be used to review and see how an assessment question could be answered.

Assessment focus point

A high priority point for the assessment.

Open book reference

Where use of an open book will be allowed for the assessment.

Real life examples

A practical real life scenario.

AAT qualifications

The material in this book may support the following AAT qualifications:

AAT Level 4 Diploma for Professional Accounting Technicians.

Supplements

From time to time we may need to publish supplementary materials to one of our titles. This can be for a variety of reasons, from a small change in the AAT unit guidance to new legislation coming into effect between editions.

You should check our supplements page regularly for anything that may affect your learning materials. All supplements are available free of charge on our supplements page on our website at:

learningmedia.bpp.com/pages/resources-for-students

Improving material and removing errors

BPP Learning Media do everything possible to ensure the material is accurate and up to date when sending to print. In the event that any errors are found after the print date, they are uploaded to the following website: learningmedia.bpp.com/pages/errata

These learning materials are based on the qualification specification released by the AAT in May 2026.

AAT Practice Assessment

The AAT practice assessments mimic the real exam and so must be attempted prior to taking the real exam. You should attempt these using a laptop/desktop computer, as this will give you a better feel for the actual AAT exam conditions.

Please note, at the end of each test you will be presented with feedback which you should review.

Use this link below to access the assessment required: https://www.aat.org.uk/learning-portal.

1 The UK tax system and ethical behaviour

Learning outcomes

1.1	**Objectives and functions of taxation**
	Learners need to know:
	• That HMRC are responsible for administering, collecting, and enforcing taxes in the UK
	• The sources of UK tax law and guidance
	• The objectives of tax digitalisation
	Learners need to understand:
	• The objectives of a tax system:
	  - Raise revenue
	  - Wealth redistribution
	  - Influence behaviour

1.2	**Tax planning, tax avoidance, tax evasion and money laundering**
	Learners need to understand:
	• The meaning of:
	  - Tax planning
	  - Tax avoidance
	  - Tax evasion
	  - Money laundering
	• The General Anti-Abuse Rule (GAAR)
	  - Purpose
	  - Circumstances for application
	  - Consequences of application
	• The consequences of dishonest conduct by tax agents:
	  - Notice
	  - Penalties
	Learners need to be able to:
	• Identify:
	  - Tax planning
	  - Tax avoidance
	  - Tax evasion
	  - Money laundering
	• Identify appropriate actions to take when unethical or illegal behaviour is identified

Assessment context

This chapter provides you with important background information about tax in the UK, and helps you to distinguish between illegal and legal tax measures. The topics covered in this chapter are likely to be examined in task 1 of your assessment for around 6 marks.

Qualification context

You will not see these rules outside of this unit.

Business context

A tax practitioner needs to know the duties and obligations the taxpayer owes to HMRC.

A tax practitioner needs to know and understand the detailed tax rules.

A tax practitioner needs to adhere to AAT's ethical standards when giving tax advice and dealing with clients.

Chapter overview

The UK tax system and ethical behaviour

Objectives and functions of taxation

- HMRC are responsible for administering, collecting and enforcing
- **Sources of UK tax law**
  - Legal force
  - Legislation - acts of parliament and statutory instruments
  - Case law - provides guidance on how legislation is interpreted
  - No legal force
  - HMRC guidance
- Objectives of tax digitalisation
- Objectives of a tax system
  - Raise revenue
  - Wealth redistribution
  - Influence behaviour

Tax planning, tax avoidance, tax evasion and money laundering

- Tax planning, tax avoidance, tax evasion
- Money laundering
- General anti-abuse rule
- Dishonest conduct by tax agents

Introduction

In this chapter we will introduce the main principles of taxation in the UK, and explain the sources of tax law and guidance in the UK. We will then consider three important concepts: tax avoidance, tax evasion and tax planning, and the important differences between them. Finally we will consider money laundering, and the objectives of tax digitalisation.

1 Objectives and functions of taxation

1.1 The purpose of taxation

Governments will collect taxation for a number of reasons:

The primary reason will be to **raise money for the Government** to use in **providing infrastructure** such as roads **and services** such as the National Health Service.

Taxes can also be used as a means of **redistributing wealth** from rich to poor, ensuring poorer people have an adequate standard of living and access to vital services.

Taxes can also be used to **control the economy**. In times of recession, taxes are cut to encourage people to spend money and stimulate the economy. In times of boom, taxes are raised to discourage people from spending money and causing the economy to overheat and crash.

Taxes can also be used to **encourage and discourage various types of activity**. For example, the Government wants us to save for our old age so we are not dependent on the state so paying into a pension saves you tax. Smoking will be harmful for you in the long run causing costs to the National Health Service so the Government taxes it. This results in higher prices for consumers discouraging them from smoking.

1.2 The UK tax system

1.2.1 His Majesty's Revenue & Customs

KEY TERM

> **HM Revenue and Customs (HMRC):** The UK Government department responsible for collecting, paying, administering and enforcing taxes.

1.2.2 Tax year

KEY TERM

> **Tax year:** The **tax year** runs from 6 April to the following 5 April. It is also known as the **fiscal year** or the **year of assessment**. Tax is calculated on the income earned, wealth transferred, and gains realised in the tax year.

The year of assessment 2026/27 runs from 6 April 2026 to 5 April 2027.

Some taxpayers will have to complete a tax return and pay tax under the self-assessment system. However, most taxpayers will have all their tax deducted at source. There is therefore no requirement for these taxpayers to complete a return.

1.3 Sources of UK tax law and guidance

1.3.1 Legislation

KEY TERM

> **Legislation:** Laws created by the Government. These include Acts of Parliament and Statutory Instruments.

The Government creates statute law. Statute laws consist of:

KEY TERM

> **Acts of Parliament:** These are created via MPs debating in Parliament. There are a number of Acts that give the main rules for each of the UK taxes. These are updated each year by the

annual **Finance Act**. Periodically they will be rewritten from scratch. This Course Book includes the provisions of the Finance Act 2026.

Statutory Instruments (SI): These are created by civil servants acting on behalf of the **Chancellor of the Exchequer**. They include the detailed rules for the operation of UK taxes. An SI will be laid before Parliament and becomes law if no objections are raised.

1.3.2 Case law

A taxpayer and HMRC may disagree over the interpretation of the legislation.

Either party may appeal to the tax tribunal. The tax tribunal is independent of the Government and will listen to both sides of the argument before making a decision.

A judge will rule in favour of one party.

Cases decided by the courts provide guidance on how legislation should be interpreted, and collectively form a second source of tax law known as case law.

You will not be expected to quote the names of decided cases in your assessment but you may need to know the principle decided in a case. Where relevant, this will be noted within this Course Book.

KEY TERM

Case law: Decisions of the Tax Tribunal about the interpretation of tax statutes which serve as a further source of tax law.

1.3.3 HMRC guidance

HMRC publishes a range of guidance material to advise taxpayers as to how it interprets the law, for example statements of practice and extra statutory concessions. Much of this information can be found on HMRC's website www.hmrc.gov.uk.

HMRC guidance does not have legal force and could be challenged in court by a taxpayer.

1.4 Objectives of tax digitalisation

KEY TERM

Tax digitalisation: The process by which tax authorities use digital technologies to collect, process, manage and monitor tax information electronically, replacing or reducing paper-based and manual tax systems.

HMRC has published a Transformation Roadmap which sets out the government's vision for a more efficient, modernised and automated tax system.

The objectives are:

- Improving day-to-day performance and the customer experience - enabling taxpayers to complete routine tasks online or in the app
- Closing the tax gap - the difference between the amount of tax that should be paid and the amount actually collected by the government
- Reform and modernisation of the tax system. By investing in IT infrastructure, HMRC will have an improved picture of a customer's tax affairs and compliance risks closer to real-time

Tax digitalisation in the UK is being achieved through Making Tax Digital (MTD). Under MTD, VAT-registered businesses, and certain unincorporated businesses and landlords are required to keep their records digitally, and submit regular updates to HMRC.

The objectives are:

(a) Enhanced compliance - by using digital software, businesses and individuals can reduce errors in their tax reporting

(b) Improved business management - MTD aims to simplify the way taxpayers manage their tax affairs, making it easier to keep track of income and expenses

(c) Regular updates - by submitting quarterly updates, taxpayers have a more current view of their financial situation. Tax liabilities, payments made, and submissions due can be seen in real time.

2 Tax avoidance, tax evasion, tax planning, and money laundering

KEY TERM

Tax evasion: Illegal means by which taxpayers attempt to minimise their tax liability.

Tax avoidance: Interpreting legislation to reduce a tax liability in a way that it was not intended to be applied. This is not illegal but may involve finding loopholes in the law and is often considered unethical.

Tax planning: A legal and ethical means by which taxpayers can minimise their tax liability, using the law as it was intended to be used.

2.1 Tax evasion

Tax evasion is always illegal. It is when people or businesses deliberately do not declare and account for the taxes that they owe. It includes the hidden economy, where people conceal their presence or taxable sources of income or over-state their expenses.

Tax evasion can result in fines/imprisonment.

2.2 Tax avoidance

Tax avoidance involves bending the rules of the tax system to gain a tax advantage that Parliament never intended. It often involves contrived, artificial transactions that serve little or no purpose other than to produce this advantage. It involves operating within the letter – but not the spirit – of the law. Most tax avoidance schemes simply do not work, and those who engage in them can find they pay more than the tax they attempted to save once HMRC has successfully challenged them.

2.3 Tax planning

Tax planning involves using tax reliefs for the purpose for which they were intended. For example, claiming tax relief on capital investment, or saving via ISAs or for retirement by making contributions to a pension scheme. However, tax reliefs can be used excessively or aggressively by others than those intended to benefit from them or in ways that clearly go beyond the intention of Parliament. Where this is the case, it is right to take action, because it is important that the tax system is fair and perceived to be so. (HMRC, 2015)

Typical tasks in the assessment might ask you to define any of the above and to decide whether a particular scenario is an example of tax evasion/ tax avoidance or tax planning.

Activity 1: Tax avoidance and tax evasion

The following acts have been committed by one of your clients.

Action 1: A customer invoice was omitted from their business accounting records in order to push the income into the taxable profits of the following tax year.

Action 2: The client has transferred income generating assets into her husband's name as he pays a lower rate of tax on the investment income.

Required

Which of these actions amounts to tax evasion?

	✓
Action 1 only	
Action 2 only	
Both actions	
Neither action	

2.4 Reporting suspicions

A practising accountant often acts for taxpayers in their dealings with HMRC and situations can arise where the accountant has concerns as to whether the taxpayer is being honest in providing information to the accountant for onward transmission. They must use their professional judgement and uphold the ethical standards of the AAT.

If a client evades tax, for example by making a material error or omission in a tax return, the accountant must first try to make the client change it and disclose their error or omission. If the client does not correct the error, omission or failure when advised, the accountant should cease to act for the client, inform HMRC of this cessation (without informing them of the reason in order to maintain client confidentiality) and consider making a money laundering report (see below).

2.5 Money laundering

KEY TERM

> **Money laundering:** The process by which the proceeds of crime are converted into assets which appear to have a legitimate origin.

Where there is a suspicion of tax evasion, the accountant should consider making a report to their firm's money laundering reporting officer (or the National Crime Agency if the accountant is a sole practitioner).

Accountants who suspect, or are aware of, tax evasion by a client may be committing an offence if they do not report their suspicions. Furthermore, the accountant must not disclose to the client or a third party that a money laundering report has been made. Doing so would constitute a criminal offence of 'tipping-off'.

2.6 The General Anti-Abuse Rule (GAAR)

KEY TERM

> **General Anti-Abuse Rule (GAAR):** A mechanism that allows tax authorities to counteract tax advantages arising from abusive tax arrangements that, while technically legal, are designed primarily to avoid tax and go against the spirit or intent of the law.

The GAAR aims to promote fairness in the tax system by preventing taxpayers from exploiting loopholes or engaging in artificial schemes that reduce tax liabilities in ways not intended by law.

The primary objective of the GAAR is to deter taxpayers from entering into abusive arrangements, and to deter would-be promoters from promoting such arrangements. An abusive arrangement is one which cannot reasonably be regarded as a reasonable course of action in relation to the relevant tax provisions.

If an arrangement is deemed to be abusive, HMRC can make a just and reasonable adjustment to counteract the tax advantage.

2.7 Dishonest conduct by tax agents

KEY TERM

> **Tax agent:** An accountant or firm of accountants that is authorised to act on behalf of a tax-payer in dealing with tax matters, including preparing tax returns, providing tax advice, and communicating with HMRC.

A small minority of tax agents act dishonestly. Legislation allows HMRC to:

- Investigate dishonest conduct by tax agents
- Charge civil penalties
- Publish details of tax agents who have acted dishonestly

When HMRC has evidence of dishonest conduct they will issue a conduct notice that sets out the evidence they have. They can then:

- Ask for access to working papers
- Charge penalties if they do not get access to working papers
- Charge a penalty for dishonest conduct between £5,000 and £50,000
- Publish details about the agent if they are charged a penalty of more than £5,000

Chapter summary

- Governments collect taxation to raise finance, redistribute wealth, control the economy and encourage or discourage certain activities.
- HMRC is responsible for the administration of tax.
- The tax year runs from 6 April in one year to 5 April in the next year.
- Some of the rules governing tax are laid down in legislation, while some are laid down in case law.
- HMRC provides guidance about how tax law works.
- The objectives of tax digitalisation are to allow taxpayers to see tax liabilities, payments made, and submissions due in real time, to reduce the number of careless errors in tax returns, and improved business management.
- It is important to be able to distinguish between tax evasion (illegal) and tax planning / avoidance (legal).
- If an accountant is concerned that a client is evading tax, they should ask the client to disclose the error or omission. If the client refuses, they should cease to act for the client, notify HMRC that they are ceasing to act (without giving a reason) and consider making a money laundering report.
- The general anti-abuse rule counteracts abusive tax arrangements. HMRC can make a just and reasonable adjustment to counteract the tax advantage.
- HMRC can ask for access to the working papers of dishonest tax agents. If found to be dishonest HMRC can levy penalties, and publish details of the agents.

Activity answers

Activity 1: Tax avoidance and tax evasion

The correct answer is:

	✓
Action 1 only	✓
Action 2 only	
Both actions	
Neither action	

Action 1 is tax evasion as it involves deliberately misleading HMRC to delay a legitimate tax charge.

Action 2 is tax planning.

Test your learning

1 Tax avoidance is illegal and can lead to fines/imprisonment.

Required

Show whether this statement is true or false.

Tick ONE box.

Tax avoidance is illegal and can lead to fines/imprisonment.

	✓
True	
False	

2 **Identify whether the statement below is true or false.**

All taxpayers are sent a tax return each year by HM Revenue & Customs.

	✓
True	
False	

3 **The tax administration within the UK is undertaken by:**

Tick ONE box.

	✓
The Chancellor of the Exchequer	
Companies House	
HM Revenue & Customs	
Members of Parliament	

4 **Indicate with ticks which TWO of the following have the force of law.**

	✓
Acts of Parliament	
HMRC statements of practice	
Statutory instruments	
Extra statutory concessions	

5 **Who should a sole practitioner make a report to if they suspect a client of money laundering?**

Tick ONE box.

	✓
HMRC	
Nearest police station	
National Crime Agency	
Tax tribunal	

6 An ISA is a special bank account where cash may be saved and any interest earned is not subject to tax. David invests his redundancy money in an ISA. David is engaged in:

Required

Tick ONE box.

	✓
Tax planning	
Tax avoidance	
Tax evasion	
Not possible to say until decided by a judge	

7 The government levies higher tax charges on company cars with high CO2 emissions. The purpose of this is to redistribute wealth.

Required

	✓
True	
False	

8 Jermaine has saved a large amount of tax by timing the disposal of assets so that they are spread across several tax years to make use of annual exemptions.

Required

This arrangement would probably be caught by the General Anti-Abuse Rule (GAAR)

	✓
True	
False	

2 Calculation of income tax

Learning outcomes

2	**Calculate income tax and national insurance contributions (NICs)**
2.1	**Calculate taxable income** Learners need to understand: 2.1.1 that the tax year is the period from 6 April in one year to the following 5 April 2.1.2 that tax years are expressed as the two calendar years included in the tax year; eg 2026/27 2.1.3 that individuals are assessed on their taxable income for a tax year 2.1.4 income included in total/net income • employment • pension (including state pension) • trading • property • savings • UK dividends 2.1.5 that all income is included gross in the income tax computation 2.1.6 the classification of income into: • non-savings • savings • dividend 2.1.7 the treatment of jointly owned income-generating assets 2.1.8 exempt income: • prizes/lottery wins/betting wins • income from Individual Savings Accounts (ISAs) • interest on National Savings Certificates • income fully covered by the rent a room scheme 2.1.9 income that does not need to be included: • trading allowance full relief • property allowance full relief 2.1.10 that every individual is entitled to a personal allowance each tax year 2.1.11 the circumstances under which the personal allowance is abated 2.1.12 that adjusted net income is reduced by the gross amount of: • personal pension contributions • gift aid donations

	2.1.13 the marriage allowance • impact on the personal allowance • conditions that must be met
	Learners need to be able to: 2.1.14 calculate: • trading income allocated to a tax year in straddle periods • total/net income • gross personal pension contributions • gross gift aid donations • adjusted net income • the personal allowance • taxable income
2.2	**Calculate income tax payable** Learners need to understand: 2.2.1 that different rates of tax apply to different types of income: • non-savings • savings • dividend 2.2.2 that the income tax liability must be calculated on non-savings income first, then savings income and lastly dividend income 2.2.3 income tax nil rate bands • personal savings allowance • dividend allowance 2.2.4 amounts that reduce the income tax liability: • marriage allowance received • property business finance costs 2.2.5 amounts that increase the income tax payable • high income child benefit charge 2.2.6 amounts that reduce the income tax payable: • pay as you earn (PAYE) deductions taken at source • construction industry scheme (CIS) deductions taken at source
	Learners need to be able to: 2.2.7 calculate the • adjusted tax bands due to gross gift aid donations or personal pension contributions • marriage allowance received • income tax liability • high income child benefit charge • income tax payable

Assessment context

Task 5 in your assessment is about the calculation of income tax for 14 marks. You can expect to see short 1-2 mark questions which are multiple choice, or fill in the blank style questions. Take care to notice whether you are being asked to calculate the tax for a taxpayer resident in England and Northern Ireland, Wales or Scotland as different rates apply.

Qualification context

You will not be tested on these areas outside of this unit.

Business context

Calculating income tax payable is one of the main tasks that a tax adviser will perform for their client.

Chapter overview

Calculation of income tax

Tax year: 6 April to 5 April eg 2026/27: 6 April 2026 to 5 April 2027

Net income

Non-savings
- Employment
- Self-employment
- Property
- Pensions

Savings
- Interest
- Tax amounts received in year

Dividends
- Tax amounts received in year

Exempt
- Don't tax!
- ISAs (limits)
- Damages
- Winnings
- Scholarships

Jointly held assets
- 50:50 by default, or
- Elect to split income based on actual interests

Taxable income

- Net income less personal allowance

Personal allowance
- Usually £12,570
- Restricted for high earners
  - Deduct ½ (ANI – 100,000)
  - Max restriction to nil
  - ANI: Adjusted net income
  - Net income less personal pension contributions and or Gift Aid payments

Marriage allowance
- Spouses and civil partners can transfer £1,260 of personal allowance
- Recipient obtains relief by way of a tax reducer at 20% of the amount transferred
- Both individuals must be either basic rate or non-taxpayers

Introduction

In this chapter we are going to look at the income tax computation and discover what makes up **taxable income**. An individual may have income from a number of sources, for example from employment, or from investments such as savings or property. We need to identify which of these are taxable, and then add them all together to get our **total or net income**, the amount that we will potentially have to pay tax on.

We'll find out how to calculate the actual employment and property income figures themselves in later chapters, for now we'll focus on **savings and dividend income**. We'll also identify some **exempt** income that will never be taxed.

Most taxpayers are given a **personal allowance**, an amount they are allowed to earn before they pay tax. We will deduct this personal allowance from the net income to leave us with our **taxable income**, the amount we will actually pay tax on.

The calculation of income tax will appear complex at first. There is a set of basic rules but these can be applied in many different combinations depending on a taxpayer's circumstances, meaning there are many different scenarios for you to get to grips with.

In this chapter we will consider some, but not all, of the possible scenarios. The more examples you study and questions you attempt the more familiar you will become with how the rules operate.

1 Taxable income

The first step in the calculation of an individual's income tax payable is to calculate their taxable income. In other words, the amount of their income which is subject to income tax.

1.1 The income tax computation

The **income tax computation** is used to calculate an individual's **income tax liability**.

The income tax liability is the total amount of income tax the taxpayer is due to pay for the tax year. Remember that the tax year runs from 6 April in one year to the following 5 April. The 2026/27 tax year runs from 6 April 2026 to 5 April 2027.

KEY TERM

Total/net income: The total amount of income from all taxable sources before deducting any allowances or reliefs.

Income tax: A UK tax charged on most types of income earned by individuals.

In this section we will calculate taxable income. We will then consider how to calculate the income tax liability on the taxable income in section 2.

The calculation of taxable income looks like this:

Assessment focus point

Proforma income tax computation

	Non-savings income £	Savings income (excluding dividends) £	Dividends £	Total £
Employment income	X			X
Pension income	X			X
Trading income	X			X

	Non-savings income £	Savings income (excluding dividends) £	Dividends £	Total £
Property income	X			X
Interest received		X		X
Dividends from UK companies	–	–	X	X
Total/net income	X	X	X	X
Less personal allowance	(X)	–	–	(X)
Taxable income	X	X	X	X

Note. Total and net income are actually two different concepts but in your syllabus the terms can be used interchangeably. We will use net income for the rest of the chapter.

You will see there are three columns representing three types of income. We will consider the implications of this in the following section.

Some income will be paid over to the taxpayer **net of tax**, meaning tax has already been deducted at source. An example of this would be a salary payment from an employer paid net of PAYE. This represents an estimate of the tax the taxpayer is likely to have to pay.

We use the income tax computation to calculate the correct amount of tax that a taxpayer should be paying for the year. We therefore need to include all income **gross** of tax, before these estimated amounts of tax have been deducted.

When the tax liability has been calculated then the individual is allowed to deduct the tax already paid for the tax year. This may or may not be the correct amount.

This could leave the taxpayer having to make an additional tax payment or claim a tax repayment.

1.2 Non-savings, savings, dividend and exempt income

Different tax rates apply to the three different types of income.

Note. That exempt income is income that is never charged to income tax.

1.2.1 Non-savings income

KEY TERM

Non-savings income: Any income subject to income tax that is not classified as savings income or dividend income. This includes employment, pension, trading and property income.

This is all income other than interest and dividends. It includes the following:

- Income from employment (see Chapter 4 Employment income)
- Income from property (see Chapter 3 Property income)
- Income from pensions, including the state pension
- Trading income from self-employment, or a share of partnership profits (see Chapters 5 to 8)

1.2.2 Savings income

KEY TERM

Savings income: Any interest received that is subject to income tax.

This is interest received. Note it is taxed on an actual basis. If interest is received in the tax year, it is taxed. If it is accrued but not received, it is not taxed.

We simply add together all the interest received in the tax year from all sources and then insert the total into the savings column in the tax computation.

Most taxpayers will not have to pay income tax on interest received unless their interest income is above the **personal savings allowance** (see later in this chapter).

Illustration 1: Savings income

Gerry receives the following interest:

	£
Lloyds Bank	80
Nationwide Building Society	400
Government interest (gilts)	100

These amounts would be added together to calculate the total interest to be included in the savings column of the tax computation.

	Gross £
Lloyds Bank	80
Nationwide Building Society	400
Government interest (gilts)	100
Total	580

1.2.3 Dividend income

KEY TERM

Dividend income: Any dividends received that are subject to income tax.

Taxpayers are taxed on the amount of dividends received in a tax year.

Illustration 2: Dividend income

Maria receives a dividend of £900. This is the gross amount that needs to be included in the computation of net income.

Most taxpayers will not have to pay income tax on dividend received unless their dividend income is above the **dividend allowance** (see later in this chapter).

1.2.4 Exempt income

KEY TERM

Exempt income: Income that is not subject to UK income tax.

Assessment focus point

Certain income is exempt from income tax. Do not include it in your total of taxable income.

If you are typing in an answer and there is exempt income in the question, state that this is exempt or if there is an exempt box to click, make sure you do this – there will be a mark here.

Exempt income includes the following:

Individual savings accounts (ISAs)

- These are special savings accounts a taxpayer can invest in.
- Individuals may invest up to £20,000 in an individual savings account (ISA) in the tax year 2026/27. This could be in the form of cash, shares, unit trusts or insurance policies. Investors may use their entire allowance on one type of investment (eg the whole £20,000 could be invested in cash) or a combination of different investments.
- Dividend income from shares and interest income received from cash invested in an ISA are free of income tax. Capital growth is also free of capital gains tax.
- An ISA may be opened by someone 16 years old and over if it only contains cash.
- ISAs containing investments other than cash may only be opened by someone at least 18 years old.

Others

- prizes, lottery winnings, betting winnings
- interest on National Savings Certificates
- income fully covered by the rent a room scheme (see property income chapter 3)

Certain other income also does not need to be included in the income tax computation:

- trading income that is fully covered by the trading allowance (see chapter 5)
- property income that is fully covered by the property allowance (see chapter 3)

Activity 1: Taxable and exempt income

Foster receives the following income:

	£
Building society interest	40
Dividend from an ISA investment	900
Rent (not covered by rent a room)	6,000
Non-ISA dividends	450

Required

Complete the following table.

Use the picklist options to list the sources of income under the appropriate headings (exempt, non-savings, savings or dividend income).

Record the amounts received under the appropriate column heading (exempt, non-savings, savings and dividends).

You do not need to total the columns.

Exempt income	Exempt income £	Non-savings income £	Savings income £	Dividend income £
▼				
Non-savings income				
▼				
Savings income				
▼				
Dividend income				
▼				

Picklist

- Building society interest
- ISA dividend
- Non-ISA dividend
- Rent

1.3 Computation of taxable income

We will now revisit the full income tax computation we looked at in Section 1.1.

1.3.1 Net income

In a tax year, all income must be brought together and totalled.

The income is split into three columns representing the three types of income subject to tax:

- non-savings income
- savings income
- dividend income

This gives us net income.

KEY TERM

Net income: An individual's total income calculated prior to deducting the personal allowance.

1.3.2 Taxable income

KEY TERM

Personal allowance: The amount of income an individual can earn in a tax year without paying income tax.

Taxable income: Any income subject to income tax after deducting all allowances and reliefs.

The personal allowance of £12,570 is then usually deducted from the total/net income to give the taxable amount.

The personal allowance is initially available to all taxpayers, including children.

The personal allowance is reduced for taxpayers who have income in excess of £100,000. The allowance can be potentially reduced to nil (see section 1.4 below).

It is usually most beneficial to deduct the personal allowance against non-savings income before savings income then dividend income.

Illustration 3: Taxable income

In 2026/27, Joe has trade profits of £3,000 and receives bank interest of £17,500 and dividends of £500. Joe's taxable income for 2026/27 is:

	Non-savings income £	Savings income £	Dividends income £	Total £
Trade profits	3,000			3,000
Bank interest		17,500		17,500
Dividends			500	500
Net income	3,000	17,500	500	21,000
Less personal allowance	(3,000)	(9,570)	–	(12,570)
Taxable income	–	7,930	500	8,430

Activity 2: Taxable income

Quentin earns a salary of £3,000 in 2026/27. He receives rental income of £1,000, building society interest of £3,750 and a dividend of £5,000.

Required

Prepare a computation of taxable income for 2026/27, clearly showing the distinction between the different types of income.

	Non-savings income £	Savings income £	Dividend income £	Total £
Employment income				
Property income				
Building society interest				
Dividend income				
Net income				
Less personal allowance				
Taxable income				

1.3.3 Marriage allowance

KEY TERM

Marriage allowance: An allowance that lets a lower-earning spouse or civil partner transfer an amount of their personal allowance to their partner.

It is possible for married couples and civil partners to transfer part of their personal allowance to their spouse or civil partner in certain circumstances. The amount that can be transferred is £1,260.

The lower-earning transferor spouse or civil partner loses £1,260 of their personal allowance.

The receiving spouse or civil partner remains at £12,570. Relief is obtained by reducing their tax liability by 20% of the amount transferred. This cannot lead to a tax repayment.

The conditions which must be met are:

- the couple must be married or in a civil partnership for all or part of the tax year
- both individuals must be either basic rate or non-taxpayers
- an election must be made within four years of the end of the tax year

1.4 Jointly owned assets

In the UK, there is independent taxation, which means that income from spouses and civil partners is kept separate. Where a taxpayer owns an income-generating asset jointly with their spouse or civil partner, for example a rental property, or a bank account, or shares in a company that are generating dividends, there are rules governing how the income will be split.

(a) By default, the income will be split equally (50:50) between the two parties, regardless of their actual interests

(b) Alternatively, an election may be made to split the income based on their actual interests in the property.

See section 2 for an illustration showing how this fits into the income tax computation.

1.5 Restricting the personal allowance

1.5.1 The basic calculation

If an individual has adjusted net income in excess of £100,000 then the personal allowance must be reduced.

It is reduced by £1 for every £2 adjusted net income the taxpayer has over the £100,000 limit.

The personal allowance may be reduced to £0 if adjusted net income is greater than or equal to £125,140.

Formula to learn

Restriction = 0.5 × (Adjusted net income – £100,000) .

KEY TERM

Abatement of the personal allowance: The gradual reduction of an individual's UK personal allowance once their adjusted net income exceeds a specific threshold.

Adjusted net income: Total income (before the deduction of the personal allowance), minus gross gift aid donations and gross personal pension contributions. This figure is used to determine whether the taxpayer's personal allowance is abated and whether they need to pay the high income child benefit charge.

Illustration 4: Personal allowance restriction

In 2026/27, Kelvin has gross employment income of £98,000 and receives building society interest of £1,500 and dividends of £5,000. Kelvin's net income for 2026/27 is:

	Non-savings income	Savings income	Dividend income	Total
	£	£	£	£
Net income	98,000	1,500	5,000	104,500

The total is above the adjustment threshold of £100,000 so we must reduce the personal allowance.

	£
Net income	104,500
Less income limit	(100,000)
Excess	4,500
Personal allowance	12,570
Less half excess (4,500/2)	(2,250)
Adjusted personal allowance	10,320

The taxable income is therefore:

	Non-savings income	Savings income	Dividend income	Total
	£	£	£	£
Net income	98,000	1,500	5,000	104,500
Less personal allowance	(10,320)	–	–	(10,320)
Taxable income	87,680	1,500	5,000	94,180

Activity 3: Personal allowance restriction

Karen has net income of £107,000 (all non-savings income).

Required

What personal allowance does Karen receive for 2026/27, and what is her taxable income?

Her personal allowance is **£** ____________

Her taxable income is **£** ____________

1.5.2 Charitable donations/pension payments

If a taxpayer makes Gift Aid or personal pension scheme contributions in the year (see section 2), then they are allowed to deduct the payments from net income before calculating the restriction on the personal allowance.

Both of these payments are made net by the taxpayer but it is the gross amount that is deducted from the net income. We will consider this in detail in the next chapter.

Total income after deducting Gift Aid and personal pension contributions is called **adjusted net income**.

Note. Gift Aid and personal pension contributions are only deducted from total income for the purpose of calculating the personal allowance; they are not deducted from income in the tax computation.

Illustration 5: Personal allowance restriction with Gift Aid payment

As per Illustration 4 in 2026/27, Kelvin has gross employment income of £98,000 and receives building society interest of £1,500 and dividends of £5,000. However, he now makes a gross payment to charity of £1,000 under Gift Aid. Kelvin's net income for 2026/27 is still:

	Non-savings income	Savings income	Dividend income	Total
	£	£	£	£
Net income	98,000	1,500	5,000	104,500

The total is above the adjustment threshold of £100,000 so we must reduce the personal allowance. However, as he has made a payment to charity under Gift Aid we are allowed to reduce the net income before calculating the restriction:

	£
Net income	104,500
Less gross Gift Aid payment	(1,000)
Adjusted net income	103,500
Less income limit	(100,000)
Excess	3,500
Personal allowance	12,570
Less half excess (3,500/2)	(1,750)
Adjusted personal allowance	10,820

The taxable income is therefore:

	Non-savings income £	Savings income £	Dividend income £	Total £
Net income	98,000	1,500	5,000	104,500
Less personal allowance	(10,820)	–	–	(10,820)
Taxable income	87,180	1,500	5,000	93,680

Activity 4: Personal allowance with personal pension payment

Karen, who has net income of £107,000, now makes a personal pension payment of £2,000 gross.

Required

What personal allowance will Karen receive? What is her taxable income?

Her personal allowance is **£** ________

Her taxable income is **£** ________

We will revisit Gift Aid and personal pension payments in section 2.

1.6 Tax planning

Individuals will pay different rates of tax depending on the level of their income. If possible, married couples and civil partners should consider whether cash balances yielding interest and shares yielding dividends could be held by taxpayers paying the lower rate of tax or having unused personal allowances (see section 2).

Other matters to consider:

- taxpayers could invest in products that yield exempt income such as ISAs or National Savings Certificates.
- taxpayers could make payments into personal pension schemes or payments to charity under Gift Aid to preserve their entitlement to the personal allowance (see section 2).

2 Calculate income tax payable

Having calculated an individual's taxable income, the next stage is to calculate their income tax payable.

2.1 Calculation of income tax liability

KEY TERM

Income tax liability: The total amount of gross income tax due to HMRC, before accounting for any payments made.

Income tax payable: The amount of income tax that needs to be paid to HMRC after accounting for any tax already collected at source (eg PAYE)

Pay As You Earn (PAYE): A UK system where employers deduct income tax and national insurance contributions from employees' wages and pay it directly to the government.

Construction Industry Scheme (CIS): A system where contractors deduct tax from payments made to subcontractors and pass it to HMRC. The deductions count as an advance payment towards the subcontractor's income tax and national insurance.

Income tax is calculated at different rates depending on the type and level of income the taxpayer has.

The various rates for 2026/27 are summarised in the diagram below. This data will be provided for you in the taxation tables in your assessment. Note that these rates are applicable to English and Northern Irish taxpayers. Please see later in the chapter for information regarding devolved taxes for Scottish and Welsh taxpayers.

The taxable income we calculated in the previous chapter is taxed in the following order:

(a) Non-savings income

(b) Savings income

(c) Dividend income

So, on the diagram we move from left to right.

Illustration 6: Calculation of tax liability (England and Northern Ireland)

Taxable income	Non-savings	Savings	Dividends	
	45%	45%	39.35%	Additional rate
125,140	40%	40%	35.75%	Higher rate
37,700	20%	20%	10.75%	Basic rate
0				

Note. We have different **tax bands**.

The basic rate band covers income from £1 to £37,700.

The **higher rate band** covers income from £37,701 to £125,140.

The **additional rate band** covers income over £125,140.

These bands may be adjusted for taxpayers who make payments to charity under Gift Aid or pay into a personal pension scheme.

In addition to these bands, there is a **personal savings allowance** that applies to savings income and a **dividend allowance** that applies to dividend income.

We apply these rates to give us our **income tax liability**.

KEY TERM

Basic rate band: The first £37,700 of taxable income. The basic rate band may be extended by the gross amount of any Gift Aid donations and personal pension contributions paid by the taxpayer.

Higher rate band: Taxable income from £37,701 to £125,140. The upper limit to the higher rate band may be extended by the gross amount of any Gift Aid donations and personal pension contributions paid by the taxpayer.

Additional rate band: Income in excess of £125,140 is taxed here.

Don't forget that an employed taxpayer will have had income tax deducted from their salary before it has been paid to them under the PAYE system. In addition, certain construction workers have tax deducted at source under the construction industry scheme (CIS)s These represens an estimated prepayment of income tax for the year. We deduct this from the income tax liability to see whether there is any further **income tax payable** for the year.

It is possible that the taxpayer has paid too much tax. If they have there will be **income tax repayable**.

Assessment focus point

Read the requirements very carefully to see if you are being asked to calculate **income tax liability** or **income tax payable.** You will lose marks or waste time if you calculate the wrong one.

2.2 Taxation of non-savings income

Non-savings income is taxed first. The rates shown here are for taxpayers resident in England and Northern Ireland. The non-savings rates for Scottish and Welsh taxpayers are different (see later in this chapter).

- It is taxed initially in the basic rate band at 20%.
- It is then taxed in the higher rate band at 40%.
- Finally, it is taxed in the additional rate band at 45%.

Illustration 7: Non-savings income

Nathan, who lives in England, has taxable income of £185,000 (>£125,140 therefore no personal allowance) consisting entirely of non-savings employment income. PAYE of £65,000 has been deducted.

The non-savings income uses all the basic rate band of £37,700, the next £87,440 of income falls into the higher rate band and the excess above that falls into the additional rate band.

The income tax liability is:

	Income tax £
Non-savings income	
37,700 × 20%	7,540
87,440 × 40%	34,976
59,860 × 45%	26,937
185,000	
Income tax liability	69,453
Less PAYE	(65,000)
Income tax payable	4,453

2.3 Savings income

Once we have taxed non-savings income we then move on to tax savings income.

We begin taxing savings income in the bands at the point where we finished taxing the non-savings income. In the previous illustration (Illustration 2) Nathan would pay tax on any savings income in the additional rate band as he has already used his basic rate and higher rate band.

Savings income is taxed as follows:

- At 20% on any savings falling in the basic rate band
- At 40% on any savings falling in the higher rate band
- At 45% on any savings falling in the additional rate band

However, there is a further complication in that taxpayers will potentially receive the personal savings allowance. This represents savings income that is taxed at 0%. Taxpayers receive the personal savings allowance as follows:

A basic rate taxpayer (one who has adjusted net income of less than £50,270) receives a personal savings allowance of £1,000.

A higher rate taxpayer (one who has adjusted net income greater than £50,270 but no more than £125,140) receives a personal savings allowance of £500.

An additional rate taxpayer (one who has adjusted net income greater than £125,140) does not receive a personal savings allowance.

(You will note these thresholds represent the relevant bands plus the personal allowance where this is available so for example the basic rate test is £37,700 plus £12,570 equals £50,270, the higher rate test is £125,140 plus £0 as no personal allowance would be available for a taxpayer with £125,140 of income.)

KEY TERM

Personal savings allowance: The amount of savings income that an individual can earn in a tax year without paying income tax..

Illustration 8: Savings income example 1

Sasha, who lives in England, has net income of £42,690 (before the personal allowance) and taxable income of £30,120. Of this, £18,920 is non-savings income and £11,200 is savings income.

Her net income is less than £50,270 so she is a basic rate taxpayer. She is therefore entitled to a personal savings allowance of £1,000.

Her non-savings income will use up some of the basic rate band. As a basic rate taxpayer, she will pay income tax on her savings income in excess of the personal savings allowance at 20%.

The income tax liability is:

	Income tax £
Non-savings income	
18,920 × 20%	3,784
Savings income	
1,000 × 0% (personal savings allowance)	0
10,200 × 20% (11,200 – 1,000)	2,040
Income tax liability	5,824

Illustration 9: Savings income example 2

Dave, who lives in England, has net income of £91,570 (before the personal allowance) and taxable income of £79,000. Of this, £70,000 is non-savings income and £9,000 is savings income.

His net income is greater than £50,270 but less than £125,140 so he is a higher rate taxpayer. He is therefore entitled to a personal savings allowance of £500.

His non-savings income will use up all of the basic rate band. He will therefore pay income tax on his savings income in excess of the personal savings allowance at 40%.

The income tax liability is:

	Income tax £
Non-savings income	
37,700 × 20%	7,540
32,300 × 40% (70,000 – 37,700)	12,920
Savings income	
500 × 0% (personal savings allowance)	0
8,500 × 40% (9,000 – 500)	3,400
Income tax liability	23,860

Illustration 10: Savings income example 3

Frank, who lives in Northern Ireland, has net income of £180,000. He receives no personal allowance, so his taxable income is also £180,000. Of this, £100,000 is non-savings income and £80,000 is savings income.

His net income is greater than £125,140 so he is an additional rate taxpayer. He is therefore not entitled to a personal savings allowance.

His non-savings income will use up all of the basic rate band. He will therefore pay income tax on his savings income initially at 40% and then 45%.

The income tax liability is:

	Income tax £
Non-savings income	
37,700 × 20%	7,540
62,300 × 40% (100,000 – 37,700)	24,920
Savings income	
25,140 × 40% (125,140 – 37,700 – 62,300)	10,056
54,860 × 45% (80,000 – 25,140)	24,687
£180,000	
Income tax liability	67,203

Activity 5: Income tax liability

In 2026/27 Jules, who is single and lives in Northern Ireland, has employment income of £39,070 and building society interest of £9,000.

Required

Calculate the income tax liability.

	Non-savings income £	Savings income £	Total £

Tax

	Non-savings income £	Savings income £	Total £
			£

	Non-savings income £	Savings income £	Total £

2.4 Dividend income

Once we have taxed non-savings income and savings income, we then move on to tax dividend income.

As before, we begin taxing dividend income in the bands at the point where we finished taxing the savings income.

Dividend income is taxed as follows:

- At 10.75% on any dividend income falling in the basic rate band
- At 35.75% on any dividend income falling in the higher rate band
- At 39.35% on any dividend income falling in the additional rate band

However, there is a further complication in that taxpayers will receive the dividend allowance. This represents dividend income that is taxed at 0%. All taxpayers receive a dividend allowance of £500 regardless of their level of net income.

KEY TERM

Dividend allowance: The amount of dividend income that an individual can receive in a tax year without paying income tax. Alternative term: Dividend nil rate band (DNRB).

Illustration 11: Dividend income

Douglas, who lives in England, has net income of £165,000. Of this, £120,000 is non-savings income, £20,000 is savings income and £25,000 is dividend income.

Douglas is clearly an additional rate taxpayer so he will not receive a personal savings allowance. However, he is entitled to the dividend allowance.

The non-savings income of £120,000 uses all the basic rate band and some of the higher rate band. The £20,000 interest uses the remaining higher rate band of £5,140, leaving a balance of £14,860 remaining to tax at the additional rate of 45%. The first £500 of dividend income is taxed at 0% because of the dividend allowance. The balance of dividend income of £24,500 is therefore taxed at the additional rate of 39.35%.

The income tax liability is:

	Income tax £
Non-savings income	
37,700 × 20%	7,540

	Income tax £
82,300 × 40%	32,920
120,000	
Savings income	
5,140 × 40%	2,056
14,860 x 45%	6,687
20,000	
Dividend income	
500 × (dividend allowance)	0
24,500 × 39.35%	9,641
25,000	
Income tax liability	58,844

Activity 6: Income tax payable

Arthur, who lives in Northern Ireland, has a salary of £125,000 (PAYE £42,000). He received bank interest of £10,000 and dividends of £10,000.

Required

Calculate the income tax payable for 2026/27.

	Non-savings income £	Savings income £	Dividend income £	Total £
Employment income				
Bank interest				
Dividends				
Net income				
Personal allowance				
Taxable income				
				£
Non-savings income				

	Non-savings income £	Savings income £	Dividend income £	Total £
Savings income				
Dividend income				
Tax liability				
Less PAYE				
Tax payable				

Activity 7: Income tax payable with marriage allowance

Amber, who lives in England, is employed on a salary of £37,000 per year. Her husband Sean has taxable trading income of £10,000 in 2026/27.

Sean makes a marriage allowance election.

Required

What is Sean's remaining personal allowance, and what is Amber's income tax payable?

2.5 Extending the bands

KEY TERM

Gift aid donations: Donations to charity made under the Gift Aid scheme, which is a UK Government scheme that allows charities to claim back basic-rate income tax on donations made by UK taxpayers.

Gross gift aid donations: The total amount donated to a charity, including both the amount paid by the individual and the basic0rate tax relief added by the Government.

Personal pension contributions: Contributions to a private (non-workplace) pension scheme.

Gross personal pension contributions: Total contributions to a private (non-workplace) pension scheme, including both the amount paid by the individual and the basic-rate tax relief added by the Government.

Assessment focus point

You will not be assessed on extending the tax bands for personal pension contributions or gift aid donations for Scottish taxpayers in your assessment. The information below focusses on English and Northern Irish taxpayers.

Certain donations to UK registered charities or payments into personal pension schemes are eligible for tax relief.

Essentially, the income the taxpayer puts into the pension scheme/gives to charity is not taxable. The taxpayer therefore saves the tax they would have paid on that income.

Different taxpayers will therefore be entitled to relief at different rates.

Most taxpayers are employees who have already paid their tax via PAYE. By giving money to charity/paying into a pension they are therefore entitled to a refund of tax already paid on this income. Most taxpayers pay tax at 20% so making a payment of £100 would entitle them to a repayment of £20.

It would be onerous for the taxpayer and the Government if everyone who made such a payment had to apply to the Government for a tax refund, so to simplify the administration payments are always made **net** of basic rate (20%) tax. The charity/pension will then reclaim the 20% tax from HMRC on behalf of all its donors in one go, saving much time and effort.

The taxpayer has therefore obtained relief at 20% as the charity/pension receives the full 100% but it has only cost the taxpayer 80%. This is effectively the same as the taxpayer giving the charity/pension 100% and then claiming the 20% tax back from the Government that they have already paid on that income.

If the taxpayer does pay tax at 20% then no further action is required on their part.

Higher rate (40%) taxpayers are entitled to an additional 20% (40% – 20%) relief on their gross donation/pension contribution. Additional rate taxpayers are entitled to an additional 25% (45% – 20%) relief on their gross donation/pension contribution.

Additional (20% or 25%) relief is given for charitable donations/pension contributions made by higher/additional rate taxpayers by a process known as 'extending the bands'. This moves income that would have been taxed at a higher rate into a lower rate band, effectively giving the taxpayer a discount on their tax bill.

The basic rate upper limit becomes:

> 37,700 + (payments × 100/80) – income is moved out of higher rate into basic rate saving 20% (40% – 20%)

The higher rate limit becomes:

> 125,140 + (payment × 100/80) – income is moved out of additional rate into higher rate saving a further 5% (45% – 40%). This combined with the basic rate extension above gives the taxpayer a 25% saving (20% + 5%).

Assessment focus point

If a taxpayer makes a payment to charity under Gift Aid or makes a payment into a personal pension scheme, gross up the amount paid by 100/80 and then add this total to the basic rate and higher rate band before calculating the tax liability.

Double check that the figure has not been given to you gross in the question. If it is already gross don't gross it up again.

Illustration 12: Gift Aid donation

Gustav lives in England, and has taxable income (all non-savings) of £50,000 in 2026/27.

Assuming that Gustav does not make any Gift Aid donations or personal pension contributions in 2026/27 his income tax liability will be:

	£
37,700 × 20%	7,540
12,300 × 40%	4,920

	£
50,000	12,460

Now think about the situation where Gustav makes a Gift Aid donation of £8,000 in 2026/27. The Gift Aid donation will have been paid net of 20% tax. This means that the gross amount of the payment is £8,000 × 100/80 = £10,000 and Gustav's basic rate band must be extended by £10,000. His income tax liability is calculated as follows:

	£
37,700 × 20%	7,540
10,000 (extended basic rate band) × 20%	2,000
2,300 × 40%	920
50,000	10,460

Extending the basic rate band means that £10,000 more income is taxed at the basic rate and therefore £10,000 less income is taxed at the higher rate. The difference between the tax liabilities with and without the Gift Aid donation is £10,000 × (40 – 20%) = £2,000. The total tax relief is:

	£
Basic rate relief given by net payment (10,000 – 8,000)	2,000
Higher rate relief given by extending basic rate band	2,000
Total tax relief (which equates to 40% of the gross donation)	4,000

Activity 8: Tax liability with Gift Aid donation

In 2026/27, Charlie has employment income of £100,000. He wishes to make a donation of £8,000 (net) to charity. Charlie lives in England.

Required

For 2026/27, calculate Charlie's:

(a) Taxable income

£ ______

(b) Tax liability if he does not make the donation.

£ ______

(c) Tax liability if he does make the donation.

£ ______

(d) Total tax saved if he does make the donation.

£ ______

Remember that a personal pension contribution or Gift Aid payment is deducted from total income for the purpose of calculating the restriction on the personal allowance. It is the **gross** payment that is deducted (payment × 100/80).

2.6 Payroll giving and occupational pension schemes

A taxpayer may also donate to charity via their employer. Under payroll giving, the taxpayer requests that their employer pay some of their salary directly to charity.

A taxpayer may contribute to an occupational pension scheme. This is a pension scheme provided by the employer. Contributions will be deducted directly from the employee's salary.

The taxpayer will obtain tax relief on both of these payments. As they are deducted from salary, they reduce the taxpayer's taxable income and thus their tax liability. See chapter 4 for further details about the calculation of taxable income from employment.

Taxpayers will save at either 20%, 40% or 45% depending on their level of income.

There is no need to extend the basic rate band for these payments.

2.7 High income child benefit tax charge

KEY TERM

High income child benefit charge: A UK tax charge that requires higher-earning individuals (or their partners) to pay back some or all of the child benefit that they receive, depending on their income level. Child benefit is a tax-free Government support paid to anyone responsible for a child.

Child benefit is a tax-free benefit that UK individuals with children can claim. However, where the adjusted net income of a claimant or their partner exceeds £60,000, the high income child benefit tax charge applies, which effectively claws it back.

The charge is 1% of the child benefit for every £200 of adjusted net income in excess of £60,000, up to a maximum of 100%.

As a reminder, adjusted net income is net income less gross personal pension contributions and gross gift aid donations.

Where there are two partners (including a couple who are not married, but living together as spouses or civil partners), the charge is levied on the partner who has the highest income.

Illustration 13:

Beata and Jacob are a married couple living in England with three children. Jacob earns a salary of £30,000. Beata earns a salary of £75,000. Beata makes donations to charity under the Gift Aid scheme of £150 each month. Jacob claims child benefit of £3,150 per year.

Required

Calculate Beata's income tax liability.

Solution

Evan though Jacob claims the child benefit, the high income tax charge falls on Beata as she is the higher earner.

	£
Employment income	75,000
Less: personal allowance	(12,570)
Taxable income	62,430

Tax

39,950 (W1) × 20%	7,990
22,480 × 40%	8,992
	16,982

Add: high income child benefit tax charge (W2)	1,985
Tax liability	18,967

(W1) Basic rate band

	£
Basic rate band	37,700
Add: gross Gift Aid (£150 × 12 × 100/80)	2,250
Revised basic rate band	39,950

(W2) High income child benefit tax charge

	£
Net income	75,000
Less: gross Gift Aid (£150 × 12 × 100/80)	(2,250)
Adjusted net income	72,750
Less: child benefit threshold	(60,000)
Excess	12,750
12,750 / 200 × 1% (round down)	63%
Child benefit tax charge: 63% × £3,150	1,985

2.8 Tax Reducer for interest paid

KEY TERM

Property business finance costs: Interest on mortgages, loans and overdrafts used to fund a property business, plus fees and other incidental costs for getting or repaying mortgages or loans.

In chapter 3 we will look at property income. Where a loan or mortgage is used by an individual to purchase a residential property which is let out, relief is obtained for the interest paid by way of a tax reducer (not as a deduction from the rent itself).

Relief is only available at the basic rate, even if the individual is a higher or additional rate taxpayer.

Illustration 14:

Jas, who lives in Northern Ireland, has the following income in 2026/27:

	£
Employment income	50,000
Property income	20,000

Jas took out a mortgage to purchase the rental property. Her repayments in 2026/27 were £8,400, of which £4,000 was interest, and the balance was capital repayment.

Required

Calculate Jas's income tax liability for 2026/27

Solution

	£
Employment income	50,000
Property income	20,000
Net income	70,000
Less: PA	(12,570)
Taxable income	57,430

Tax

37,700 × 20%	7,540
19,730 × 40%	7,892
	15,432
Less: tax reducer (£4,000 × 20%)	(800)
Tax liability	14,632

2.9 Devolved taxes

The Scottish Parliament and Welsh Government have the power to vary the rate of income tax payable by Scottish and Welsh taxpayers on non-savings income. The rates of Scottish and Welsh devolved taxes are provided to you in your assessment in the reference material available on screen.

2.9.1 Scotland

Taxpayers living in Scotland pay Scottish income tax. It is paid to the Scottish Government. It is only paid in relation to non-savings income. Scottish taxpayers pay the same rate as the rest of the UK (detailed above) in relation to their savings and dividend income.

The rates are as follows:

	Taxable income	Scottish tax rate
Personal allowance	Up to £12,570	0%
Starter rate	£12,571 to £16,537	19%
Basic rate	£16,538 to £29,526	20%
Intermediate rate	£29,527 to £43,662	21%
Higher rate	£43,663 to £75,000	42%
Advanced rate	£75,001 to £125,140	45%
Top rate	Over £125,140	48%

The calculation of taxable income is the same as detailed in the sections above. In addition, the personal allowance is the same, including restrictions where adjusted net income is more than £100,000.

2.9.2 Wales

The UK government has reduced the main rates of tax by 10% for Welsh taxpayers, who then also pay the additional Welsh income tax. The personal allowance and tax bands for Welsh taxpayers are the same as for other UK taxpayers.

The Welsh rate of income tax is 10% for 2026/27. This means that Welsh taxpayers pay the same rates of income tax as English and Northern Irish taxpayers.

2.10 Tax planning

Even if both people in a marriage/civil partnership pay tax at the same rate they should consider transferring assets between each other to ensure they get the maximum benefit from the savings allowance and the dividend allowance. For example, if each person is paying tax at higher rate, they will each receive a personal savings allowance of £500. If one party owns all the invested cash and is in receipt of £1,000 of interest, then £500 of it will be above the allowance and will be taxable. If half of the cash is transferred to the other party, then they will both be in receipt of £500 which will be covered by their personal savings allowance and together they will not pay tax.

People should also consider making charitable payments or payments into pensions to reduce their tax liability or to preserve the higher personal savings allowance. Again, with couples it makes more sense for the taxpayer paying tax at the higher rate to make the payment.

Chapter summary

- There are three types of income in the income tax computation: non-savings, savings and dividend.
- Non-savings income includes employment income, property income, trading (or business) income and pension income.
- Savings income is interest received.
- Dividend income is dividends received.
- Exempt income includes income from individual savings accounts (ISAs), prizes/lottery/betting wins, interest on National Savings Certificates, and income fully covered by the rent a room scheme.
- Income from jointly held assets is split 50:50 by default, but an election can be made to split it based on actual ownership.
- Income that is fully covered by the trading allowance or property allowance does not need to be included in the income tax computation.
- Tax computations must be prepared for a tax year.
- All the components of an individual's income are added together to arrive at 'net income'.
- Net income less the personal allowance gives 'taxable income'.
- The personal allowance is deducted first from non-savings income, then from savings income and finally from dividend income. It is reduced by £1 for every £2 that the individual's net income exceeds the income limit of £100,000.
- The net income figure for comparison to the income limit for the personal allowance is reduced by gross Gift Aid donations and personal pension contributions.
- A lower-earning individual is able to make a claim to transfer up to £1,260 of their personal allowance to their spouse or civil partner where both individuals are either basic or non-taxpayers. The recipient obtains relief by way of a 20% tax reducer (not by increasing their own personal allowance).
- Income is categorised into different types: non-savings, savings and dividend. Each type of income suffers different rates of tax, depending on whether the income falls into the basic or higher rate bands or over the additional rate threshold.
- Non-savings income is taxed first (at 20%, then 40%, then 45%) then savings income (at 20%, then 40%, then 45%) and finally dividend income (at 10.75%, then 35.75%, then 39.35%).
- A personal savings allowance is available at £1,000 for a basic rate taxpayer, £500 for a higher rate taxpayer and £0 for an additional rate taxpayer. Savings income falling into the allowance is taxed at 0%. The allowance uses up the basic rate and higher rate band.
- A dividend allowance of £500 is available to all taxpayers. Dividends falling into this band are taxed at 0%. The allowance uses up the basic rate and higher rate bands.
- Gift Aid donations and personal pension contributions are paid net of basic rate (20%) tax.
- Extend the basic rate band by the gross amount of any Gift Aid donations and/or personal pension contributions paid by the taxpayer. This gives further tax relief to higher and additional rate taxpayers.
- Payments made to charity via payroll deduction or pension contributions made to an occupational scheme are simply deducted from salary.
- Tax deducted under the PAYE system and the construction industry scheme (CIS) is deducted in computing tax payable and can be repaid if it is greater than the taxpayer's liability.
- Interest paid on loans taken out to purchase residential properties which are let out is allowed as a basic rate tax reducer.
- The high income child benefit tax charge claws back the child benefit received by individuals or their partners who have adjusted net income in excess of £60,000. The charge is 1% of the child benefit for every £200 of adjusted net income in excess of £60,000. The charge is levied on the partners with the higher adjusted net income irrespective of which partner claimed the benefit.

Activity answers

Activity 1: Taxable and exempt income

Exempt income	Exempt income £	Non-savings income £	Savings income £	Dividend income £
ISA dividend	900			
Non-savings income				
Rent		6,000		
Savings income				
Building society interest			40	
Dividend income				
Non-ISA dividend				450

Activity 2: Taxable income

	Non-savings income £	Savings income £	Dividend income £	Total £
Employment income	3,000			3,000
Property income	1,000			1,000
Building society interest		3,750		3,750
Dividend income			5,000	5,000
Net income	4,000	3,750	5,000	12,750
Less personal allowance	(4,000)	(3,750)	(4,820)	(12,570)
Taxable income	nil	nil	180	180

Activity 3: Personal allowance restriction

Her personal allowance is **£** 9,070

Her taxable income is **£** 97,930

Working

	£
Personal allowance	12,570
Less 0.5 × (107,000 – 100,000) =	(3,500)
Adjusted personal allowance	9,070
Net income	107,000
Personal allowance	(9,070)
Taxable income	97,930

Activity 4: Personal allowance with personal pension payment

Her personal allowance is **£** 10,070

Her taxable income is **£** 96,930

Working

	£
Net income	107,000
Less personal pension payment	(2,000)
Adjusted net income	105,000
Personal allowance	12,570
Less 0.5 × (105,000 – 100,000)	(2,500)
Adjusted personal allowance	10,070
Net income	107,000
Personal allowance	(10,070)
Taxable income	96,930

Activity 5: Income tax liability

	Non-savings income £	Savings income £	Total £
Employment income	39,070		39,070
Building society interest		9,000	9,000
Net income	39,070	9,000	48,070

	Non-savings income £	Savings income £	Total £
Personal allowance	(12,570)		(12,570)
Taxable income	26,500	9,000	35,500
Net income < £50,271 therefore £1,000 personal savings allowance available			

Tax

	Non-savings income £	Savings income £	Total £
			£
Non-savings income			
26,500 × 20%			5,300
Savings income			
1,000 × 0% (personal savings allowance)			0
8,000 × 20%			1,600
35,500			
Tax liability			6,900

Activity 6: Income tax payable

	Non-savings income £	Savings income £	Dividend income £	Total £
Employment income	125,000			125,000
Bank interest		10,000		10,000
Dividends			10,000	10,000
Net income	125,000	10,000	10,000	145,000
Personal allowance	(Nil)			(Nil)
Taxable income	125,000	10,000	10,000	145,000
				£
Non-savings income				

	Non-savings income £	Savings income £	Dividend income £	Total £
£37,700 x 20%				7,540
£87,300 x 40%				34,920
£125,000				
Savings income				
£140 x 40%				56
£9,860 x 45%				4,437
£10,000				
Dividend income				
£500 x 0%				0
£9,500 x 39.35%				3,738
£10,000				
Tax liability				50,691
Less PAYE				(42,000)
Tax payable				8,691

Activity 7: Income tax payable with marriage allowance

Sean's personal allowance for 2026/27 is:

	£
Personal allowance	12,570
Less: transferred to Amber	(1,260)
Remaining personal allowance	11,310

Amber's tax liability is as follows:

	£
Employment income	37,000
Less: personal allowance	(12,570)
Taxable income	24,430

Tax

24,430 × 20%	4,886
Less: marriage allowance (£1,260 × 20%)	(252)

Tax liability	4,634

Note that the marriage allowance is given as a tax reducer at 20%. It does not increase the personal allowance for the recipient spouse or civil partner.

Activity 8: Tax liability with Gift Aid donation

(a) £ 87,430

Working

Taxable income

	Non-savings income £
Employment income	100,000
Less personal allowance (income ≤ 100,000 no restriction)	(12,570)
Taxable income	87,430

(b) £ 27,432

Working

	£
37,700 × 20%	7,540
49,730 × 40%	19,892
87,430	
Tax liability	27,432

(c) £ 25,432

Working

Tax liability with the donation

	£
Gross donation is (8,000 × 100/80)	10,000
Basic rate extends to (10,000 + 37,700)	47,700
47,700 × 20%	9,540
39,730 × 40%	15,892
87,430	
Tax liability	25,432

(d) £ 4,000

Working

Tax saving (27,432 – 25,432)	= extra 2,000

which is 20% of the gross donation	
(8,000 × 100/80 = 10,000 @ 20%)	
Total relief:	
Obtained at source: (10,000 – 8,000)	2,000
Reduction in tax liability (above)	2,000
Total	4,000
ie 40% of gross donation of 10,000	

Test your learning

1 **Classify the following types of income by ticking the correct box:**

	Non-savings income ✓	Savings income ✓	Dividends ✓
Employment income			
Dividends			
Property income			
Bank interest			
Pension income			
Interest on government stock			

2 **Complete the table below to show the amount of income that would be included in a tax return for 2026/27. If your answer is zero, please put a '0'.**

	Amount received £	Amount in tax return £
Building society interest	240	
Interest on an individual savings account	40	
Dividends	160	
Interest from government gilts	350	

3 In 2026/27 Joe has employment income of £30,000 and receives dividends of £300 and premium bond winnings of £500.

Required

Use the table below to show his taxable income for 2026/27.

	Non-savings income £	Dividend income £	Total £

Premium bond winnings are exempt from income tax.

4 Pratish receives property income of £3,000 and building society interest of £9,000 in 2026/27.

Required

Use the table below to show his taxable income for 2026/27.

	Non-savings income £	Savings income £	Total £

The personal allowance is deducted first from non-savings income and then from savings income. The full personal allowance was available but not used as taxable income was less than £12,570.

5 Jesse has employment income of £112,200 in 2026/27. He also received building society interest of £5,000, a prize of £50 in an internet competition and dividends of £4,000.

Required

Use the table below to show Jesse's taxable income for 2026/27.

	Non-savings income £	Savings income £	Dividend income £	Total £

6 **At what rates is income tax charged on non-savings income for English taxpayers?**

Tick ONE box.

0%, 20%, 40% and 45%	
40% and 45%	
20% only	
20%, 40% and 45%	

7 In 2026/27 Albert, who lives in England, has a salary of £17,520, £2,000 of building society interest and £3,000 of dividends.

Required

Albert's income tax liability is:

£

8 In 2026/27 Harry, who lives in England, has a salary of £140,000, has received building society interest of £20,000, and dividends of £30,000.

Required

Harry's income tax liability is:

£

9 **Explain how tax relief is given on Gift Aid donations.**

10 Sase, who lives in Northern Ireland, has the following income and outgoings in 2026/27

	£
Business profits	39,600
Building society interest received	2,000
Dividends received	12,000
Gift Aid donation paid	1,600

Required

Compute Sase's income tax payable for the year.

11 Vince is a higher rate taxpayer and makes a Gift Aid donation of £15,000 in 2026/27.

Required

What is Vince's basic rate band in 2026/27?

Tick ONE box.

£37,700	
£52,700	
£56,450	
£62,700	

12 Emma and Gabi jointly own a rental property which generates £40,000 of income per year. Emma owns 60% of the property, and Gabi owns 40%. They have not made any elections in relation to the rental income.

Required

How will the income be shared between them?

	✓
50% each	
60% taxed on Emma, 40% taxed on Gabi	
100% on Emma	
100% on Gabi	

13 Joe and Sophie are married. Their income is as follows:

	Joe £	Sophie £
Employment income	37,000	10,000
Trading income	5,000	-
Interest income	4,000	1,000

Sophie intends to make a marriage allowance claim.

Required

How would Joe's income tax calculation be affected by the marriage allowance claim?

	✓
His personal allowance will be reduced by £1,260	
His personal allowance will be increased by £1,260	
His income tax liability will be reduced by £252	
A marriage allowance claim is not possible	

14 Alison and Kevin have three children, and Alison claims child benefit of £3,150 in 2026/27. Alison has trading income of £20,000. Kevin is employed on a salary of £79,000 and makes personal pension contributions of £400 per month.

Required

How much is the high income child benefit charge?

£ [ ]

15 Jenny, who lives in Scotland, has the following sources of income:

	£
Salary	80,000
Bank interest	10,000
Dividends	5,000

Required

Calculate Jenny's income tax liability for 2026/27.

3 Property income

Learning outcomes

2	**Calculate income tax and national insurance contributions**
2.6	**Calculate income from property** Learners need to understand: 2.6.1 that the cash basis is the default basis 2.6.2 the circumstances in which the accruals basis may be used 2.6.3 that income and expenses from all properties are pooled 2.6.4 how to identify allowable and disallowable expenses • wholly and exclusively • property available for letting • interest costs • replacement furniture • mileage allowances 2.6.5 when claiming the property allowance instead of expenses is appropriate 2.6.6 how losses on property may be relieved 2.6.7 rent a room relief: • gross rental income above the threshold • gross rental income below the threshold • impact on property income assessment • impact on losses • shared property
	Learners need to be able to: 2.6.8 calculate profit and losses from property: • cash basis • accruals basis • property allowance • rent a room relief • losses

Assessment context

In the AAT practice assessments, property income is tested as part of task 4 for 3 marks.

Qualification context

You will not see these areas again in your AAT qualification outside of this unit.

Business context

Property may be an additional source of income for some people. For others, it will be their livelihood. Anyone investing in property needs to understand the tax implications.

Chapter overview

Property income

Property income

- Pool all UK rents
- If receipts ≤ £150,000 use cash basis
- If receipts > £150,000 use accruals basis
- Relief for losses (carry forward v future property income)

Expenses

- Wholly & exclusively
- Interest costs not allowed (basic rate tax reducer instead)
- Replacement furniture (not original cost)
- Flat rate mileage allowance available

Rent a room relief

- Where let furnished accommodation as part of main residence
- £7,500
- Applies automatically where rent <£7,500
- Claim required where rent >£7,500

Property allowance

- If gross property income< £1,000 => automatically exempt (or elect to disapply)
- If gross property income> £1,000, expenses deducted instead, or elect for property allowance

Tax planning

- Transfer ownership of property to spouse/CP paying lower rate of tax

Introduction

Before we can calculate income tax payable for the tax year we need to calculate a taxpayer's total income. This consists of the grand total of their income from various sources. One source of income included in this total would be the income realised from letting out property. This chapter looks at how we calculate the taxable value of this income.

1 Property income

1.1 What is property income?

KEY TERM

Property income: All income derived from renting out land and/or buildings.

Landlord: The person letting out the property.

Tenant: The person letting the property.

1.2 Basis of assessment

KEY TERM

Cash basis: The default method of calculation of property income for an individual. Under the cash basis the property income received less the property expenses paid are taxable. Rather than using the accruals basis.

A landlord normally uses the cash basis to calculate property income for the current tax year (although they can opt to use accruals basis if they wish).

Under the cash basis, property income = receipts – allowable expenses paid. This is taxed as non-savings income.

The exception to this rule is if the landlord receives > £150,000 in rents in one tax year, in which case they will have to use the accruals basis. Unless told otherwise you should assume the landlord receives ≤ £150,000 and uses the cash basis.

Illustration 1: Cash basis

Susie bought a property on 6 September 2026. She began letting the property immediately for an annual rent of £36,000 payable in advance in 3-monthly instalments due on 6 September, 6 December, 6 March and 6 June. Susie's tenant makes all rental payments on time.

Rental income is taxed using the cash basis. This means the income which is received from the letting between 6 September 2026 and 5 April 2027 is taxed in 2026/27. During the tax year 2026/27 Susie receives £36,000 × $^3/_{12}$ ie £9,000 on 6 September 2026, 6 December 2026 and 6 March 2027 and is therefore taxed on £9,000 × 3 = £27,000.

1.3 Allowable deductions from property income

The landlord may deduct all incidental expenses, also calculated on a **cash basis,** ie only deducting those which have actually been paid. These must be revenue in nature, this means regular ongoing costs giving a short-term benefit, for example insurance. Capital costs are not deductible; these are one-off expenses that give a long-term benefit, for example installing central heating.

The following costs would be allowable if paid by the landlord:

- Advertising, accountancy and insurance
- Business rates and council tax
- Bad debts
- Management and agent's fees

- Fixed rate deductions for motor vehicles (see below)

1.3.1 Wholly and exclusively

In order to be allowable, expenses need to be incurred wholly and exclusively for the purposes of the property business. This rule applies whether using the cash or accruals basis. However, where an identifiable part of an expense is wholly and exclusively incurred for the purposes of the property business, that part can be deducted. For example, if a property is used partly as private accommodation, and partly let, the costs may be apportioned.

1.3.2 Property available for letting

Where a taxpayer incurs expenses for the purposes of a property business before the business starts, they may be able to claim a deduction once the letting begins where:

- expenses are incurred within seven years before the date the property business is started, and
- the expenses would have been allowed as a deduction had they been incurred after the property business started.

Capital allowances work in a similar way.

1.3.3 Interest costs

Where interest is paid in relation to a loan or mortgage used to purchase a residential property, the interest is not deductible when calculating the taxable property income. Instead, relief is obtained as a basic rate tax reducer when calculating the individual's income tax liability.

Illustration 2: Mortgage interest

Alice, who lives in England, lets out a residential property throughout 2026/27 for a gross rent of £2,000 per month. Her expenses are maintenance costs of £1,500 for the year, and mortgage interest of £6,000 for the year.

Her only other income is her salary of £40,000.

Required

Calculate Alice's income tax liability for 2026/27.

Solution

	Non savings £
Employment income	40,000
Property income (£2,000 × 12) - £1,500	22,500
Net income	62,500
Less: personal allowance	(12,570)
	49,930

37,700 × 20%	7,540
(49,930 - 37,700) × 40%	4,892
	12,432
Less: tax reducer for mortgage interest (£6,000 × 20%)	(1,200)
Tax liability	11,232

1.3.4 Replacement furniture

There is no relief available when the landlord first buys furniture and equipment for the property.

When these assets are replaced the landlord may claim the full cost of the replacement in the tax year in which the replacements were bought.

The following assets would qualify for replacement furniture relief:

- Movable furniture or furnishings, such as beds or sofas
- Televisions
- Fridges and freezers
- Carpets and floor coverings
- Curtains
- Linen
- Crockery or cutlery
- Beds and other furniture

If an asset is replaced with a better asset then only the cost of a similar replacement would be allowable.

Note that replacement of integral features such as bathrooms and central heating systems would be covered by the repair rules below.

1.3.5 Mileage allowances

Under both the cash and accruals basis, where a landlord incurs expenditure in relation to a vehicle that is used for the property business, they can choose to deduct either the actual motor expenses that relate to the business use (including capital allowances), or claim a flat rate expense based on the business mileage.

The flat rates (from April 2026) are:

Vehicles	First 10,000 business miles	Additional business miles
Cars or vans	55p	25p
Motorcycles	24p	24p

Once a claim for fixed rate mileage has been made, this same method must be used every year in relation to that vehicle.

1.3.6 Repair expenditure

Sometimes it is difficult to distinguish between revenue and capital expenses. A good example would be repair costs. If the costs constitute regular costs required to maintain the property in its current condition then these would be allowable, for example decorating and routine maintenance.

If the repair represents an improvement then it is not allowable, for example if the landlord installed a second bathroom in the property. Note also that if the building is bought in a dilapidated state then the initial costs incurred to make it usable again would also be capital and not allowed.

1.4 Accruals basis

To recap:

- a landlord in receipt of > £150,000 of rental income **cannot** use the cash basis and
- any landlord in receipt of ≤ £150,000 may opt out of the cash basis.

In this case they would instead use the accruals basis.

KEY TERM

Accruals basis: An alternate method of calculating property income whereby accrued property income less accrued allowable expenses give the property income to be taxed.

1.5 More than one property – pooling income and expenses

Income and expenses from different properties are pooled to give a single total for property income.

	£
Total property income received	X
Total allowable deductions paid	(X)
Profit/(loss)	X/(X)

Profits and losses on different properties are thus automatically offset.

Illustration 3: Property pooling calculation

Bahrat lets two properties in 2026/27.

Property 1 was bought in June 2026 and let unfurnished from 1 July 2026 at an annual rent of £18,000 per annum, payable monthly on the first of the month. Buildings insurance of £9,000 was paid for the year to 30 June 2027. This was payable on a quarterly basis from 1 July 2026 onwards. £1,200 was spent in June 2026 on advertising for tenants.

Property 2 became vacant on 5 April 2026. Bahrat then spent £7,500 on repairing the leaking roof in the property. The unfurnished property was let again with effect from 1 March 2027 for £24,000 per annum, payable monthly in advance. Buildings insurance of £1,800 was paid on 6 April 2026 for the year to 31 March 2027.

Bahrat's property income for 2026/27 is:

	£	£
Rental income – Property 1		
(10/12 × £18,000) (1 July to 1 Apr)		15,000
Rental income – Property 2		
(2/12 × £24,000)		4,000
Less: Buildings insurance		
Property 1 (1 July, Oct, Jan, Apr)	9,000	
Property 2	1,800	
Advertising for tenants	1,200	
Repairs	7,500	
		(19,500)

	£	£
Overall property loss		(500)

Pooling income and expenses on all let properties effectively allows a loss on one property to be set against income from other properties.

1.6 Losses

If the overall result is a profit it is taxable in the current year.

If the overall result is a loss, carry it forward to use against property income in the future. The loss can carry forward indefinitely until it is used.

Activity 1: Property income

Fiona owns a property that she lets furnished on a short-term basis. In the year ended 5 April 2027, she received rents of £8,400 and incurred the following expenses:

	£
Agent's commission	360
Redecoration	500
Insurance paid in advance on 1 January	
– year to 31 December 2026	400
– year to 31 December 2027	500
Repairs	1,200

Repairs include £300 to replace a broken window; the balance was to install a brand new window. There had been no window here before but Fiona decided the new window would offer views that would encourage future lettings.

She also replaced a single bed with a double bed. The double bed cost £400. An equivalent single bed would have cost £300.

Fiona has a property loss brought forward of £500.

Required

How much is assessable on her as property income in 2026/27?

£ [ ]

2 Property allowance

KEY TERM

Property allowance: The amount of property income that an individual can earn in a tax year without paying income tax.

If gross receipts from property ≤ £1,000

- this income is automatically exempt due to the property allowance, unless
- the taxpayer elects to disapply the property allowance in which case they calculate the property income as normal: ie receipts – allowable expenses paid

If gross receipts from property > £1,000

- the taxpayer calculates the property income as normal: ie receipts – allowable expenses unless
- they elect to apply the property allowance, in which case they calculate the property income as receipts – £1,000

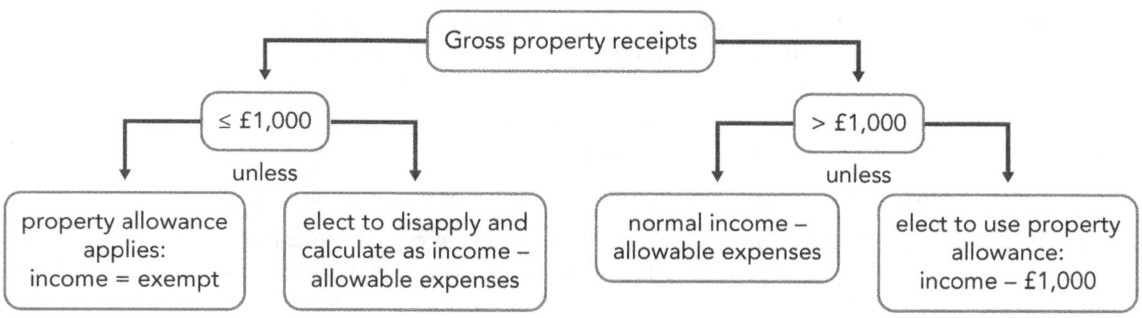

In either case the deadline for an election is the first anniversary of the 31 January following the tax year for which the election is being made.

Eg the deadline for an election for tax year 2026/27 is 31 January 2029.

Activity 2: Property allowance

Charlotte lets out her flat for £800 when she goes away on holiday and incurs expenses of:

(1) £200

(2) £900 due to extensive damage caused by the tenants

Thomas lets out his house when he is seconded to another office for a month. He receives £1,500 of income and incurs advertising and cleaning expenses of:

(1) £300

(2) £1,050

Required

Advise Charlotte and Thomas as to whether or not they should make an election and how much rental income they will be taxed on in each scenario.

3 Rent a room relief

KEY TERM

> **Rent a room scheme:** A UK Government scheme that allows individuals to earn an amount of tax-free income from letting furnished accommodation in their own home.

Where an individual lets out furnished accommodation in their only or main residence, for example a lodger, rent a room relief is available.

The rent a room limit is £7,500, or where the accommodation is let jointly, £3,750.

Where gross rents are less than £7,500, rent a room relief applies automatically and the rental income is exempt from tax. Alternatively, if allowable expenses would exceed rents, rent a room relief can be disapplied so that an allowable loss crystallises.

Where gross rents exceed £7,500, a claim needs to be made for rent a room relief to apply. This would only be beneficial where allowable expenses are less than £7,500.

4 Tax planning

Property income is **non-savings** income and is taxed depending on the taxpayer's level of income.

Spouses or civil partners or couples cohabiting or friends or relatives may own property either jointly or individually. One party may be paying tax at a higher rate than the other. If this is the case it makes sense to have the property owned by the taxpayer who is paying tax at the lower rate as they will then receive the income and it will be taxed at a lower rate reducing the overall tax liability.

One party may therefore need to transfer property to another.

If one of the parties has no income then the property should be transferred to them so they can offset their personal allowance against the income. This will enable them to use a personal allowance that would otherwise have been wasted.

Assets including cash can be transferred between spouses and civil partners without causing inheritance tax or capital gains tax problems. If the parties are not married or in a civil partnership it may cause tax issues. For the planning to be effective the asset or cash to buy an asset must be transferred with 'no strings attached', the spouse receiving the asset has total control over it and makes no promises to return the asset at a later date or pay the income generated to the other party. Clearly you must trust the other party before following this course of action!

HMRC will disregard transactions which appear to be artificial and undertaken purely for a tax advantage so for the planning to work there must be some other purpose for the transaction, for example a wife with a husband who is not working could gift a property to him so that he has a source of income of his own and some independence.

Chapter summary

- Property income is all income derived from letting out land and buildings.
- It is calculated on a cash basis by default for a tax year and taxed as non-savings income.
- The accruals basis must be used by taxpayers with rental income exceeding £150,000. A claim may be made for taxpayers with income below £150,000 to use the accruals basis.
- Income and expenses on different properties are pooled to give a grand total. A net positive result will be taxable. A net negative result is a loss that may be carried forward and offset against property income in the future.
- Expenditure is allowable if it is incurred wholly and exclusively for the purposes of the property business.
- Interest costs, such as mortgage interest, are not allowable as a deduction from the gross property income. Instead, relief is given as a basic rate tax reducer.
- Where a landlord first purchases furniture for a property, no relief is available. However, relief is available for the cost of replacement furniture.
- Where motor expenses are incurred relating to the property business, the individual may either claim the actual expenses that relate to the business, or alternatively a fixed rate mileage deduction.
- The property allowance is £1,000. Where gross rents are less than £1,000, the allowance exempts the income. Alternatively, the allowance can be disapplied and allowable expenses deducted instead. Where gross rents are more than £1,000, the default position is that the property allowance does not apply and allowable expenses are deducted. However, where allowable expenses are less than £1,000, a claim may be made to use the property allowance instead.
- The rent a room relief limit is £7,500. It is available where an individual lets out a furnished room in their main residence.
- Couples should ensure properties are owned by the spouse/civil partner who is paying tax at a lower rate or has an unused personal allowance.

Activity answers

Activity 1: Property income

£ 5,940

Working

Workings (not provided in the assessment)

	£
Rents	8,400
Less expenses commission	(360)
Replacement cost of equivalent single bed	(300)
Redecoration	(500)
Insurance (payment made on 1 January 2027)	(500)
Repairs to existing window	(300)
Property income	6,440
Less property losses brought forward	(500)
	5,940

Activity 2: Property allowance

	Assessable income	Make election (Y/N)
Charlotte		
	Nil (Income ≤ £1,000)	N
	£100 loss (Income ≤ £1,000 but better off making election and deducting expenses)	Y
Thomas		
	£500 (better to make election and deduct property allowance £1,500 – £1,000)	Y
	£450 (better to ignore property allowance and deduct expenses as normal)	N

Test your learning

1 David buys a property for letting on 1 August 2026 and grants a tenancy to Ethel from 1 December 2026 at £3,600 per annum, payable quarterly in advance.

Required

The rental income taxable in 2026/27 is:

£ [ ]

2 John pays buildings insurance premiums for 12 months in advance on 1 October each year to cover all his rental properties. His gross rental income from all of his properties is £50,000. He pays £4,800 in 2025 and £5,200 in 2026.

Required

What amount for building insurance would be allowed against his rental income for 2026/27?

£ [ ]

3 Harry owns a property which he lets for the first time on 1 July 2026 at a rent of £4,000 per annum, payable monthly in advance.

The first tenants left on 28 February 2027 and the property was re-let to new tenants on 4 April 2027 at a rent of £5,000 per annum, payable yearly in advance.

Harry's allowable expenditure was £1,000 in 2026/27.

Required

What is his taxable rental income for 2026/27?

£ [ ]

4 Ben and Polly are married and live in England. Polly earns a salary of £200,000 a year meaning she pays tax at 45%, Ben has trading income of £20,000 meaning he pays tax at 20%. They are planning to buy an investment property which they will let out for £12,000 a year.

Required

To minimise their tax liability the property should be [▼]

Picklist

- Held in Ben's name
- Held in Polly's name
- Held in trust
- Held jointly by Ben and Polly

5 **Property losses may be:**

	✓
Carried back one year and offset against property income only	
Offset against net income in the current year	
Carried forward for one year only and offset against property income	
Carried forward indefinitely and offset against property income only	

6 Nigel lets out the spare room in his London home to a lodger for a rent of £8,000 per year. His allowable expenses in relation to the letting are £3,000. Nigel does not make any elections in relation to the rental income.

Required

What is the taxable rental income for the year?

	✓
£8,000	
£5,000	
£500	
Nil	

7 Liv had the following income and expenses in relation to a rental property for 2026/27.

	£
Rental income	50,000
Mortgage interest	14,500
Motor expenses (N1)	3,000
New sofas	1,500
Replacement curtains	750
Brought forward property loss	600

(N1) the motor expenses relate to the use of Liv's car. Liv drove 12,000 miles for business purposes in the year. £3,000 represents the proportion of the actual costs incurred relating to these journeys. Liv elected to use flat rate expenses where possible.

Required

What is Liv's taxable property income for 2026/27?

4 Employment income

Learning outcomes

2.4	Calculate income from employment
	Learners need to understand 2.4.1 the basis of assessment: • receipts basis • rules for directors
	2.4.2 exempt benefits: • beneficial loans • bicycles/safety equipment • counselling • medical/eye tests • mileage payments at the approved mileage rate • mobile phone • overnight expense allowance • parking • pension contributions • pool cars • relocation • staff entertaining • staff suggestion schemes • training • transport to work • trivial benefits • workplace childcare • workplace electric vehicle charging points • workplace meals • working from home • workplace sporting/recreational facilities
	2.4.3 assessable benefits general rules: • cost to employer • employee contributions • time apportionment

	2.4.4 assessable benefits special rules:
	• company cars
	• private fuel
	• vans
	• mileage payments above the approved mileage rate
	• beneficial loans
	  - average
	  - strict

	2.4.5 allowable deductions: • wholly exclusively and necessarily in performance of duties • pension contributions • charity donations • relevant professional fees and subscriptions • travel expenses • mileage payments below the approved mileage rate
	Learners need to be able to: 2.4.6 calculate: • salary • bonus • benefits • allowable deductions • employment income
3.1	Employed v self-employed
	Learners need to understand: 3.1.1 the importance of identifying status
	3.1.2 the factors used to determine status: • degree of control • mutual obligations • provision of equipment • degree of financial risk/ability to profit • ability to provide a substitute • level of integration • the employment rights provided.
	Learners need to be able to: 3.1.3 identify: • factors indicating employment • factors indicating self-employment • a valid conclusion on employment or self-employment • the consequences of the conclusion

Assessment context

Benefits are highly examinable. Make sure you can calculate and explain them.

In AAT's practice assessments, task 3 is about income and national insurance contributions from employment for 14 marks. The questions on employment income are a mixture of short 1 - 2 mark multiple choice, true/false, fill in the blank, select from a drop down list style questions, and included:

- identifying taxable and exempt benefits,
- calculating the taxable value of several benefits,
- Identifying allowable deductions
- Identifying the basis of assessment of salary and bonus
- Identifying which benefits would generate greater taxable income
- Identifying which benefit is not taxable

Qualification context

You will not see the information in this chapter outside of this unit.

Business context

Calculation of employment income will often form a large part of the preparation of income tax returns, which is one of the main tasks a personal tax adviser will complete.

Chapter overview

Employment income

Employment income

Types
- Salaries
- Bonuses
- Benefits

Basis
- Normal rules
  Earlier of
  - Earned
  - Received
- Rules for directors
  Earlier of
  - Payment
  - Entitlement
  - Credited in accounts
  - AP end if determined before AP end
  - Date determined if after AP end

Admin
- PAYE

Employment versus self-employment
- Control?
- Have to accept work?
- Provide further work?
- Provide equipment?
- Hire helpers?
- Risk?
- Responsibility?
- Opportunity to profit?
- Work when choose?
- Wording?

Taxable Benefits

Vans and fuel
- £4,170 charge
- £798 fuel benefit
- Nil benefit for zero emission vans

Cars and fuel
- List price × CO2%
- Dependent on electric range for electric/hybrids
- Max 37%
- Fuel £29,200

Loans
- (Loan × official rate) – interest paid
- Average loan or actual loan
- Exempt if ≤ £10,000
- Taxed on amounts written off

Exempt
- Job-related accommodation
- Canteen
- Removal exp (£8,000)
- Car parking
- Pool cars
- Nurseries
- Employer pension contributions
- Sports facilities
- Counselling on redundancy
- Staff parties (max £150)
- Incidental expenses (£5/£10)
- Mileage allowance
- Mobile phones
- £6/week home working
- Bus subsidies
- Buses
- Bicycles
- Long service awards
- Staff suggestion schemes
- Training

Introduction

Before we can calculate the income tax that an individual will pay we have to calculate their total income.

Their total income will be made up of income from different sources; for example, a person renting out property will have **property income**, while a person who is employed will have **employment income**.

Different types of income are calculated in different ways.

In this chapter we are going to look at how to calculate employment income.

Note that a great deal of the information in this chapter is provided in the assessment in the tax reference material.

1 Employment income

KEY TERM

Employment income: This is the type of income received by someone who holds an office or employment. It is calculated using the detailed rules we will be considering in this chapter.

It is usually clear whether someone is employed or self-employed. If you work for the same person every working day for a regular salary then you are employed. If you are, say, a plumber who performs jobs for different people, then you are probably self-employed.

However, in certain circumstances it is not obvious whether a taxpayer is an employee or self-employed. It is important to classify the relationship correctly otherwise the wrong tax rules would be applied.

HMRC would consider whether the taxpayer has a **contract of service** or **a contract for services**.

A contract of service means the taxpayer works for the other party over a period of time, performing different tasks as they are assigned to them. The relationship is ongoing. This makes them employed.

A contract for services means the taxpayer has agreed to perform a specific task or tasks. Once these tasks have been completed the relationship is at an end. This makes them self-employed.

If it is not clear whether we have a contract of service or contract for services then HMRC would consider the following:

(a) The degree of control exercised over the person doing the work – control implies an employment relationship

(b) Whether they must accept further work – obligation implies employment

(c) Whether the other party must provide further work – obligation implies employment

(d) Whether they provide their own equipment – using someone else's equipment implies an employment relationship

(e) Whether they hire their own helpers or a substitute – hiring their own helpers or a substitute suggests autonomy meaning they are self-employed

(f) What degree of financial risk they take – self-employment is more risky than employment

(g) Whether they can profit from sound management – self-employed people will benefit directly from good decisions they make

(h) The level of integration that they have in the organisation - the more integrated they are, the more likely they are to be deemed to be an employee

(i) The employment rights provided - employment rights, for example sick pay, would indicate employment.

Tutorial note. Items 2 and 3 in the list above are often referred to as mutual obligations - the mutual obligation of the employer to provide work and the employee to accept it.

1.1 Consequences of the conclusion

It is important to correctly classify the worker as employed or self-employed because the tax treatment of the two alternatives is different. For example:

(a) Income tax and Class 1 national insurance contributions are collected at source by the employer for employees, whereas self-employed individuals pay income tax and Class 4 national insurance contributions via self-assessment.

(b) Class 1 NIC rates are higher than Class 4 NICs.

(c) If the individual is deemed to be an employee, then the employer should pay Class 1 national insurance contributions.

(d) Expenses that are allowable as a deduction for people who are self-employed may not be allowed as a deduction for employees (employees have a 'wholly, exclusively and necessarily' test)

(e) Self-employed individuals may need to register for VAT depending upon the level of their turnover, but employment income is not taxable for VAT.

(f) Self-employed individuals do not have the same legal employment rights as employees, for example statutory sick pay, and holiday pay.

The following sections in this chapter explain the taxation of employees. If the conclusion of the above tests is that the individual is self-employed, the taxation of sole traders is covered in chapters five to nine.

2 Taxation of employment income

2.1 Types of income

A taxpayer will be taxed on any amounts deriving from an office or employment performed wholly or partly in the UK including:

- Salaries, bonuses and commissions
- Non-cash benefits, for example a company car

2.2 Basis of assessment

These rules identify the tax year that income is taxed in. There are normal rules and additional rules that apply to directors only.

2.2.1 Normal rules

KEY TERM

Receipts basis: The standard method for taxing employment income, meaning earnings are taxed in the tax year that they are received, not when earned.

A taxpayer will be assessed on amounts received in the current tax year (6 April 2026 - 5 April 2027).

Earnings are treated as received at the earlier of:

- The time when payment is made
- The time when a person becomes entitled to payment of the earnings

Illustration 1: Basis of assessment

Joy is employed by R plc. She is entitled to the payment of a bonus of £2,000 on 31 March 2027, although she does not receive it until 25 April 2027.

Joy will be taxed on the bonus in 2026/27 because she is entitled to payment on 31 March 2027.

If the bonus payment to Joy was calculated based on the results of R plc for 31 March 2027 but she was not entitled to it at that date, she would be taxed on receipt of the bonus in 2027/28, or on the date she actually becomes entitled to it, if earlier.

Activity 1: Basis of assessment

Rudolph is an employee of Mabuse Ltd. He earns a salary of £28,000 (paid monthly on the last working day of each month) but on 1 November 2026 he is promoted and his salary increases to £35,000. The company also pays him a bonus relating to the year ended 31 March 2026 of £3,000 on 15 May 2026. The bonus for the year ended 31 March 2027 of £4,000 is paid on 13 May 2027.

Required

(a) What is Rudolph's taxable salary for 2026/27?

£ ______

(b) What is Rudolph's taxable bonus for 2026/27?

£ ______

2.2.2 Rules for directors

Special rules apply to company directors. Their earnings are treated as being received on the earliest of:

- The time when payment is made.
- The time when a person becomes entitled to payment of the earnings.
- The time when the amount is credited in the company's accounting records.
- The end of the company's period of account (if the amount has been determined by then).
- The time the amount is determined (if after the end of the company's period of account).

2.3 Deduction of tax by employers

Employers have an obligation to deduct income tax and employee Class 1 NIC from payments they make to their employees under the **Pay As You Earn (PAYE) system**. Employees therefore receive their salary net of tax.

Most employees will have the correct amount of tax deducted by their employers so there will be no need for them to complete a tax return or make further payments of tax.

In your assessment salaries will be quoted gross. This means you are given the figure before tax and NIC has been deducted. You will then be provided with information as to the amount of income tax deducted under PAYE.

3 Taxable benefits

KEY TERM

> **Assessable benefits:** Non-cash benefits provided to employees such as company cars or private medical insurance.

Certain perks provided by employers represent benefits taxable on employees. The rules on these are set out in legislation called the benefits code.

There are specific rules applying to certain benefits, for example cars. If there is no specific rule then employees will be taxed on the **cost to the employer** of providing the benefit.

As a general rule:

- There is no taxable benefit if there is no private benefit to the employee (eg no benefit for the use of a projector in class by a BPP tutor)
- Time-apportion the benefit if it is not available for the whole tax year
- Deduct any contributions made by the employee from the benefit

3.1 Cars

A car provided by the employer that is available for private use gives rise to a benefit. If fuel is provided for private motoring there will be an additional benefit.

Note that HMRC considers commuting to work and back as private use so in practice if an employee uses a car belonging to their employer they will normally be taxed on this as a benefit. The exception to this would be a **pool car** (see later).

3.1.1 Car benefit

The starting point for calculating a car benefit is the list price of the car. A percentage of that list price is the taxable benefit.

The price of the car is calculated as follows:

- List price when new*, plus optional extras costing at least £100
- Deduct capital contributions made by employee (capped at £5,000)

* Ignore any discounts that have been obtained; it is the published list price which is relevant.

The percentage used varies, depending on the CO_2 emissions or the electric range for hybrid cars.

Assessment focus point

CO_2 g/km	Electric range (miles)	Electric/hybrid	All engines
Nil		4%	
1 to 50	130 or more	4%	
1 to 50	70 - 129	7%	
1 to 50	40 - 69	10%	
1 to 50	30- 39	14%	

CO_2 g/km	Electric range (miles)	Electric/hybrid	All engines
1 to 50	Less than 30	16%	
51 to 54			17%
55 to 59			18%
60 to 64			19%
65 to 69			20%
70 to 74			21%
75 or more			Calculation: Minimum 21% Maximum 37%

Note that the above percentages will be provided to you in your tax tables.

Formula provided

For cars that emit CO_2 of 75g/km or more, the taxable benefit percentage starts at 21% and increases by 1% for every 5 g/km (rounded down to the nearest multiple of 5) by which CO_2 emissions exceed 75 g/km, up to a maximum of 37%.

Illustration 2: Car benefit percentage

Working for a car with CO_2 emissions > 74 g/km

The relevant CO_2 percentage for a car with 168 g/km CO_2 emissions is calculated as follows:

Round down to 165

165 – 75 = 90

Divided by 5 = 18

Add basic 21 + 18 = 39% (this will be capped at 37%)

The maximum car benefit percentage cannot exceed 37%.

The benefit is apportioned if the car is not available for the whole year or cannot be used for a period of at least 30 days (for example if being repaired).

The benefit is reduced by any payment the user must make for the private use of the car (as distinct from a one-off capital contribution to the cost of the car which would be deducted from the price before applying the percentage).

Pool cars are exempt. A car is a pool car if all the following conditions are satisfied:

- It is used by more than one employee/director and not ordinarily used by one of them to the exclusion of others.
- Any private use is incidental to business use.
- Not normally kept overnight at or near the residence of an employee.

3.1.2 Fuel benefit

Where fuel is provided for private miles (including commuting) there is a further benefit in addition to the car benefit.

The taxable benefit is a percentage of a base figure. The base figure for 2026/27 is £29,200 (see tax tables).

The percentage is the same percentage as is used to calculate the car benefit.

> **Assessment focus point**
>
> Exceptionally there is no reduction in benefit for partial contributions made by the employee – don't get caught out by this! There is always a benefit unless the employee pays for all private fuel.

There is no benefit if the employee pays for all private fuel.

Illustration 3: Car and fuel benefit

An employee was provided with a new car costing £15,000 (the list price) on 6 June 2026. During 2026/27, the employer spent £900 on insurance, repairs and the vehicle licence. The firm paid for all fuel (£2,300) without reimbursement. The employee was required to pay the firm £25 per month for the private use of the car. The car has CO_2 emissions of 97 g/km.

The total taxable benefit for 2026/27 in respect of the car and fuel is calculated as follows:

	£
List price £15,000 × 25% (21% + (95 – 75)/5)	3,750
£3,750 × (10/12)	3,125
Less contribution (10 × £25)	(250)
	2,875
Fuel benefit £29,200 × 25% × (10/12)	6,083
Total taxable benefit	8,958

If the contribution of £25 per month had been towards the fuel, the contribution would not be deducted, making the benefit assessable £250 greater. Conversely, if the cost of private fuel was fully reimbursed by the employee, then there would have been no fuel benefit at all.

Activity 2: Car and fuel benefit

Damon who works for Stuart Ltd earns £52,500 (PAYE £21,000) and has use of a company car, a Jaguar S-Type 2.5. The CO_2 emissions rate is 127 g/km. The car has a list price of £60,000 but the employer negotiated a discount and bought it for £57,000. The company fitted accessories (CD player and child safety seat) at a cost of £900.

Damon is required to pay £100 per month towards the running costs of the car (excluding fuel). The company meets all Damon's fuel costs in 2026/27 which amounted to £3,500.

Required

(a) What is Damon's taxable benefit for 2026/27?

£ [ ]

(b) **What is the benefit if Damon left the company on 1 January 2027 and returned the car on that date?**

3.2 Vans

There is a £4,170 charge when vans are available to employees for private use.

> **Assessment focus point**
>
> Note that, unlike company cars, a home to work journey does not qualify as private use for a van.

If the van has CO_2 emissions of 0, then the benefit is nil.

There is an additional £798 charge if fuel is made available for private use.

3.3 Mileage payments

Where an employee uses their own vehicle for work purposes, and receives a mileage payment from their employer, the amount received is taxable, but a deduction is allowed based on HMRC's approved mileage rate. Where the amount received is more than the approved amount, the excess is taxable. Where the amount received is less than the approved amount, the shortfall is allowed as a deduction from their other employment income.

HMRC's approved rates are as follows:

Cars or vans	First 10,000 miles	55p per mile
	Over 10,000 miles	25p per mile
Additional passengers in cars or vans		5p per mile per passenger
Motorcycles		24p per mile
Bicycles		20p per mile

Illustration 4: Statutory mileage

Owen drives 14,000 business miles in the tax year using his own car.

	£
Statutory limit: 10,000 × 55p	5,500
4,000 × 25p	1,000
	6,500

Required

You are required to calculate the taxable benefit/allowable deduction assuming:

(a) He is reimbursed 55p a mile

(b) He is reimbursed 25p a mile

Solution

(a)

	£
Amount received (14,000 × 55p)	7,700
Less statutory limit	(6,500)
Taxable benefit	1,200

(b)

	£
Amount received (14,000 × 25p)	3,500
Less statutory limit	(6,500)
Allowable deduction	(3,000)

Activity 3: Statutory mileage

Jen drives 15,000 miles in the tax year.

(a) Choose the correct option and insert the numerical value.

If Jen's employer pays her 30p per mile she [▼] £ [ ]

Picklist

- Is taxed on
- May deduct

(b) Choose the correct option and insert the numerical value.

If Jen's employer pays her 50p per mile she [▼] £ [ ]

Picklist

- Is taxed on

- May deduct

3.4 Beneficial loans

There is a benefit when an employer gives an employee an interest-free loan or when the employer charges less than a commercial interest rate.

The benefit is the difference between the interest that should have been charged, using the official rate of interest of 3.75% for tax year 2026/27 (given in the exam), and the interest paid by the employee.

Formula to learn

Where the size of the loan has changed during the year, the interest is calculated on either of the following:

- The average loan outstanding in the year
- The loan outstanding on a month by month basis ('strict method')

The average method is usually used but either the taxpayer or HMRC can elect to use the month by month 'strict' calculation.

There is no benefit if the total of all loans made to the employee in the year is £10,000 or less. If this limit is broken then all loans are taxed, not just the excess over £10,000.

An employee will always be taxed on the value of a loan written off by the employer even if the loan was below the £10,000 limit.

Illustration 5: Beneficial loan

At 6 April 2026, a low interest loan of £30,000 was outstanding to a director, who repaid £20,000 on 6 January 2027. The remaining balance of £10,000 was outstanding at 5 April 2027. Interest paid during the year was £250.

The benefit under both methods for 2026/27, assuming that the official rate of interest was 3.75% throughout 2026/27, is calculated as follows:

Average method

	£
3.75% × (30,000 + 10,000) ÷ 2	750
Less interest paid	(250)
Taxable benefit	500

Strict method

	£
£30,000 × $^{9}/_{12}$ × 3.75%	844
(6 April 2026 – 6 January 2027)	
£10,000 × $^{3}/_{12}$ × 3.75%	94
(7 January 2027 – 5 April 2027)	
	938
Less interest paid	(250)
Taxable benefit	688

Therefore, the taxable benefit will be £500.

Activity 4: Beneficial loan

At 6 April 2026, a taxable cheap loan of £40,000 was outstanding to an employee earning £12,000 a year, who repaid £25,000 on 7 July 2026. The remaining balance of £15,000 was outstanding at 5 April 2027. Interest paid during the year was £250.

Assume the official rate of interest was 3.75%.

Required

Complete the following sentences:

The benefit calculated under the average method is £ ______

The benefit calculated under the strict method is £ ______

The taxpayer would be taxed on £ ______

4 Exempt benefits

KEY TERM

> **Exempt benefits:** Employer-provided benefits that employees do not pay tax on because HMRC grants an exemption.

The following benefits are not taxable. Much of this information is provided in the reference material in the assessment.

(a) Canteen offering free or discounted food available to all staff. A benefit would arise if the canteen was only available to selected staff members. The benefit would be the cost to the company net of payments made by the employee.

(b) Qualifying relocation expenses up to £8,000 when the employee has to move house because of their job. Qualifying costs include legal and removal costs as well as purchasing replacement goods such as curtains and carpets. Excess payments over the £8,000 would be taxable.

(c) Car parking spaces near place of work.

(d) Use of pool cars.

(e) Workplace nurseries (crèches) - The crèche must be operated by the employer.

(f) Contributions by an employer into an approved pension scheme.

(g) Sport and recreational facilities available generally for the staff. These must be provided directly by the employer. If the employer pays for facilities provided by an external supplier then this will create a taxable benefit.

(h) Outplacement counselling services to employees made redundant who have been employed full time for at least two years. The services can include counselling to help adjust to the loss of the job and to help in finding other work.

(i) Annual staff events up to a maximum of £150 per head. If this limit is exceeded then the full cost is taxable.

(j) Incidental expense of £5 per night if working away from home (telephone calls, laundry etc). The limit is £10 if working abroad. These amounts may be aggregated if working away a number of days; for example, if working away for three days then the limit for the period would be £15. If this limit is exceeded, then the whole amount is taxable.

(k) Mileage allowances at the approved mileage rate (see above).

(l) Mobile phones – these are exempt if a single phone is provided. A benefit would apply to additional phones provided to the employee.

(m) Subsidies paid to bus services used by employees for commuting.

(n) Any employer-reimbursed costs of home working

(o) Provision of buses for nine or more employees for commuting.

(p) Provision of bicycles and cycling safety equipment for commuting.

(q) Awards under staff suggestion schemes up to £5,000.

(r) Work-related training.

(s) Trivial benefits - where the cost to the employer of providing the benefit does not exceed £50. If it exceeds £50, the full amount will be taxable. There is a maximum of £300 per year for directors.

(t) Loans to employees where the aggregate value of all loans outstanding throughout the year is £10,000 or less.

(u) Bicycles and associated safety equipment provided it is mainly used for commuting to work.

(v) Workplace electric vehicle charging points

(w) One medical check up per year

5 Allowable deductions

KEY TERM

Allowable deductions (from employment income): Expenses that employees can deduct from their taxable employment income. They must be incurred wholly, exclusively, and necessarily in the performance of their duties.

Certain expenses may be deducted from employment income before tax is applied.

Assessment focus point

The general rule for allowable deductions states that expenses must be incurred '**wholly, exclusively and necessarily**' (HMRC, 2014) in the performance of duties. This means that if the employee could perform their duties without incurring the expense then it is not deductible as it is not strictly necessary.

The following are specific allowable deductions:

- Fees and subscriptions to relevant professional bodies.
- Travelling and other expenses incurred in the performance of duties.
- Contributions to an approved occupational pension scheme; an occupational scheme is one provided by the employer.
- Donations to charity under payroll deduction scheme.
- Mileage payments received below the approved mileage rate (see above).

5.1 Expenses

Employees will incur expenditure performing their job. They may or may not be reimbursed by their employer for these expenses. Certain business expenses are allowable:

- Wholly, exclusively and necessarily incurred in the performance of the duties of the employment;
- Qualifying travel expenses; or
- Professional fees and subscriptions.

The treatment of these expenses depends upon whether the employee is reimbursed for the expenditure by their employer or not.

5.1.1 Employee incurs expenditure without reimbursement

If the employee bears the cost of the expense themselves without reimbursement from their employer then they would simply deduct the expense from their employment income.

Illustration 6: Expenses not reimbursed

Paul earns a salary of £35,000 a year. He has to pay his £500 subscription to the Chartered Institute of Taxation. Paul's employer does not reimburse him for this expense.

Paul's employment income calculation would be as follows:

	£
Salary	35,000
Less expenses	(500)

	£
Employment income	34,500

5.1.2 Employee incurs expenditure and is reimbursed by employer, or employer pays directly

The payment or reimbursement of expenses is exempt (ie no need to include in earnings) if they are fully allowable and the employee would therefore otherwise be able to claim a deduction.

Illustration 7: Reimbursed expenses

Paul earns a salary of £35,000 a year. His employer reimburses him for his £500 subscription to the Chartered Institute of Taxation.

The subscription is exempt income as it is a reimbursed allowable expense, so it is not included in the calculations of earnings.

	£
Salary	35,000
Reimbursed expenses (exempt)	nil
Employment income	35,000

5.1.3 Expenses with a private and business element

Strictly, if an expense has a 'private' and 'business' component, then it is not exclusively used in the duties of employment and will not be allowed (for example if a phone is used for work purposes and privately, then no deduction can be claimed for the line rental, although the cost of the business calls would be allowed).

In practice, HMRC will allow taxpayers to apportion costs where there is a business and a private element. The business use will be an allowable expense, and deductible for the employee on their tax return. If the allowable element is clearly identifiable, the exemption will apply.

5.1.4 Travel expenses

Travelling expenses are deductible; if the employer reimburses this is an exempt benefit. As noted above, if expenses are not reimbursed then the taxpayer may deduct the expense.

Only business travelling is allowable. Normal commuting from home to office is not included.

An exception is where an employee is seconded to a **temporary workplace** for less than 24 months; here commuting from home is allowable.

KEY TERM

Temporary workplace: A workplace at which the employee expects to be for no more than 24 months.

5.2 Contributing to a pension

An employee may save tax by paying into a pension.

We saw, in chapter 2, how individuals obtained relief for payments into a **personal** pension scheme (by extending the tax bands by the grossed up personal pension contribution).

Individuals obtain relief for **occupational** pension scheme contributions by way of an allowable deduction from their employment income.

5.2.1 Maximum contributions

Formula to learn

The maximum tax relief available for pension contributions each year is the higher of:

- £3,600
- Earnings for the year

Additional contributions are permitted but no tax relief will be available on these.

5.2.2 Tax relief

Effectively the taxpayer's income is being reduced by the payment into the pension scheme so they are no longer paying tax on the top level of their income. They therefore save the tax they would have paid on this income. This saving will be at their applicable tax rates depending on their level of income. For a taxpayer resident in England, a 20% taxpayer saves tax of 20p for every £1.00 contribution, a 40% taxpayer saves tax at 40p for every £1.00, while a 45% taxpayer would save 45p for every £1.00.

The method of relief is different depending on the type of pension scheme.

KEY TERM

Personal pension scheme: is a scheme organised by the taxpayer. Contributions are made net of basic rate tax (20%). As we saw in Chapter 2 - Calculation of Income Tax, additional relief is available for higher and additional rate taxpayers by **extending the basic and higher rate bands**.

Occupational pension scheme: is a scheme provided by an employer. Contributions are deducted directly from earnings. PAYE is then applied to just the remaining income. This is called a **net pay arrangement**.

Occupational pension contributions: Contributions to a workplace pension scheme.

Net pay arrangements: Where an employer deducts an employee's occupational pension contributions from the employee's earnings before they deduct income tax.

5.2.3 Employer contributions

An employer may also contribute to either an occupational scheme or a personal scheme on behalf of the employee.

Employer contributions are not taxable benefits on the employee.

There is no limit on the amount of contributions an employer can make.

5.3 Donations to charity

Employees may request that their employer pays some of their salary to an approved charity of their choice.

The donation is deducted from gross salary before PAYE is applied. It therefore saves the taxpayer tax at their highest marginal rate of tax.

This is sometimes called a 'Payroll deduction scheme' or '**Give-As-You-Earn**' (**GAYE)**.

KEY TERM

Payroll deduction scheme: Set up by an employer to enable employees to make tax-deductible donations to charity.

Chapter summary

- It is important to distinguish between income from employment and self-employment. The basic question is whether the person is employed under a contract of service, or performs services under a contract for services.
- An employee's earnings comprise wages or salary and bonuses and benefits.
- Money earnings are received on the earlier of the time payment is made and when the employee becomes entitled to payment. There are special rules for directors.
- The taxable benefit on a car is a percentage of the car's list price. This varies with carbon dioxide emissions/electric range and fuel type. There is an additional benefit if fuel is provided.
- The private use of a pool car is an exempt benefit.
- There is a taxable benefit for private use of a van (but home to work travel is not treated as private use) plus a further benefit if private fuel is provided.
- Employer loans written off give rise to a taxable benefit. For loans there is a benefit equal to the excess of official rate of interest over interest actually charged.
- There are certain exempt benefits which are not taxable for employees.
- A deduction is given to employees for using their own vehicle for business travel if any mileage allowance paid is less than the statutory rates. Any excess is taxable.
- Employees are generally allowed a deduction for travel costs incurred in the performance of their duties, or incurred in travelling to and from home to a temporary workplace. Temporary is taken to be not exceeding 24 months.
- Occupational pension schemes are employer-run schemes. No taxable benefit arises in respect of employer contributions made to pension schemes.
- Employee contributions to an occupational pension scheme are deducted from the employee's taxable earnings before tax is applied.
- Individuals can make pension contributions up to the higher of:
  - The basic limit (£3,600 – 2026/27)
  - Earnings for the year
- Employees can make charitable donations under an employer's payroll deduction scheme. Such payments are deductible in arriving at taxable earnings.
- For other employment-related expenses to be deductible, such expenses must be 'wholly, exclusively and necessarily' (HMRC, 2014) incurred 'in the performance of' the employee's duties.

Activity answers

Activity 1: Basis of assessment

(a) £ 30,916

(b) £ 3,000

Working

	£
Salary:	
6 April 2026 to 31 October 2026 – $^{7}/_{12}$ × 28,000	16,333
1 November 2026 to 5 April 2027 – $^{5}/_{12}$ × 35,000	14,583
Total salary	30,916
Bonus received between 6 April 2026 and 5 April 2027	3,000

Activity 2: Car and fuel benefit

(a) £ 26,731

Workings

	£
List price + accessories (60,000 + 900)	60,900
31% (W) × £60,900	18,879
Less employee contributions (12 × £100)	(1,200)
Car benefit	17,679
Plus fuel benefit (£29,200 × 31%)	9,052
Total benefit	26,731

(W)		Round down to 125	
		Relevant emissions percentage:	
	125 – 75	=	50
	Divide by 5	=	10
		Add basic	21
			31%

(b) £20,048

Working

Workings (not provided in the CBT)

	£
31% × £60,900 × $^{9}/_{12}$	14,159
Less employee contributions (9 × £100)	(900)
Car benefit	13,259
Add fuel benefit (£29,200 × 31% × $^{9}/_{12}$)	6,789
Total benefit	20,048
Alternatively, £26,731 (the benefit figure from part a) × $^{9}/_{12}$	20,048

Activity 3: Statutory mileage

(a) If Jen's employer pays her 30p per mile she | may deduct | £ 2,250

Working

Mileage calculation

Mileage calculation			£
Receives	15,000 × 0.30		4,500
Approved HMRC rates	10,000 × 0.55	5,500	
	5,000 × 0.25	1,250	(6,750)
Deductible			(2,250)

(b) If Jen's employer pays her 50p per mile she | is taxed on | £ 750

Working

Mileage calculation

Mileage calculation		£
Receives	15,000 × 0.50	7,500
Approved HMRC rates (as above)		(6,750)
Taxable		750

Activity 4: Beneficial loan

The benefit calculated under the average method is £ | 781 |

The benefit calculated under the strict method is £ | 547 |

The taxpayer would be taxed on £ | 547 |

Working

Average method	£
3.75% × (40,000 + 15,000) ÷ 2	1,031
Less interest paid	(250)
Benefit	781

Alternative method (strict method)	£
£40,000 × $^{3}/_{12}$ (6 April – 6 July) × 3.75%	375
£15,000 × $^{9}/_{12}$ (7 July – 5 April) × 3.75%	422
	797
Less interest paid	(250)
Benefit	547

The taxpayer would opt for the strict method.

Test your learning

1 **Fill in the missing words.**

Someone is regarded as self-employed if they have a contract [ ], whereas if they have a contract [ ], they will be regarded as an employee.

2 **Fill in the missing words.**

Expenses are allowable if they are incurred [ ], [ ] and [ ] in the performance of the duties of employment.

3 Brian uses his own car to travel 8,000 business miles in the tax year. Brian's employer reimburses him with 35p per mile travelled. The approved mileage rate for the first 10,000 business miles travelled is 55p per mile.

Required

The amounts that are taxable (deductible) in calculating employment income are (both minus signs and brackets can be used to indicate negative numbers):

£ [ ]

4 A taxable fuel benefit is reduced by any reimbursement by the employee of the cost of fuel provided for private mileage.

Required

Tick ONE box.

True	
False	

5 There is no benefit on the first £10,000 of an interest-free loan.

Required

Tick ONE box.

True	
False	

6 Gautown was supplied with a hybrid car by his employer throughout 2026/27. The list price of the car was £24,000, its CO_2 emissions were 38g/km and its electric range was 50 miles.

Required

The taxable benefit arising in respect of the car is:

£ [ ]

7 Buster is the Managing Director of Buster Braces Ltd and is supplied with a Bentley car which cost £72,000. It has CO_2 emissions of 138g/km and was provided to Buster on 6 April 2026. All running costs are borne by the company. Buster is also provided with a mobile phone for private and business use. The cost of provision of the phone to Buster Braces Ltd is £750 in 2026/27.

Required

The total taxable benefits are:

£ [ ]

8 For each of the following benefits, tick whether they would be taxable or exempt if received by an employee in 2026/27:

Item	Taxable ✓	Exempt ✓
Write off loan of £8,000 (only loan provided)		
Payments by employer of £500 per month into registered pension scheme		
Provision of one mobile phone		
Provision of a company car for both business and private use		
Removal costs of £5,000 paid to an employee relocating to another branch		

5 Trading income

Learning outcomes

3.2 Badges of trade

Learners need to understand:

3.2.1 the importance of identifying whether a trade exists

3.2.2 the badges of trade:

- profit-seeking motive
- the number of transactions
- the nature of the asset
- existence of similar trading transactions or interests
- changes to the asset
- the way the sale was carried out
- the source of finance
- interval of time between purchase and sale
- method of acquisition

Learners need to be able to:

3.2.3 identify:

- factors indicating a trade exists
- factors indicating a trade does not exist
- a valid conclusion on whether or not a trade exists
- the consequences of the conclusion

2.5	**Calculate trading income for sole traders and partners** Learners need to understand: 2.5.1 that the cash basis is the default basis 2.5.2 the circumstances in which the accruals basis may be used 2.5.3 how to adjust accounting profit for tax purposes • wholly and exclusively • capital v revenue expenditure • appropriations of profit by the owner • approved mileage allowance • business expenses paid for by owner • donations • entertaining • fines and penalties • gifts • interest payable leasing of assets • legal fees • payments to family members • private use • removal of inventory for owner use • trade and non-trade debts written off or recovered 2.5.4 when claiming the trading allowance instead of expenses is appropriate	

Assessment context

Adjustment of profits is highly examinable.

Qualification context

You will not see the information in this chapter outside of this unit.

Business context

Adjusting trading profit is one of the core tasks a tax adviser will have to perform for their client.

Chapter overview

Computing trading income

Adjustment to profit

Add

- Items not allowable included in the accounts
- Taxable items not included in the accounts

Deduct

- Items not taxable included in the accounts
- Allowable items not included in the accounts

Trading allowance

- If trading receipts do not exceed £1,000 trading profits are treated as nil.
- Available to individuals only.

Introduction

In this chapter we look at trading income.

We will start by looking at the rules which are used in determining whether an individual is trading or not. These rules are known as the badges of trade.

We will then look at how to calculate a taxable trading profit figure on which an individual will pay tax if they are trading

1 Is a trade being carried on?

It is important to know whether profits of an individual or company should be assessed as trading income.

For example, a person who buys and sells stamps may be trading as a stamp dealer. Alternatively, stamp collecting may be a hobby of that person. In this case, they are probably not trading.

If a trade is not being carried on, any profit arising from selling items could be exempt from tax or chargeable to capital gains tax. If a trade is being carried on, then the individual will be liable to income tax and national insurance contributions based on their trading profits.

To make this decision we use some tests known as the 'badges of trade' to determine whether an individual is trading or not.

1.1 Badges of trade

KEY TERM

Badges of trade: A set of criteria used by HMRC to determine whether an activity constitutes trading.

The following tests are used by the courts when distinguishing trading from investment or capital transactions and have evolved over the years as a result of the outcome of many court cases arguing trade versus investment:

1.1.1 Subject matter

Some items are commonly held as an **investment**, for example, works of art and antiques. A subsequent disposal may produce a gain of a capital nature rather than a trading profit. However, where the subject matter of a transaction is such that it would not normally be held as an investment (for example, 1,000,000 rolls of toilet paper), it is presumed that any profit on resale is a trading profit.

1.1.2 Ownership

Consider the length of ownership of the asset. The purchase of items followed by sale soon afterwards indicates trading. Conversely, if items are held for a long time before sale there is less likely to be a trade.

1.1.3 Frequency of transactions

A series of similar transactions indicates trading. Conversely, a single transaction is unlikely to be considered as a trade.

1.1.4 Improvement expenditure

If work is done to make an asset more marketable, or steps are taken to find purchasers, there is likely to be a trade. For example, when a group of accountants bought, blended and recasked a quantity of brandy, they were held to be taxable on a trading profit when the brandy was later sold. Advertisement of the goods for sale is also a factor which makes it more likely there is a trade.

1.1.5 Reason for sale

Where objective criteria clearly indicate that a trade is being carried on, the taxpayer's intentions are irrelevant. If, however, a transaction (objectively) has a dual purpose, you should consider the taxpayer's intentions. For example, the taxpayer could buy a property, restore it and sell it. You need to consider whether it was purchased purely for resale, which would indicate trade, or did the taxpayer buy it with the intention of making it their home and then changed their mind – not trade.

1.1.6 Motive for profit

If an item is bought with the intention of selling it at a profit, a trade is likely to exist.

1.1.7 Existence of similar trading transactions or interests

The existence of similar trading transactions or interests would suggest that a trade exist. If an accountant sold a car, it would be unlikely to constitute a trade as there is no direct link between their existing interests and the sale. However, if a car mechanic sold a car there is a direct link between their existing trade and the sale. It would be likely that the sale of the car would be a trading transaction.

1.1.8 The source of finance

If an asset is acquired using short term finance, a trade is likely to exist. This is particularly the case where it will be necessary to dispose of the asset to repay the funds.

1.1.9 Method of acquisition

If goods are acquired unintentionally, for example, by gift or inheritance, their later sale is unlikely to constitute trading.

For the remainder of this chapter, we will assume that the badges of trade have been applied, and it has been concluded that the individual is trading.

2 Adjustment of profits

KEY TERM

Adjustment of profits: The adjustment of the accounting profits to comply with tax legislation.

Whether the business is unincorporated (sole trader or partnership) or incorporated (limited company) the tax computation will start with the **adjustment of profits. This is a vital area for all business types**. Many of the rules are the same for unincorporated businesses and for companies, with some differences highlighted in this chapter.

The exception to using an adjustment to profit approach is if a sole trade business has trading receipts during a tax year of less than £1,000 when the **trading allowance** will be used. This is covered in more detail in the Trading allowance section below.

2.1 Taxable trading profits

Taxable trading profits are not the same as accounting profits. The trader arrives at the profit for the year in the accounts by taking income and deducting various trading expenses. However, the trader is unlikely to follow tax rules in arriving at this profit as, for example, there are some costs for which tax legislation does not allow a tax deduction, even though the taxpayer quite legitimately deducts them for accounting purposes.

KEY TERM

Cash Basis: An accounting method where income and expenses are recorded only when they are actually received or paid.

Accruals Basis: An accounting method where income and expenses are recorded when they are earned or incurred, regardless of when the money is actually received or paid.

	Cash basis	Accruals (GAAP) basis
Automatic?	Automatic for unincorporated businesses from 2024/25	Election required on self-assessment tax return for the year

	Cash basis	Accruals (GAAP) basis
Taxable receipts	All amounts received, including from the sale of capital assets (except cars, and certain items such as buildings and land)	All trade-related revenue items which are receivable in the accounting period
Allowable deductions	Amounts paid, including the cost of capital items (except cars, and certain items such as buildings and land)	Revenue expenses payable (capital expenditure is disallowable – see below)

2.2 General rule for expenditure

KEY TERM

Expenditure wholly and exclusively for trade purposes: Expenditure that is incidental to the trade and that does not have a dual purpose.

Non-deductible expenditure: Expenses that cannot be deducted from a business's income when calculating taxable profit. If these expenses have been deducted in the accounting profit, they will need to be added back. Alternative term: Disallowable expensiture.

Deductible expenditure: Expenses that can be deducted from a business's income when calculating taxable profit. If these expenses have been deducted in the accounting profit, no adjustment will be required. Alternative term: Allowable expenditure.

Expenditure incurred not wholly and exclusively for business purposes is disallowed.

2.3 Specific expenses

2.3.1 Capital expenditure including depreciation

KEY TERM

Capital expenditure: Expenditure on the purchase or improvement of non-current assets.

Revenue expenditure: All other expenditure incurred by a business that is not capital expenditure.

Capital expenditure is one-off expenditure leading to the creation or improvement of an asset (eg an item of plant).

Revenue expenditure is regular ongoing expenditure required in the day to day running of the business (eg paying the gas bill).

Usually, revenue expenditure is allowable: it can be deducted from income before tax is calculated.

Capital expenditure under the accruals basis

Capital expenditure is not allowable under the accruals basis, so must be added back if it has been charged in the statement of profit or loss. This includes any purchase cost of an asset which has incorrectly been charged to the statement of profit or loss (including any associated legal fees), depreciation and any profit/ loss on disposal of a fixed asset. Capital allowances (see later) may sometimes be claimed on capital expenditure.

Repair expenditure can cause problems:

- Maintaining an asset (ie keeping it in its current condition) is allowable.
- Improving an asset is not allowable as this is, in fact, capital expenditure.

However, where a repair is made which brings an asset up to date with what would now be considered industry norm this is considered to be a repair and is an allowable expense. An example of this would be replacing a single-glazed window with a double-glazed equivalent.

There are special rules where assets are repaired following acquisition:

- If the repairs are to make the asset usable, they are treated as part of the capital expense (eg repairs to an unseaworthy ship), so disallowable
- If the repairs merely improve the appearance of an asset, they are allowable as a revenue expense (eg refurbishing a cinema).

Capital expenditure under the cash basis

Under the cash basis, capital expenditure is generally allowed. This means that capital allowances are not generally available under the cash basis as relief has been obtained by way of a trading deduction instead. However, see below in relation to cars.

There are exceptions to this general rule (that capital expenditure is allowed) as follows:

- Capital payments related to cars are not a deductible expense. Capital allowances are available in relation to cars (see chapter 6). Note that vans and motorcycles are not cars, and therefore capital expenditure on these would be allowed (and capital allowances would not be available).
- Capital payments related to buildings and land are not a deductible expense. Structures and buildings allowances are also not available (see chapter 6).
- Depreciation is not allowable.

Activity 1: Capital versus revenue

Identify whether the following expenses are revenue or capital in nature by ticking the relevant button.

	Revenue	Capital
Paying employee wages	O	O
Paying rent for premises	O	O
Buying machinery	O	O
Buying a van	O	O
Building an extension to shop	O	O
Paying for repairs to car	O	O

2.3.2 Private expenditure of the owner

Strictly, expenditure incurred partly for private purposes and partly for business purposes has a dual purpose and is not deductible. However, HMRC sometimes allows taxpayers to apportion the expenditure between the part that is wholly for business purposes, and therefore deductible; and the part that is wholly for private purposes, and therefore not deductible. This is the same treatment under both the cash and accruals basis.

Under both the cash and accruals basis, if the owner has extracted profits by way of a 'salary' from the business and has incorrectly deducted this in their accounts, it must be added back as it constitutes drawings and is not tax deductible. In addition, the owner's Class 4 national insurance contributions and any personal legal and professional fees are not tax deductible.

If the owner pays a salary to a family member then only the reasonable salary is allowable. Any excess salary over a reasonable amount must be added back.

Under the accruals basis, goods taken from stock by the proprietor of a business should be treated as if they had been sold for their market value. If correctly accounted for as drawings, this will require an adjustment for the profit, whereas if the cost is still reflected in cost of sales, the full selling price will need to be added back. The AAT have confirmed that a question would specifically state if an adjustment to cost of sales for the goods taken has been made so, if a question does not make it clear, the selling price should be added back.

Under the cash basis, a 'just and reasonable amount' (eg the cost of the stock), should be added to taxable profit where goods are taken for the proprietor's own use.

Illustration 1: Private use expenditure

A sole trader who runs his business from home incurs £500 on heating and lighting bills. 30% of these bills relate to the business use of his house. £500 has been deducted in arriving at the accounts profit.

Required

How much should be added back in the calculation of taxable trading profits?

Solution

The 30% relating to business use is allowable. Therefore, 70% × £500 = £350 must be added back to the accounts profit as disallowable expenditure. This is the same treatment under either the cash or accruals basis.

Assessment focus point

In the assessment, you may need to calculate adjusted profits for a sole trader/partnership (unincorporated business) or a company (incorporated business).

The calculation is basically the same as a sole trader using the accruals basis; however, there are no private adjustments for a company.

Everybody who works for a company (including a director) is an employee, so any benefit they receive is taxed on them as part of their employment income.

The cost is part of the company's cost of employing the workforce it needs to perform its trade, and is therefore allowable.

2.4 The treatment of various other items

The table below details various types of allowable and **disallowable expenditure**, with mention of any differences between unincorporated businesses (sole traders and partnerships) under either the cash or accruals basis, and incorporated businesses (companies) where necessary.

Allowable expenditure	Disallowable expenditure	Comments
	Fines and penalties	HMRC usually allows parking fines incurred in parking an employee's car whilst on the employer's business. Fines relating to the owner of the business are, however, never allowed. Similarly, a company would not be able to deduct fines relating to directors.
Incidental costs of obtaining loan finance		This deduction does not apply to companies because they get a deduction for the cost of borrowing in a different way. We look at this later in this Course Book.

Allowable expenditure	Disallowable expenditure	Comments
	Depreciation or amortisation	In specific circumstances, a company can deduct these amounts, but this is outside the scope of this assessment.
	Any salary or interest paid to a sole trader or partner	
	The private proportion of any expenses incurred by a sole trader or partner	The private proportion of a director's or employee's expenses is, however, deductible.
Irrecoverable debts incurred in the course of a business. Specific provisions for irrecoverable debts	General provisions for irrecoverable debts (and other general provisions)	Loans to employees written off, despite being specific, are not allowable. Under the cash basis there is automatic bad debt relief as the receipt should not be recorded until it is received.
Staff entertaining	Non-staff (eg customer/supplier) entertaining	
Gifts for employees Gifts to customers as long as they: • Cost no more than £50 per donee per year • Carry a conspicuous advertisement for the business; and • Are not food, drink, tobacco or vouchers exchangeable for such goods Gifts to a small local charity if they benefit the trade	All other gifts including donations to national charities. Charitable gifts by companies are referred to as 'qualifying charitable donations (QCDs)'.	QCDs are charitable gifts by companies on which tax relief is given. These are covered later in this Course Book.
Subscriptions to a professional or trade association	Political donations	

Allowable expenditure	Disallowable expenditure	Comments
Legal and professional charges relating directly to the trade	Legal and professional charges relating to • Capital items (disallowed under accruals basis, allowed under cash basis) • Purchase/renewal of a long lease • Purchase of short lease (50 years or less) • Breaches of law/ regulations • Settling tax disputes	Deductible items include: • Charges incurred defending the taxpayer's title to non-current assets • Charges connected with an action for breach of contract. • Normal charges for preparing accounts and assisting with the self-assessment of tax liabilities • Charges for trade debt collection • Expenses for the renewal (not the original grant) of a lease for less than 50 years
Interest on loans taken out for trade purposes	Interest on overdue tax	These rules are for unincorporated businesses. Companies have different rules for interest. We look at these later in this Course Book.
	15% of with CO_2 emissions in excess of 50g/km under the accruals basis (fully allowed under the cash basis).	

Activity 2: Calculation of add back

A sole trader, who uses the accruals basis, charged the following expenses in computing their accounts profit:

	£
Fine for breach of Factories Act	1,000
Cost of specialist tax consultancy work relating to the trader's personal tax liability	2,000
Salary for the sole trader	15,000
Leasing cost of car (CO_2 emissions 55g/km)	3,000

Required

Calculate how much must be added back in computing taxable trading profits.

Tick ONE box.

	✓
£17,450	
£16,000	
£18,450	
£11,450	

Activity 3: Entertainment and gifts

Decide which of the items in the entertainment account below should be added back in computing taxable trading profits.

Expenditure	£	✓
Staff tennis outing for 30 employees	1,800	
2,000 t-shirts with firm's logo given to race runners	4,500	
Advertising and sponsorship of an athletic event	2,000	
Entertaining customers	7,300	
Staff Christmas party (30 employees)	2,400	

Activity 4: Adjustment of profits (ii)

Hugo Drax, a sole trader, has the following statement of profit or loss:

	£
Sales	100,000
Cost of sales	(50,000)
Gross profit	50,000
Add other income:	
Bank interest	4,000
Less expenses:	
Depreciation	(5,000)
Entertaining clients	(100)
Office costs	(2,000)
Staff wages and salaries	(15,000)
Hugo's personal council tax bill	(1,000)

	£
Net profit	30,900

Salaries include £5,000 paid to Hugo and £10,000 paid to his wife. His wife's salary is reasonable in respect of the work she performs in the business.

Required

Complete the table below showing the calculation of adjusted trading profits before capital allowances. Complete the narrative by using the items in the picklist below the table.

Adjustment to profit	£	£
Net profit per the accounts		
Add back		
▼		
▼		
▼		
▼		
Total added back		
Deduct		
▼		
Adjusted profits before capital allowances		

Picklist

- Bank interest
- Cost of sales
- Council tax
- Depreciation
- Entertaining
- Gross profit
- Office costs
- Sales
- Staff wages

3 Trading allowance

KEY TERM

Trading allowance: A tax exemption that allows an individual to earn a specified amount of trading income per tax year without paying tax on it and, in many cases, without needing to register for Self Assessment.

From 2017/18, the trading allowance was introduced to simplify the calculation of trading profits for smaller sole traders.

If a sole trader has trading receipts (under the accruals basis) for a tax year which do not exceed the trading allowance of £1,000, the trading profits are treated as nil and there is no charge to income tax as a result of the trade. An election can be made for the trading allowance rules not to apply if, for example, the deduction of allowable costs would instead give rise to a trading loss.

If the sole trader has trading receipts exceeding the £1,000 trading allowance, then the usual adjustment to profits approach will be used to calculate trading profits as explained above. If the sole trader would prefer, perhaps if allowable costs were small, then an election can be made to deduct the £1,000 trading allowance from trading receipts in order to calculate the taxable trading profits instead of deducting allowable expenses.

Assessment focus point

Please refer to the reference material at the end of this Course Book to see which elements of this chapter will be available to you as a pop-up in the live assessment.

Chapter summary

- The badges of trade give guidance as to whether a trade is being carried on.
- Where a trader elects to use the accruals basis, revenue expenses are generally allowable expenses for computing taxable trading profits but capital expenses are not (unless relieved through capital allowances – see later chapter).
- The main disallowable items that you must add back in computing taxable trading profits under the accruals basis are:
  - Entertaining (other than staff entertaining)
  - Depreciation charges (deduct capital allowances instead)
  - Fines
  - Legal fees relating to capital items
  - Wages or salary paid to a business owner
  - The private proportion of any expenses for a sole trader/partner (not applicable to a company)
- The default position is for the cash basis to apply. Under the cash basis taxable receipts include all amounts received, including from the sale of capital assets, less amounts paid, including the cost of capital assets. There are exceptions to this rule which have been detailed above.
- Deduct non-trading income/capital profits included in the accounts from the accounts profit to arrive at taxable trading profits.
- If a sole trader has trading receipts for the tax year not exceeding the trading allowance of £1,000, the trading profits are treated as nil.

Activity answers

Activity 1: Capital versus revenue

The correct answers are:

- Paying employee wages - **Revenue**
- Paying rent for premises - **Revenue**
- Buying machinery - **Capital**
- Buying a van - **Capital**
- Building an extension to shop - **Capital**
- Paying for repairs to car - **Revenue**

Activity 2: Calculation of add back

The correct answer is:

	✓
£17,450	
£16,000	
£18,450	✓
£11,450	

The fine will not be deductible and will therefore need to be added back as will the cost of the specialist tax consultancy work as it is incurred in the individual's personal capacity as a taxpayer and therefore the costs do not relate to the trade. The payment of a salary to the proprietor of a business is not deductible because it is just a method of extracting a profit from the business and that profit is taxable in the normal way as part of the taxable trading profits. 15% of leasing costs of car with CO_2 emissions exceeding 50g/km are disallowable. Add back 1,000 + 2000 + 15,000 + (15% × 3,000) = £18,450.

Activity 3: Entertainment and gifts

The correct answer is:

Expenditure	£	✓
Staff tennis outing for 30 employees	1,800	
2,000 t-shirts with firm's logo given to race runners	4,500	
Advertising and sponsorship of an athletic event	2,000	
Entertaining customers	7,300	✓
Staff Christmas party (30 employees)	2,400	

Activity 4: Adjustment of profits (ii)

Adjustment to profit	£	£
Net profit per the accounts		30,900

Adjustment to profit	£	£
Add back		
Depreciation	5,000	
Entertaining	100	
Staff wages	5,000	
Council tax	1,000	
Total added back		11,100
Deduct		
Bank interest		(4,000)
Adjusted profits before capital allowances		38,000

Test your learning

1 **Which TWO of the following expenses are allowable when computing taxable trading profits under the accruals basis?**

	✓
Legal fees incurred on the acquisition of a factory to be used for trade purposes	
Heating for factory	
Legal fees incurred on pursuing trade receivables	
Acquiring a machine to be used in the factory	

2 A sole trader incurs the following expenditure on entertaining and gifts.

	£
Staff entertaining	700
50 Christmas food hampers given to customers	240
Entertaining customers	900
	1,840

Required

How much of the above expenditure is allowable for tax purposes?

£ [ ]

3 **For each of the following expenses, show whether they are allowable or disallowable by ticking the relevant boxes.**

	Allowable ✓	Disallowable ✓
Parking fines incurred by the owner of the business		
Parking fines incurred by an employee while on the employer's business		
Parking fines incurred by the director of a company while on company business		
Legal costs incurred in relation to acquiring a 10-year lease of property for the first time		
Legal costs incurred in relation to the renewal of a lease for 20 years		
Gifts of calendars to customers, costing £4 each and displaying an advertisement for the company		
Gifts of bottles of whisky to customers, costing £12 each		

4 Herbert, a self-employed carpenter who uses the accruals basis, makes various items of garden furniture for sale. He takes a bird table from stock and sets it up in his own garden. The cost of

making the bird table amounts to £80, and Herbert would normally expect to achieve a mark-up of 20% on such goods.

Required

Identify the adjustment Herbert needs to make to the accounts for tax purposes, assuming he has reflected in the accounts the deduction for the cost of making the table.

Tick ONE box.

	✓
£80 must be deducted from the accounts profit	
£80 must be added back to the accounts profit	
£96 must be deducted from the accounts profit	
£96 must be added back to the accounts profit	

5 Trude works from home as a self-employed hairdresser. She incurs £450 on heating and lighting bills and this amount is deducted in her accounts. 20% of this expenditure relates to the business use of her home.

Required

How much of the expenditure is disallowable for tax purposes?

£ [ ]

6 The following sole traders have income and expenditure for 2026/27 as stated below:

	Zack	Mythili	Rohan	Arthur
Trading receipts	800	800	1,500	1,500
Allowable expenses	200	900	800	1,100

Required

Calculate the taxable trading profits for the sole traders, assuming they make any beneficial claim available to them.

	Taxable trading profits
Zack	
Mythili	
Rohan	
Arthur	

7 Pratish trades as a car mechanic. His most recent accounts show a profit of £38,000. In arriving at this figure, he deducted entertaining expenses of £2,000 and depreciation of £4,000. Capital allowances of £3,500 are available for tax purposes.

Required

Using the proforma layout provided, calculate the taxable trading profit.

The starting figure has already been entered for you.

6 Capital allowances

Learning outcomes

2.5 Calculate trading income for sole traders and partners

Learners need to understand:

2.5.5 the capital allowances available to different assets:

- plant and machinery
- structures and buildings

2.5.6 the inclusion of gross or net amounts in capital allowance computations, in accordance with:

- VAT registration status
- blocked expenditure for VAT

2.5.7 within the capital allowances computation, the availability of:

- annual investment allowance (AIA)
- first year allowance (FYA)

2.5.8 the pool within the capital allowances computation in which to include asset addition and disposals:

- main/general pool
- special rate pool

2.5.9 that private use assets are included separately in the capital allowances computation

2.5.10 the writing down allowances (WDAs) available on each pool within the capital allowances computation

2.5.11 the small pools allowance

2.5.12 when balancing adjustments are required for capital allowances

2.5.13 the capital allowances available on structures and buildings

2.5.14 the impact of capital allowances (including balancing adjustments) on the tax adjusted accounting profit

Learners need to be able to:

2.5.19 calculate capital allowances for accounting periods:

- longer than 12 months
- shorter than 12 months
- equal to 12 months

5	**Prepare tax computations for trading companies**	

5.1	**Calculate taxable total profits**
	Learners need to understand:
	5.1.3 trading income
	• capital allowances available on plant and machinery
	• annual investment allowance (AIA)
	• full expensing
	• first year allowance (FYA)
	• additions and disposals in the main/general pool
	• additions and disposals in the special rate pool
	• writing down allowances (WDAs)
	• The inclusion of gross or net amounts in capital allowance computations, in accordance with:
	  - VAT registration status
	  - blocked expenditure for VAT
	• small pools allowance
	• balancing adjustments in the pools
	• balancing adjustments on fully expensed assets
	• capital allowances available on structures and buildings	

	Learners need to be able to: 5.1.13 calculate capital allowances for accounting periods: • longer than 12 months • shorter than 12 months • equal to 12 months	

Assessment context

All the rules in this chapter are highly examinable and could be examined in a variety of different combinations. Make sure you can deal with any scenario the assessment throws at you. Some students find the task on capital allowances quite challenging, so you must make sure you practise plenty of tasks to feel comfortable with applying your knowledge of this topic. In addition, you must ensure you know what information is available in your reference material.

Capital allowances will be tested as part of Task 2 in the assessment for around 6 marks.

Qualification context

You will not see these rules outside of this unit.

Business context

In practice, capital allowances are a significant form of tax relief for reducing a taxpayer's tax liability.

The government often uses capital allowances to encourage businesses to invest in new plant and machinery.

Chapter overview

Capital allowances

Plant and machinery

Capital v Revenue
- Capital
  - Claim relief over several periods via capital allowances
- Revenue
  - Claim all relief this period

Main pool
- Full Expensing FYA at 100%
  - Expenditure on new P&M (not cars) by companies only
- AIA £1,000,000
  - Time apportion if not 12m period
- 14% WDA (18% prior to 1/6 April 2026)
- 100% FYA
- 40% FYA

Small pools allowance = £1,000

Cars
- CO_2 0g/km
  - 100% FYA
- CO_2 ≤50g/km
  - Pooled
  - 14% WDA
  - No AIA
- CO_2 > 50g/km
  - Special rate pool
  - 6% WDA
  - No AIA

Private use assets
- Restricted relief
- Sole trader only

Disposals
- Pooled
  - Balancing charge only (unless ceasing to trade
- Separate assets
  - Balancing charge or allowance
- Proceeds restricted to cost

Interaction with VAT
- Use VAT-exclusive cost if business is VAT-registered (except cars)
- Use VAT-inclusive cost for businesses that are not VAT registered (and cars)

Structures and buildings

Qualifying expenditure
- Construction/ acquisition from builder of qualifying assets
- Qualifying property includes offices, shops, factories, bridges
- Cost of land and acquisition expenses excluded
- Enhancing/renovating existing property can qualify

Writing down allowance
- 3% straight line once brought into use
- Apportioned in periods of acquisition and disposal
- SBAs claimed are added to seller's sale proceeds in gain computation

Introduction

This chapter looks at the difference between capital and revenue expenditure; and how to get tax relief for the different types of expenditure by either treating them as an expense, or plant and machinery or a structure or building for capital allowances.

1 Capital and revenue expenditure

KEY TERM

Capital expenditure: One-off expenditure that will bring benefits to the business over a number of years (eg purchase of machinery).

Revenue expenditure: Regular ongoing expenditure that only brings benefit in the period in which the expenditure is made (eg payment of electricity bill).

Revenue expenditure, generally, may be deducted against taxable profits before they are taxed (but we saw in the previous chapter that not all revenue expenditure is automatically allowable).

It may be possible to claim capital allowances on some capital expenditure where a deduction has not been available against trading profits. Remember that, where an unincorporated business uses the cash basis, most capital expenditure is allowed as a deduction from trading profits, so capital allowances will not be available. The main exception to this is cars.

Capital allowances are just the tax version of accounts depreciation. They are calculated to replace the depreciation charged in the accounts.

Both individuals (sole traders and partners) and companies may claim capital allowances.

2 Expenditure qualifying for capital allowances

KEY TERM

Plant and machinery: Assets used by a business to carry out its trade. These are items that perform a function within the business rather than forming part of the building or structure.

Capital allowances: An allowance that can be deducted when calculating a business's taxable profits, related to certain types of capital expenditure.

Plant and machinery is something which has a function within the trade as opposed to being part of the setting where the business takes place. Essentially, plant and machinery is any capital item used in the business other than buildings. For example, equipment, furniture, machinery and vehicles are all examples of plant and machinery.

Assessment focus point

There is much case law determining what is allowable as plant and machinery and what is not. The AAT have confirmed that the very detailed rules on this do not form part of your syllabus but, for information, some examples include:

- Moveable office partitions are plant – but fixed partitions are not.
- Decorative items (eg paintings) in hotels are plant.

The more common items you will see in the assessment are:

- Cars, vans and lorries
- Furniture
- Computers

Capital expenditure on buildings (part of the setting of a business) did not historically qualify for any type of capital allowances. However, a structures and buildings allowance is now available for qualifying expenditure on new commercial structures and buildings for contracts entered into on/after 29 October 2018.

We will first consider the capital allowances available on plant and machinery and then, later in this chapter, we will consider the capital allowances available on structures and buildings.

3 Allowances on plant and machinery

3.1 When and how capital allowances are given

Allowances are computed by reference to the period for which accounts are drawn up.

They are deducted from the taxable profits of the period.

They include all additions and disposals occurring in the relevant accounting period. Expenditure must be of a capital nature.

Assessment focus point

For traders who prepare accounts using the cash basis, relief for most capital expenditure is given as a trading deduction (instead of capital allowances). However, no deduction is available for expenditure on cars, so capital allowances are available for this expenditure.

For traders who prepare accounts using the accrual basis, no trading deduction is available for capital expenditure, so capital allowances will be claimed much more widely.

3.2 General pool for capital allowances

Most expenditure on plant and machinery is put into a 'pool' of assets known as the **general (or main) pool**. This includes expenditure on cars with CO_2 emissions of 1g/km to 50g/km.

3.3 Annual investment allowance

KEY TERM

Annual investment allowance (AIA): A capital allowance that enables a business to deduct 100% of the cost of qualifying plant and machinery up to an annual limit from its taxable profits in the year the expenditure is incurred.

Open book reference: Capital allowances

Section 15 of your reference material provides information about capital allowances. Ensure you are aware of the information which is (and is not) provided to you in your exam. The reference material is reproduced at the end of this Course Book.

A business can claim an annual investment allowance (AIA), giving 100% tax relief on its expenditure on plant and machinery.

A business can claim AIA on the first £1,000,000 of expenditure on plant and machinery in a 12month period of account.

The AIA is not available for expenditure on cars.

The amount of the AIA is scaled up/down for long/short periods of account.

Note. Companies cannot have a corporation tax period that is longer than 12 months.

Activity 1: Annual investment allowance

Delson starts a business on 1 January 2027, preparing accounts using the accrual basis. In the nine-month period to 30 September 2027, he incurs the following expenditure:

		£
15 January 2027	Manufacturing equipment	650,000
16 January 2027	Computer equipment	60,000
7 May 2027	Office furniture	30,000
13 May 2027	Delivery vans	20,000
20 June 2027	Car	19,000

Required

Delson can claim an annual investment allowance of:

£ [ ]

Workings (on-screen free text area provided in the assessment as part of larger question)

Assets eligible are:

		£

3.4 First year allowances (FYAs)

KEY TERM

> **First year allowances (FYAs):** A capital allowance that enables a business to claim an immediate deduction for the cost (or part of the cost) of qualifying plant and machinery in the year the expenditure is incurred.

These are special allowances given in addition to the AIA.

100% first year allowances (FYAs) are available on expenditure incurred on:

- Zero emission cars

You must give FYAs at 100% to the assets that are eligible for them. Do not use the AIA against them.

KEY TERM

> **40% first year allowances (FYAs):** From 1 January 2026, a new 40% first year allowance (FYA) is available to all businesses.
>
> - Available only on new and unused plant and machinery (not second hand)
> - Not available on cars
> - Not available on special rate pool expenditure (see later).
>
> The 40% FYA will in practice only be utilised for expenditure not covered by the available AIA.

FYAs are never time apportioned for short or long accounting periods. The remaining 60% of expenditure does not qualify for a WDA in the same period, it is added to the TWDV carried forward at the end of the period, and WDAs can then be claimed in the following period.

Open book reference: Capital allowances

The capital allowances section of your reference data, which you can access in your assessment, is in section 15. It reminds you of the assets on which the FYA is available and the CO_2 emissions for cars and their respective capital allowance treatment.

3.5 Writing-down allowances

KEY TERM

Writing-down allowances (WDA): The annual tax deductions a business can claim on the unrelieved expenditure in its capital allowance pools for plant and machinery. The amount is calculated by applying the WDA percentage to the remaining tax written-down value.

From 6 April 2026 (1 April 2026 for companies), a **writing-down allowance** (WDA) is given on the general pool at the rate of 14% (on a reducing balance basis). The WDA is calculated on the value of pooled plant, after adding current period additions and taking out current period disposals (as explained shortly).

The additions will include:

(a) Expenditure that qualifies for the AIA but is in excess of the maximum AIA available for the period.

(b) Cars with CO_2 emissions from 1g/km up to 50g/km. These are cars that do not qualify for 100% FYA and do not go into the special rate pool (see later). The emissions are stated clearly in the capital

Illustration 1: Basic proforma for calculating WDAs

	General pool £	Allowances £
TWDV b/f	X	
Additions (not eligible for AIA/FYA)	X	
Less disposals	(X)	
	X	
WDA @ 14%	(X)	X
TWDV c/f	X	

Note. TWDV = Tax Written-Down Value: this is the value of the pool of assets for tax purposes.

The total allowances for the accounting period can then be deducted in the adjustments to profit working.

WDAs are time apportioned for short/long accounting periods (n/12 × 14%), where n is the number of months in the trader's period of account.

Activity 2: Writing-down allowances in the general pool

Jamie prepares his accounts to 31 March using the accrual basis. At 1 April 2026, he has a balance of £10,000 on his general pool.

In the period of account to 31 March 2027, he has the following transactions:

		£
13 June 2026	buys a car (CO_2 45g/km)	18,000
31 August 2026	buys a van	29,000
30 October 2026	sells plant for	2,000
20 November 2026	buys manufacturing plant	930,000

Required

Complete the capital allowances computation for the year ended 31 March 2027.

	AIA	General pool	Total allowances

Illustration 2: 40% FYA

James' business has a tax written down value brought forward in the main pool at 1 April 2026 of £20,000. In the year ending 31 March 2027 he purchased a new item of plant and machinery for £1.5 million.

Required

What are the capital allowances available?

Solution

	FYA	AIA	Main	Allowances
TWDV b/f			20,000	
Addition	500,000	1,000,000		
AIA		(1,000,000)		1,000,000

	FYA	AIA	Main	Allowances
FYA @ 40%	(200,000)			200,000
WDA @ 14%			(2,800)	2,800
Transfer to main	(300,000)		300,000	
TWDV c/f / allowances	0	0	317,200	1,202,800

Before 6 April 2026 (1 April 2026 for companies), the WDA rate on the general pool was 18%. For accounting periods straddling 6 April (1 April 2026 for companies), a hybrid WDA is used for that period (rounded to 2 decimal places).

Illustration 3: Hybrid WDA

Becky is preparing her tax-adjusted trading profits for the year ended 30 June 2026. After additions and disposals in the period the tax written down value of her general pool on 30 June 2026 is £75,000.

Required

What is the WDA that Becky can claim on her general pool in the year ended 30 June 2026?

Solution

The year ended 30 June 2026 has nine months which fall before 6 April 2026 and three months which fall after 6 April 2026.

The hybrid WDA rate is used for that period. It is calculated as follows:

(18% x 9/12) + (14% x 3/12) = 17%

The WDA is therefore 17% x £75,000 = £12,750

3.6 WDA for small pools

KEY TERM

Small pools allowance: A capital allowance rule that enables a business to write off the entire balance of a pool if the value falls below a specified threshold.

If the balance on the general pool or special rate pool (before WDA) is less than the small pool limit at the end of the chargeable period, a WDA can be claimed up to the value of the small pool limit. This is known as a 'small pools allowance.'

This means that the pools may be written down to nil, rather than a small balance being carried forward.

The small pool limit is £1,000 for a 12-month period (pro rata for short and long chargeable periods). Note that this does not apply to any assets which are kept separate and not included in the pools.

4 Disposals

When an asset is sold in the year, we deduct the proceeds from the tax written down value of the pool brought forward. Note that if a zero-emission car, on which a 100% FYA was claimed, is sold the proceeds are deducted from the general pool.

The proceeds deducted will usually be the proceeds received on sale of the asset, however, if an asset is sold for more than its original cost, we only deduct the original cost from the pool.

Illustration 4: Disposal proceeds

On 6 April 2026, a sole trader who prepares accounts using the accrual basis, had a balance on their general pool of £47,000. Plant that had cost £7,000 was sold in the year for proceeds of:

(a) £14,000

(b) £4,000

In (a) the proceeds are more than the original cost and so only £7,000 would be deducted from the general pool balance of £47,000.

In (b) the actual proceeds are less than original cost and so the proceeds of £4,000 would be deducted from the general pool balance of £47,000.

5 Periods that are not 12 months long

The AIA limit and WDA are adjusted by the fraction: months/12.

The FYA is never adjusted.

A sole trader or partnership may have a period shorter or longer than 12 months. AIA and WDA can therefore be scaled up or down.

A company may have a corporation tax period shorter than 12 months but not longer than 12 months. AIA and WDA could therefore be scaled down but not up.

Assessment focus point

Note that the Chief Assessor has commented that short or long accounting periods are one of the scenarios which students find most challenging in this task and so you must make sure you fully appreciate the consequences of the length of the accounting period on the calculation.

Activity 3: Short period of account

Edward has been in business for a number of years, preparing accounts to 31 March using the accrual basis.

In 2026, Edward decided to change his year end to 31 December.

In the period ended 31 December 2026, Edward had the following additions:

		£
13 April	Car (CO_2 emissions 30g/km)	7,000
15 April	Plant	1,046,750

Edward sold a van for £2,000 on 7 July that had cost £3,000.

TWDV b/f at 1 April 2026 was £12,000.

Required

Complete the capital allowances computation for the period ended 31 December 2026.

	AIA	FYA 40%	General pool	Total allowances

	AIA	FYA 40%	General pool	Total allowances

6 Cessation of a business

KEY TERM

Balancing adjustment: Balancing adjustments ensure that over the life of the asset, the total tax relief given equals the actual cost to the business. Balancing adjustments will be required when:

(a) There is cessation of trade

(b) Assets are disposed of that are not in the main/general or special rate pool

(c) A disposal from the main/general or special rate pool result in a negative balance in the pool

Balancing allowance: Given when a positive balance remains at cessation or disposal of certain assets.

Balancing charge: Given when a negative balance remains at cessation or disposal of certain assets.

When a business ceases to trade, no AIAs, FYAs or WDAs are given in the final period.

Additions in the final period are added to the pool in the normal way. Similarly, any disposal proceeds (limited to cost) of assets sold in the final period are deducted from the balance of qualifying expenditure. If assets are not sold, they are deemed to be disposed of on the final day of trading for their market value. For example, a sole trader may keep a car from the business that has just ceased trading and so must deduct the market value from the pool.

If, after the above adjustments, a positive balance of qualifying expenditure remains in the pool, then a **balancing allowance** equal to this amount is given. **The balancing allowance is deducted from taxable trading profits**. If, on the other hand, the balance on the pool has become negative, a **balancing charge** equal to the negative amount is given. **The balancing charge increases taxable trading profits.**

Balancing allowances on the general pool and the special rate pool (see below) can only arise on cessation of trade, whereas balancing charges on these pools, although most commonly happening on cessation, can arise whilst trade is still in progress.

Assessment focus point

This is another scenario which the Chief Assessor has said that students find challenging.

Activity 4: Cessation of a business

Baxter, who prepares accounts using the accrual basis, normally has a June year end. On 1 July 2026, he has a TWDV in the pool of £12,000. He ceases to trade on 31 January 2027. His additions and disposals in his final period are as follows:

		£
5 September	Buys plant	2,000
12 October	Sells plant	See below

(a) If Baxter sells his plant for £15,500 then he will have a [▼] of £ [ ]

Picklist

- Balancing allowance
- Balancing charge

Workings (on-screen free text area provided in the assessment as part of larger question)

	General pool	Allowances

(b) If Baxter sells his plant for £11,500 then he will have a [▼] of £ [ ]

Picklist

- Balancing allowance
- Balancing charge

Workings (on-screen free text area provided in the assessment as part of larger question)

	General pool	Allowances

	General pool	Allowances
	–	

Notes.

1 A balancing allowance only arises in the general pool on the cessation of trade.

2 A balancing charge may arise on the general pool at any point in the business's life.

7 Assets that are not included in the general pool

We have seen above how to compute capital allowances on the general pool of plant and machinery. However, some special items are not put into the general pool. A separate record of allowances must be kept for these assets.

These assets are:

- Cars with CO_2 emissions greater than 50g/km
- Assets not wholly used for business purposes in unincorporated businesses (such as cars with private use by the proprietor)

7.1 Cars with CO_2 emissions greater than 50g/km

Open book reference: Capital allowances

Cars with CO_2 emissions in excess of 50g/km are put in a pool known as the special rate pool. The WDA rate on the special rate pool is 6% for a 12-month period calculated on the pool balance (after any additions and disposals) at the end of the chargeable period.

Activity 5: Special rate pool

Myles Ltd prepares accounts to 31 March each year and incurred the following transactions for the year ended 31 March 2027.

Date	Transaction
1.7.2026	Bought car for £17,000, CO2 emissions of 40g/km
1.10.2026	Bought car for £8,000, CO2 emissions of 60g/km

On 1 April 2026, the TWDV of plant and machinery were as follows:

	£
General pool	25,000
Special rate pool	10,000

Required

Complete the capital allowance computation for the year ended 31 March 2027.

	General pool	Special rate	Total allowances

	General pool	Special rate	Total allowances

7.2 Assets used partly for private purposes

KEY TERM

Private use assets: A business asset that is used partly for business purposes and partly for personal (private) use.

If a proprietor of a sole trader business or a partner in a partnership uses a business asset for private purposes, the following treatment applies:

- The asset is put in a separate column.
- TWDV is reduced by full amount of AIA/FYA/WDA calculated as normal.
- A balancing allowance or charge will arise at the date of disposal.
- Only the business proportion of the allowance/charge is transferred into the allowances column.

We refer to these as private-use assets.

An asset with some private use by an employee (not the business owner) suffers no restriction. The employee may be taxed on the private use as a taxable benefit, so the business is entitled to full capital allowances on such assets. This means there is never any private use restriction in a company's capital allowance computation, whether the asset is used by an employee or a director.

Assessment focus point

The Chief Assessor has noted that making private use adjustments when they are not required is a common mistake, so please ensure you check who you are calculating capital allowances for.

- If it is a sole trader or partnership - make the adjustment IF it is the sole trader or partner who is using the asset privately.
- If it is a company – do not make the adjustment.

Activity 6: Private-use assets

At 1 January 2026, Carola has two cars used in her business: a car she uses herself with a TWDV b/f of £20,000 (20% private use, CO_2 emissions 80g/km); and a car used by her employee, James, with a TWDV b/f of £16,000 (35% private use, CO_2 emissions 40g/km). Carola prepares accounts to 31 December 2026.

Carola has no other assets.

Required

(a) Calculate the capital allowances available to Carola for the year ended 31 December 2026.

Carola's capital allowances

	Main pool	Private-use asset	Total allowances

(b) **What capital allowances would Carola claim if the business instead ceased in this period and both cars were sold for £15,000 each?**

Carola would have a [▼] of £ [ ] .

Picklist

- Balancing allowance
- Balancing charge

Workings (on-screen free text area provided in the assessment as part of larger question)

	£

Note. There is no restriction for the private use of an employee.

8 Differences between unincorporated and incorporated businesses

KEY TERM

Private use asset: Has restricted capital allowances but does not apply to companies.

Period of account: The period for which a business prepares its accounts.

We have seen in this chapter that, broadly, the rules on capital allowances are the same for unincorporated businesses (sole traders and partnerships) and incorporated businesses (companies).

However, three important differences in the calculation of capital allowances are as follows:

(a) There is never a private use asset column in a company's capital allowance computation.
  - The director or employee may suffer a taxable benefit instead and so the company can deduct the allowance in full.
  - If a sole trader or partner uses a business asset for private purposes, then we restrict the capital allowances claimed on this asset.

(b) Long period of account (accounts that have been made up for more than 12 months).

- If a sole trader/partnership has a period shorter or longer than 12 months, we would scale down or scale up the calculation.
- If a company has a long period of account, we perform two capital allowances computations (see corporation tax chapter).

> **Assessment focus point**
>
> Both of these points are ones which the Chief Assessor has noted students find challenging in this task, so make sure you feel comfortable with these points.

9 Full expensing for companies

KEY TERM

> **Full expensing:** A type of first year allowance that enables companies to deduct 100% of the cost of qualifying plant and machinery from their taxable profits in the year the expenditure is incurred.

We have seen that businesses can claim a 100% first year allowance (FYA) on zero-emission cars and 40% FYA on new main pool plant and machinery. We have also seen that businesses can claim an annual investment allowance of £1,000,000 to relieve expenditure on plant and machinery in the year of purchase.

A relief known as full expensing is available to companies for expenditure on plant and machinery. The rate is 100% for assets in the main pool, and 50% for assets in the special rate pool. The 50% FYA is not examinable.

- Available to companies only (not sole traders or partnerships).
- Available only on new plant and machinery (not second hand).
- Not available on cars.

When an asset which has been fully expensed is disposed of, there is a balancing charge equal to the disposal value (ie the lower of cost and sales proceeds).

When an asset which has been relieved using the AIA is sold, the disposal value is deducted from the pool.

Therefore, it is generally preferable to use the AIA rather than full expensing (when a new asset qualifies for either allowance) because the AIA avoids the balancing charge on disposal.

> **Assessment focus point**
>
> Where expenditure on plant and machinery qualifies for both the AIA and full expensing, we would generally use the AIA to relieve the expenditure up to the AIA limit first and use the full expensing FYA to relieve the balance. This is because of the balancing charge that arises on disposal of fully expensed assets.

Activity 7: Full expensing for companies

Backwell Ltd makes up accounts for the 7 months to 31 March 2027. The brought forward value on its main pool on 1 September 2026 was £81,000. The following assets were bought and sold during the period:

		£
11 September 2026	Plant	750,000
16 December 2026	Car for salesperson	

		£
	(CO_2 emissions 49g/km)	11,000
8 February 2027	Car for finance director	
	(CO_2 emissions 62g/km)	50,000
28 February 2027	Machinery	36,000
1 March 2027	Disposed of plant (bought in 2019 for £30,000. Full expensing not available on acquisition)	32,000

Required

Calculate the capital allowances claim that Backwell Ltd can make for the period ended 31 March 2027.

The capital allowances claim that Backwell Ltd can make for the period ended 31 March 2027 is:

	AIA	FYA Full expensing	Main pool	Special rate pool	Total allowances

Assessment focus point

It is very important in an assessment capital allowance task that you spot whether the business is a company or not. You must only consider the full expensing rules if the business is a company.

Activity 8: Calculation of capital allowances

Marina, a sole trader who prepares accounts using the accrual basis, makes up accounts for the 18 months to 30 September 2027. The brought forward value on her general pool on 1 April 2026 was £481,000. She bought and sold the following assets:

		£
10 October 2026	Plant	1,410,000
10 November 2026	Car for member of the sales team	
	(CO_2 emissions 0g/km)	11,000
12 December 2026	Plant	550,000
1 September 2027	Disposed of plant (cost £30,000)	32,000

Required

Calculate the capital allowances claim that Marina can make for the period ended 30 September 2027.

The capital allowances claim that Marina can make for the period ended 30 September 2027 is calculated as follows:

	AIA	FYA 40%	FYA 100%	General pool	Total allowances

10 Interaction with VAT

Where a business purchases an asset, it is important to determine whether the VAT-inclusive, or VAT-exclusive cost should be included in the capital allowances computation.

- Where the business is VAT-registered and is therefore usually able to recover the input VAT suffered on the asset purchase, then it is the VAT-exclusive cost of the asset which is used.

In relation to cars, input VAT cannot generally be recovered, so it will be the VAT-inclusive cost which is used in the capital allowances computation.

- A business that is not registered for VAT cannot recover input VAT, so will use the VAT-inclusive cost of the assets in its capital allowances computation.

Assessment focus point

To convert a VAT-inclusive figure to a VAT-exclusive figure, multiply by 5/6.

Activity 9: Ben

Ben runs a VAT-registered floristry business. He has a tax written down value brought forward in the main pool of £26,000 at 1 April 2026. During the year ended 31 March 2027 he made the following acquisitions and disposals:

Date	Asset	Cost/proceeds (VAT-inclusive)
1 June 2026	Bought Volvo car (CO_2 emissions 30g/km)	£43,000
1 July 2026	Bought new display stand	£20,000
1 August 2026	Sold machinery	(£14,000)

Required

Calculate the capital allowances available for the year ended 31 March 2027.

11 Structures and buildings allowances

KEY TERM

Structures and buildings: The physical premises or structural elements in which the business operates. These items do not qualify as plant and machinery.

A structures and buildings allowance (SBA) is available for qualifying expenditure on new commercial structures and buildings for contracts entered into on/after 29 October 2018. Qualifying expenditure is expenditure on the construction of the building or structure itself (or the acquisition cost if bought from a developer), but not the cost of land, nor the cost of planning permission, fees and stamp taxes.

Where an existing building is renovated or converted, this expenditure may qualify (even if the underlying property was constructed prior to 29 October 2018).

Commercial structures and buildings include:

- Offices
- Retail and wholesale premises
- Factories
- Warehouses
- Walls
- Bridges
- Tunnels

Residential property or any part of a building which functions as a dwelling does not qualify for SBAs.

The allowance is given at 3% straight line, over a 33 ⅓ year period.

Each building or structure is treated separately, and enhancement expenditure is treated separately to the underlying building.

For SBAs to be claimed, the relevant asset must be in qualifying use, for example used in a trade or property letting business.

The allowance is pro-rated for accounting periods which are not 12 months in length, or where the structure of building is brought into use or sold during the period. This is in contrast to plant and machinery allowances which are given in full in the period of acquisition (with no WDA at all in the period of disposal).

There is no balancing adjustment on the sale of an SBA asset; however, an adjustment is made to the chargeable gain or capital loss arising, by adding the SBA claimed to the seller's disposal proceeds.

The new purchaser takes over the remaining allowances (based on the original cost) over the remainder of the 33 ⅓ year period. The seller and buyer both time apportion up to the date of disposal.

Assessment focus point

The Chief Assessor has confirmed that they will not be assessing that the proceeds from sale of an asset for the seller are increased by the SBAs received for chargeable gains purposes.

Activity 10: SBAs

Rose Ltd purchases a newly constructed office building from a developer for £2,050,000 (excluding land) on 1 July 2026 and brought it into use immediately. The purchase price of £2,050,000 includes £50,000 relating to solicitor's fees and other acquisition costs.

Rose Ltd prepares accounts to 31 December each year.

Required

(a) What are the maximum SBAs available to Rose Ltd in the year ended 31 December 2026?

£ ____________

Rose Ltd continued to use the office building for its trade until 30 June 2029, when it was sold to Petal plc for £2,500,000 (excluding land). Petal immediately started using the office for trading purposes.

Petal plc prepares its accounts to March each year.

Required

(b) Which TWO of the following statements are correct regarding the implications of the disposal?

	✓
Rose Ltd will not be entitled to any SBA on the building for its year ended 31 December 2029	
Rose Ltd's chargeable gain will increase by £180,000 due to the SBAs claimed	
Petal plc will claim £75,000 pa structures and buildings allowances on the office	
Petal plc will time apportion its SBA by 9/12 in its year ended 31 March 2030	

Chapter summary

- Assets that perform a function in the trade are generally plant. Assets that are part of the setting are not plant.
- Traders that prepare accounts on the cash basis can only claim capital allowances on cars. Traders who use the accrual basis can claim capital allowances on all qualifying plant and machinery.
- Most expenditure on plant and machinery goes into the general (main) pool.
- An annual investment allowance (AIA) of £1,000,000 is available on expenditure other than on cars. The limit is pro-rated for periods of more or less than 12 months.
- FYAs at 100% are available on zero emission cars.
- FYAs at 40% on new general pool additions (not cars).
- There is a writing-down allowance (WDA) of 14% on the balance of the general pool in a 12 month period and 6% on the special rate pool.
- WDAs are time-apportioned in short or long periods.
- FYAs are never time-apportioned for short or long periods.
- If the WDV on the general or special rate pool is £1,000 or less, an election can be made to write off the pool balance, known as a 'small pools allowance'.
- Balancing allowances or balancing charges will be given when the trade ceases, and when an asset is disposed of, which is not included in the general pool or special rate pool.
- Private use of assets by sole traders and partners restricts capital allowances.
- Cars are dealt with according to their CO_2 emissions:
  - 0/km – FYA at 100%
  - up to 50g/km – general pool with WDA of 14%
  - Over 50g/km – special rate pool with WDA 6%
- A 100% first year allowance (known as full expensing) is available to companies (not sole traders or partnerships) purchasing new plant and machinery (not cars) that would be in the main pool.
- Where a business is VAT-registered, use the VAT-exclusive cost in the capital allowances computation (except cars).
- Qualifying buildings constructed since October 2018 are entitled to a 3% straight-line structures and buildings allowance on cost (excluding land).

Activity answers

Activity 1: Annual investment allowance

£ 750,000

Workings (on-screen free text area provided in the assessment as part of larger question)

Assets eligible are:

		£
15 January 2027	Manufacturing equipment	650,000
16 January 2027	Computer equipment	60,000
7 May 2027	Office furniture	30,000
13 May 2027	Delivery vans	20,000
		760,000

Nine-month period.

Maximum entitlement is n/12 × £1,000,000 = £750,000,

where n = the number of months in the period of account

As the eligible assets are greater than the limit, Delson may only claim £750,000.

Note. The balance of expenditure, and the car, will be eligible for other allowances.

Activity 2: Writing-down allowances in the general pool

	AIA	General pool	Total allowances
TWDV b/f		10,000	
Additions			
Car		18,000	
Van	29,000		
Manufacturing plant	930,000		
AIA	(959,000)		959,000
Disposals		(2,000)	
		26,000	
WDA @ 14%		(3,640)	3,640
			962,640
TWDV c/f		22,360	

Activity 3: Short period of account

	AIA	FYA 40%	General pool	Total allowances
TWDV b/f			12,000	
P/e 31.12.26				
Disposal				
7.7 van			(2,000)	
AIA additions				
15.4 Plant (total £1,046,750)	750,000	296,750		
AIA £1,000,000 × 9/12	(750,000)			750,000
FYA @ 40%		(118,700)		118,700
Non-AIA addition				
13.4 car			7,000	
			17,000	
WDA @ 14% x 9/12			(1,785)	1,785
Transfer to main pool		178,050	178,050	
TWDV c/f			193,265	
				870,485

Activity 4: Cessation of a business

(a) If Baxter sells his plant for £15,500 then he will have a | balancing charge | of £ | 1,500 |

Workings (on-screen free text area provided in the assessment as part of larger question)

	General pool	Allowances
TWDV b/f	12,000	
Additions	2,000	
Disposals	(15,500)	
	(1,500)	
Balancing charge	1,500	(1,500)
TWDV c/f	–	

(b) If Baxter sells his plant for £11,500 then he will have a | balancing allowance | of £ | 2,500 |

Workings (on-screen free text area provided in the assessment as part of larger question)

	General pool	Allowances
TWDV b/f	12,000	
Additions	2,000	
Disposals	(11,500)	
	2,500	
Balancing allowance	(2,500)	(2,500)
TWDV c/f	–	

Notes.

1 A balancing allowance only arises in the general pool on the cessation of trade.

2 A balancing charge may arise on the general pool at any point in the business's life.

Activity 5: Special rate pool

	General pool	Special rate	Total allowances
Y/e 31.3.2027			
TWDV b/f	25,000	10,000	
Additions	17,000	8,000	
	42,000	18,000	
WDA 14%/6%	(5,880)	(1,080)	6,960
TWDV c/f	36,120	16,920	

Activity 6: Private-use assets

(a) Carola's capital allowances

	Main pool	Private-use asset	Total allowances
TWDV b/f	16,000	20,000	
WDA @ 15%	(2,400)		2,400
WDA @ 6%		(1,200)	960
			3,360
TWDV c/f	13,600	18,800	

Note. As there is no restriction for the private use of an employee, and it has emissions of ≤ 50g, James's car would be in the main pool. Only 80% of the allowances on Carola's car are claimed on her private use car.

The year ended 31 December 2026 has 3 months which fall before 6 April 2026 and 9 months which fall after. The hybrid rate is therefore used: (18% x 3/12) + (14% x 9/12) = 15%.

Carola's car has CO_2 emissions in excess of 50g/km so it is written down at the special rate rather than the main rate.

(b) Carola would have a [balancing allowance] of £ [5,000] .

Workings (on-screen free text area provided in the assessment as part of larger question)

	£
Carola's car	
Balancing allowance (20,000 – 15,000) × 80% =	4,000
Main pool (James's car)	
Balancing allowance (16,000 – 15,000) =	1,000
	5,000

Note. There is no restriction for the private use of an employee.

Activity 7: Full expensing for companies

The capital allowances claim that Backwell Ltd can make for the period ended 31 March 2027 is:

	AIA	FYA Full expensing	Main pool	Special rate pool	Total allowances
TWDV brought forward at 1 September 2026			81,000		
Plant	583,333	166,667			
Salesperson's car			11,000		
Finance director's car				50,000	
Machinery		36,000			
AIA (£1m x/12)	(583,333)				583,333
FYA		(202,667)			202,667
Disposals (limited to cost)			(30,000)		
			62,000	50,000	
WDA 14%/ 6% x 7/12			(5,063)	(1,750)	6,813
C/fwd/total			56,937	48,250	792,813

Activity 8: Calculation of capital allowances

The capital allowances claim that Marina can make for the period ended 30 September 2027 is calculated as follows:

	AIA	FYA 40%	FYA 100%	General pool	Total allowances
18m p/e 30 Sept 2027					
B/f				481,000	
Disposal 1.9.27 AIA acquisition				(30,000)	
10.10.26 Plant	1,410,000				
12.12.26 Plant	90,000	460,000			
AIA (see note)	(1,500,000)				1,500,000
FYA @ 40%		(184,000)			184,000
100% FYA acquisition					
10.11.26 Car			11,000		
FYA @ 100%			(11,000)		11,000
WDA @ 14% × 18/12				(94,710)	94,710
Transfer to main pool		(276,000)		276,000	
C/f				632,290	
Allowances					1,789,710

Notes.

1. The AIA limit and WDA are scaled up for the 18-month period, whereas the FYA is never scaled up or down. The limit is (£1,000,000 × 18/12). The total AIA is therefore £1,500,000.
2. This working would not be the same had it related to a company, as the 18-month period would be split into two accounting periods (a 12-month period and a 6-month period). In addition, the two purchases of plant would have been eligible for full expensing. We look at accounting periods for companies later in the Course Book.

Activity 9: Ben

	AIA	Main	Allowances
	£	£	£
TWDV b/f		26,000	
Volvo		43,000	
Display stand (£20,000 × 5/6)	16,667		
Machinery sale (£14,000 × 5/6)		(11,667)	

	AIA £	Main £	Allowances £
AIA	(16,667)		16,667
	0	57,333	
WDA @ 14%		(8,027)	8,027
TWDV c/f / allowances		49,306	24,694

Activity 10: SBAs

(a) £ 30,000

£2,000,000 × 3% × 6/12 = £30,000

The cost of acquisition excludes acquisition fees. The SBA must be time-apportioned in the year of acquisition.

(b) The correct answers are:

	✓
Rose Ltd will not be entitled to any SBA on the building for its year ended 31 December 2029	
Rose Ltd's chargeable gain will increase by £180,000 due to the SBAs claimed	✓
Petal plc will claim £75,000 pa structures and buildings allowances on the office	
Petal plc will time apportion its SBA by 9/12 in its year ended 31 March 2030	✓

Statement 1 is incorrect as the seller may claim a time-apportioned SBA in the year of disposal.

Statement 2 is correct, as Rose Ltd would have claimed (3 × 3% × £2,000,000) = £180,000 of SBAs at the date of disposal, which are added to the proceeds in its chargeable gain computation.

Statement 3 is incorrect, as SBAs are based on the original qualifying cost of £2 million.

Statement 4 is correct, as the building was brought into qualifying use by Petal plc on 1 July 2029, and therefore the WDA must be multiplied by 9/12.

Test your learning

1 An item of plant is acquired for £2,000 and sold five years later for £3,200.

Required

The amount that will be deducted from the pool as proceeds when the disposal is made is:

£ [ ]

2 Nitin, who prepares accounts to 30 September each year using the accrual basis, had a balance on his general pool of £22,500 on 1 October 2026. In the year to 30 September 2027, he sold one asset and bought one asset as follows:

Addition (eligible for AIA) 1.12.26	£171,250
Disposal proceeds on sale on 1.8.27 (less than cost)	£7,800

Required

The amount of capital allowances available for the year ended 30 September 2027 is:

£ [ ]

3 A company starts to trade on 1 July 2026, preparing accounts to 31 December 2026 and buys a car with CO_2 emissions of 45g/km costing £18,000 on 15 July 2026. The company also buys a car with CO_2 emissions of 0g/km for £5,000 on 1 September 2026.

Required

The capital allowances available in the first period of account to 31 December 2026 are:

£ [ ]

4 Abdul ceased trading on 31 December 2026, preparing his final accounts for the year to 31 December 2026.

The following facts are relevant:

General pool balance at 1.1.26	£12,500
Addition – 31.5.26	£20,000
Disposal proceeds	
(in total – proceeds not exceeding cost on any item) – 31.12.26	£18,300

Required

Identify whether the following statement is true or false. Tick ONE box.

There is a balancing charge of £14,200 arising for the year to 31 December 2026.

	✓
True	
False	

5 Raj, a sole trader who prepares accounts to 30 April each year, buys a Volvo estate car, with CO_2 emissions of 60g/km, for £30,000 on 31 March 2026. 60% of his usage of the car is for business purposes.

Required

The capital allowance available to Raj in respect of the car for y/e 30 April 2026 is:

£ [ ]

6 Barry ceased trading on 31 December 2026, having been self-employed for many years, preparing accounts under the accrual basis. On 1 January 2026, the tax written down value of his plant and machinery general pool was £7,200. On 10 November 2026, Barry purchased a computer for £1,600. All of the items of plant and machinery were sold on 31 December 2026.

6 (a) If Barry sells all the plant and machinery for £10,000 then he will have a [▼] of £ [ ].

Picklist

- Balancing allowance
- Balancing charge

Workings

(b) If Barry sells his plant for £6,000 then he will have a [▼] of £ [ ].

Picklist

- Balancing allowance
- Balancing charge

Workings

7 Peter is a sole trader who started to trade and acquired a car for both business and private purposes on 1 July 2026. He prepared his first set of accounts for the 9 months to 31 March 2027. The car purchased has CO_2 emissions of 60g/km and cost £19,000. The private mileage for the nine months ending 31 March 2027 represented 20% of his total mileage for that year.

Required

Peter can claim capital allowances for the 9 month accounting period ending 31 March 2027 of:

£ [ ]

Working

8 Xeon Ltd purchases a newly constructed office building from a developer for £1,875,000 on 1 March 2026 and starts using it on 1 April 2026. The purchase price includes acquisition costs of £75,000. Xeon Ltd has a 31 December year end.

Required

What are the maximum SBAs available to Xeon Ltd in the year ended 31 December 2026?

£ [ ]

9 A Ltd is building a new factory for £1,000,000 including £200,000 for land. A Ltd prepares its accounts to 31 December.

Required

Identify which of the following statements are true or false.

	True ✓	False ✓
If the contract for the factory is signed in 2026 and the factory brought into use in that year, an SBA will be available for the year ended 31 December 2026.		
If the factory is constructed by 1 March 2026 and brought into use in A Ltd's trade on 1 July 2026 then an SBA of £24,000 is available as SBAs are claimed in full in year of construction/ purchase.		
The eligible cost qualifying for the SBA is £1,000,000.		

10 Nailsea Ltd makes up accounts for the 3 months to 30 September 2026. The brought forward value on its general pool on 1 July 2026 was £123,000. The following assets were bought and sold during the period:

		£
11 July 2026	Zero emission car	41,000
16 July 2026	Machinery	160,000
8 August 2026	Car for managing director	

		£
	(CO_2 emissions 42g/km 10% private use)	38,000
31 August 2026	Plant	136,000
1 September 2026	Disposed of plant (cost £20,000)	15,000

Required

Calculate the capital allowances claim that Nailsea Ltd can make for the period ended 30 September 2026.

How would the allowances be calculated differently if Nailsea Ltd was a sole trader (preparing accounts using the accrual basis)?

	AIA (max £1m x 3/12 = £250,000)	FYA	100% Full expensing	General pool	Special rate pool	Private use asset	Total allowances

7 Trading profits - basis of assessment

Learning outcomes

2.1.14	Learners need to be able to calculate: • trading income allocated to a tax year in straddle periods

Assessment context

You may need to time-apportion profits from different periods of account to identify how much taxable trading profit should be included for the tax year.

Qualification context

You will not see these areas again in your studies.

Business context

Taxpayers need to know which tax year their trading profits fall into, so they can determine when their tax is due, and how much tax is due.

Chapter overview

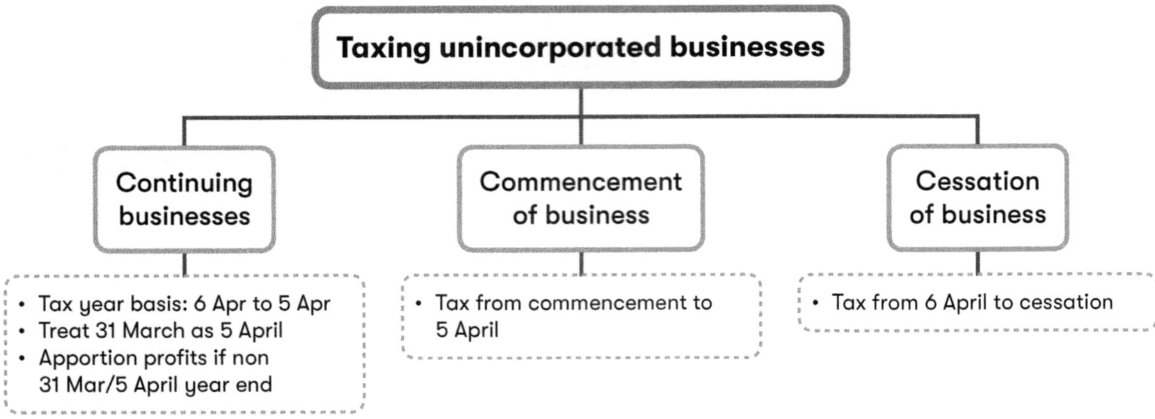

Introduction

This chapter will concentrate on computing the figure to insert as **trading profit** in the income tax computation. These rules apply to unincorporated businesses only (ie individuals in business – sole traders and partners – not companies).

A sole trader/partnership may make up their accounts for any period they choose. As we have seen in earlier chapters, we use their accounting period as the basis for our adjustment of profit and capital allowances calculations.

However, income tax is calculated with reference to the tax year (also referred to as the fiscal year or year of assessment). The 2026/27 tax year runs from 6 April 2026 to 5 April 2027.

1 Basis periods

A mechanism is needed to link the taxable trading profits (as adjusted for tax purposes and after the deduction of capital allowances) to a tax year. This mechanism is known as the basis of assessment, and the period for which profits are assessed in a tax year is called the basis period.

KEY TERM

> **Tax year basis:** The basis of assessment is known as the tax year basis. Under the tax year basis, business profits are assessed and taxed in the tax year in which they arise. Therefore, for 2026/27, businesses will need to report their profits for the period 6 April 2026 to 5 April 2027.

2 Ongoing trades

2.1 Accounting date between 31 March and 5 April

Businesses which have an accounting period which ends between 31 March and 5 April will be treated as if their accounting period aligned with the tax year.

Illustration 1:

Jodie's beauty business prepares accounts to 31 March each year.

Required

How will her business profits be assessed?

Solution

The profits for the year ended 31 March 2027 will be assessed in the 2026/27 tax year. Any profits falling in the period 1 April 2027 to 5 April 2027 will be reported in her accounts for the period to 31 March 2028 and assessed in the 2027/28 tax year.

Activity 1:

A trader prepares accounts to 5 April each year.

Required

Which year's profits will be assessed in 2026/27?

Picklist

- Year ended 5 April 2026

- Year ended 5 April 2027

2.2 Other accounting dates

Businesses which have an accounting reference date which does not align with the tax year will need to use information from two sets of accounts to prepare their tax returns. This may mean that there is little time between the end of the second accounting period to prepare and submit the tax return.

KEY TERM

Straddle periods: A period during which a taxpayer's accounting period overlaps two separate tax years.

Illustration 2:

Kristiana's book shop has a 30 June accounting date.

Required

Show how her profits will be attributed to tax years.

Solution

For the 2026/27 tax year, she will need to use information from the accounts for the years ending 30 June 2026 and 30 June 2027, and apportion profits on a pro-rata basis as follows:

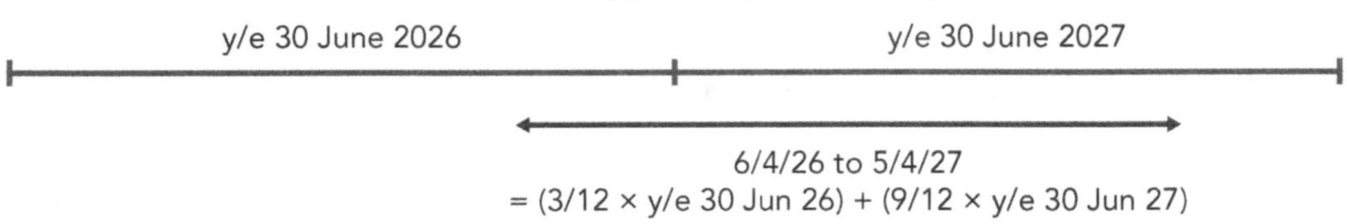

Stakeholder perspective

The 2026/27 tax return needs to be submitted by 31 January 2028, so Kristiana only has seven months after the end of the second accounting period to prepare and submit this, compared to ten months if she had an accounting period which aligned with the tax year. Consider a situation for a business with a 31 December year end, that business would only have one month after the end of the second accounting period. In this situation, HMRC would allow the business to file their tax return using estimated figures, and then amend it once the accounts have been finalised for the second period.

Activity 2:

Kristoff prepares accounts to 30 September each year. His profits are as follows:

	£
y/e 30 September 2026	45,000
y/e 30 September 2027	53,000
y/e 30 September 2028	63,000

 BPP

Required

What are Kristoff's assessable profits for 2026/27 and 2027/28?

3 Commencement of trade

When a business starts trading, it will be assessed on the period from the date of commencement to the following 5 April.

Illustration 3:

Rishi starts a new business on 1 August 2026. The tax adjusted trading profit for the first period to 31 May 2027 is £90,000.

Required

What are Rishi's assessable trading profits for 2026/27?

Solution

The assessable trading profits are based on the period from the date of commencement to the following 5 April.

1 August 2026 to 5 April 2027 = 8 months out of the total period of 10 months

8/10 × £90,000 = £72,000

Activity 3:

Chris starts to trade on 1 January 2027, and prepares a first set of accounts for the 8 months to 31 August 2027, and annually thereafter. The tax adjusted profits are as follows:

	£
p/e 31 August 2027	96,000
y/e 31 August 2028	84,000

Required

What are Chris's assessable profits for the first two tax years of trading?

4 Ceasing trade

On cessation, the assessable profits are those in the period starting on 6 April and ending on the date of cessation.

Illustration 4:

Marina ceased trading on 31 July 2028. Her tax adjusted profits were as follows:

y/e 31 March 2027	£72,000
p/e 31 July 2028	£80,000

Required

What are Marina's assessable profits for 2026/27, 2027/28 and 2028/29?

Solution

Tax year		Assessable profits
2026/27	6 Apr 26 - 5 Apr 27	£72,000
2027/28	6 Apr 27 - 5 Apr 28 12/16 × 80,000	£60,000
2028/29	6 Apr 28 - 31 Jul 28 4/16 × 80,000	£20,000

Chapter summary

- Business profits are assessed and taxed in the tax year in which they arise. For 2026/27, this is the period from 6 April 2026 to 5 April 2027.
- An accounting date between 31 March and 5 April will be treated as if it aligned with the tax year.
- Businesses which use other accounting dates will need to apportion profits from two different accounting periods.
- On commencement of trade a business is assessed on the profits arising from the date of commencement to the following 5 April.
- On cessation of trade a business is assessed on the profits arising from 6 April to the date of cessation.

Activity answers

Activity 1:

The profits for the year ended 5 April 2027 will be assessed in 2026/27.

Activity 2:

Tax year		Assessable profits
2026/27	6 Apr 2026 - 30 Sep 2026 = 6/12 × 45,000 1 Oct 2026 - 5 Apr 2027 = 6/12 × 53,000	£49,000
2027/28	6 Apr 2027 - 30 Sep 2027 = 6/12 × 53,000 1 Oct 2027 - 5 Apr 2028 = 6/12 × 63,000	£58,000

Activity 3:

Tax year		Assessable profits
2026/27	1 Jan 27 - 5 Apr 27 = 3/8 × 96,000	£36,000
2027/28	6 Apr 27 - 31 Aug 27 = 5/8 × 96,000 1 Sep 27 - 5 Apr 28 = 7/12 × 84,000	£109,000

Test your learning

1 Hermione commenced trade on 1 September 2026, preparing her first set of accounts to 31 March 2027 and annually thereafter. Her tax adjusted trading profits are as follows:

p/e 31 March 2027	£64,000
y/e 31 March 2028	£83,000

Required

What are Hermione's assessable trading profits for 2026/27?

2 Nadim runs a successful sports club. His tax adjusted trading profits are as follows:

y/e 31 May 2026	£34,000
y/e 31 May 2027	£50,000
y/e 31 May 2028	£64,000

Required

What are Nadim's assessable trading profits for 2026/27?

3 Manuel ceased trading on 31 July 2027 with profits for the final two periods as follows:

y/e 31 May 2026	£76,000
p/e 31 July 2027	£34,000

Required

What are Manuel's assessable trading profits for 2027/28?

4 Amarjat started trading on 1 February 2027. He prepared his first accounts to 30 June 2028. Taxable profits for this 17 month period were £34,000.

Required

Show the taxable profits for 2026/27 and 2027/28.

Tax year	Basis period	Taxable profits £
2026/27	to	
2027/28	to	

5 Susi started to trade on 1 December 2026. Her first accounts were prepared to 30 June 2027. Taxable profits for the first two periods of account were:

Period to 30 June 2027: £70,000

Year to 30 June 2028: £60,000

Required

Her taxable profits for 2026/27 are: £ ☐

Her taxable profits for 2027/28 are: £ ☐

8 Partnerships

Learning outcomes

2.5	**Calculate trading income for sole traders and partners** Learners need to be able to: 2.5.20 allocate profits between partners
	Learners need to understand: 2.5.15 how profits are allocated between partners • salary • interest on capital • profit sharing ratio

Assessment context

In the assessment, you may be required to compute the split of partnership profits for new, continuing and leaving partners. It will probably be tested in task 4 for 3 marks.

Qualification context

You will have seen partnerships in your accounting studies, so the basic treatment will not be a surprise to you. The tax treatment of partnerships is unique to this unit.

Business context

Partners need to know how much tax they owe to HM Revenue and Customs.

Chapter overview

Partnerships

Computing taxable trading profits

- Start with partnership profit
- Adjust as for sole trader
  - Salaries
  - Interest on capital
  - Ratios
- Split adjusted profit between partners

Dividing profit between partners

- Follow rules for period
- If rules change split period
- Salaries
- Interest on capital
- Ratios

Introduction

In this chapter we look at the profits of a partnership and how these profits are split between the individual partners. We then go on to look at how the individual partners are taxed on their share of the profits.

1 Computing taxable trading profits of partnerships

KEY TERM

Partnership: A group of self-employed people working together.

The partnership produces a statement of profit or loss for the whole business. Profits will be adjusted for tax purposes, and capital allowances will be calculated in exactly the same way as for a self-employed sole trader. This means that you must add back disallowable items. You must deduct specifically deductible items that have not been deducted in the accounts (for example, capital allowances) and also any income in the accounts that is not part of the taxable trading profit. Finally, add any amounts taxable as trading profits that have not been included in the accounts; for example, the market value of any goods taken for own use.

A particular point worth noting is that any partners' salaries or interest on capital deducted in the accounts must be added back when computing taxable trading profits of the partnership. These items are disallowable expenses because they are a form of drawings. They will be part of each partner's taxable trading profit as described below.

There is an additional stage here, though. The adjusted profits must be split between the partners.

Once profit has been split, each partner is treated as a sole trader and taxed separately.

2 Dividing taxable trading profits between partners

KEY TERM

Appropriations of profit: How the profits of a partnership are shared amongst the partners.

Once you have computed a partnership's taxable trading profit for a period of account, you must divide it between the partners concerned.

The partners may agree to share profits in any way they wish. The agreed division of profits will be set out in the partnership agreement and will always be stated for you in assessment tasks.

Method:

- First, allocate any salaries and interest on capital to the partners.
- Second, share the residue of profits between the partners in the agreed ratio.

Illustration 1: Dividing profit between the partners

Pearl and Ruby are in partnership. The partnership's taxable trading profits (as adjusted for tax purposes) for the year ended 31 March 2027 were £110,000. The partnership agreement provides for Pearl to be paid a salary of £20,000 per annum and for Ruby to be paid a salary of £30,000 per annum. Any remaining profits are divided between Pearl and Ruby in the ratio 2:1.

First allocate the partners' salaries and then divide the balance of the profit in accordance with the profit-sharing ratio:

	Total	Pearl	Ruby
	£	£	£
Salary	50,000	20,000	30,000
Profit (£110,000 – £30,000 – £20,000) 2:1	60,000	40,000	20,000

	Total	Pearl	Ruby
	£	£	£
	110,000	60,000	50,000

Pearl has taxable profits of £60,000 and Ruby has taxable profits of £50,000 for the year ended 31 March 2027. These profits will be taxable as trading income in each partner's self-assessment tax return for the tax year 2026/27.

Activity 1: Partnership profit allocation

Ron and Steve have been in partnership as farmers for many years sharing profits and losses as follows.

	Ron	Steve
Salary	5,000	Nil
Balance – profit-share ratio	3	2

During y/e 30 June 2027 the partnership made a trading profit of £60,000.

Required

Complete the table showing how the profits are allocated between the partners.

	Ron	Steve
	£	£

Workings (not provided in the assessment)

	Ron	Steve	Total
	£	£	£

3 Change in profit-sharing agreement

Sometimes the profit-sharing agreement may change during a period of account.

Here we apportion the profit before and after the change. We then split the profits before the change using the old rules, and the profits after the change using the new rules.

Do not forget interest and salaries are annual figures, so will need to be time apportioned.

Illustration 2: Change in partnership agreement

Jenny and Chris are in partnership. Taxable trading profits of the partnership for the year ended 31 March 2027 are £60,000. Until 30 September 2026 profits are shared equally. From 1 October 2026 Jenny and Chris agree that the profits should be shared in the ratio 2:1.

Show how the taxable trading profits of the year to 31 March 2027 are divided between Jenny and Chris.

Your first step should be to apportion the profits to the periods before and after the change in the profit-sharing ratio:

1.4.26–30.9.26 6/12 × £60,000 = £30,000

1.10.26–31.3.27 6/12 × £60,000 = £30,000

Next, divide these profits between the partners:

	Total £	Jenny £	Chris £
1.4.26–30.9.26 (1:1)	30,000	15,000	15,000
1.10.26–31.3.27 (2:1)	30,000	20,000	10,000
	60,000	35,000	25,000

For the year to 31 March 2027, Jenny's taxable trading profits are £35,000 and Chris's taxable trading profits are £25,000.

Activity 2: Change in profit-sharing arrangements

During the year ended 30 June 2027, the Ron and Steve partnership made profits of £90,000.

On 1 January 2027 the partners decided to change their profit-sharing arrangement.

The old arrangement had been:

	Ron	Steve
Salary	5,000	Nil
Balance – profit-share ratio	3	2

After the change both partners receive an equal share of all profits and no one receives a salary.

Required

Complete the table showing how the profits are allocated between the partners.

	Ron £	Steve £
Profit share		

Workings (not provided in the assessment)

	Ron £	Steve £	Total £

	Ron £	Steve £	Total £

4 The tax positions of individual partners

Once we have allocated profits between partners, we treat each partner as an individual sole trader.

5 Changes in partners

A partnership may continue but individual partners may choose to leave while new partners may join.

When a partner joins or leaves the partnership, treat the arrival or departure as a change in the partnership share agreement. Split the period of account into periods before and after the change and apportion profits between the partners based on whatever agreement they have come to in respect of sharing profits and losses.

Illustration 3: Partner joining partnership

Francis and Caroline have been in partnership for many years, preparing accounts to 31 December each year. Profits were shared equally until 1 June 2026, when Charles joined the partnership. From 1 June 2026 profits were shared in the ratio 2:2:1.

Profits adjusted for tax purposes are as follows.

Period	Taxable profit £
Year ended 31 December 2026	48,000
Year ended 31 December 2027	18,000
Year ended 31 December 2028	24,000

We need to calculate the taxable profits for each partner for the years ending 31 December 2026, 2027 and 2028.

We must first share the profits between the partners.

	Total £	Francis £	Caroline £	Charles £
Year ended 31.12.26				
1.1.26–31.5.26 (5/12)				
Profits 50:50	20,000	10,000	10,000	
1.6.26–31.12.26 (7/12)				
Profits 2:2:1	28,000	11,200	11,200	5,600
Total for year ended 31.12.26	48,000	21,200	21,200	5,600
Year ended 31.12.27				
Profits 2:2:1	18,000	7,200	7,200	3,600
Total for y/e 31.12.27	18,000	7,200	7,200	3,600
Year ended 31.12.28				
Profits 2:2:1	24,000	9,600	9,600	4,800
Total for y/e 31.12.28	24,000	9,600	9,600	4,800

Illustration 4: Partner leaving a partnership

Dominic, Sebastian and India have traded in partnership, sharing profits equally for many years. On 1 May 2027 India left the partnership. Profits continue to be shared equally. Accounts have always been prepared to 30 September and recent results have been:

	Profit £
Y/e 30.9.25	36,000
Y/e 30.9.26	81,000
Y/e 30.9.27	60,000

Allocate the profits of each period of account to the partners for the years ending 30 September 2025, 2026 and 2027.

	Total £	Dominic £	Sebastian £	India £
Y/e 30.9.25	36,000	12,000	12,000	12,000
Y/e 30.9.26	81,000	27,000	27,000	27,000
Y/e 30.9.27				
1.10.26–30.4.27 (7/12)	35,000	11,667	11,667	11,666
1.5.27–30.9.27 (5/12)	25,000	12,500	12,500	–

	Total	Dominic	Sebastian	India
	£	£	£	£
	60,000	24,167	24,167	11,666

Activity 3: Change in partnership personnel

M and G began a partnership many years ago, sharing profits and losses equally. On 1 December 2026, G retired and B joined as a new partner. M and B share profits in the ratio of 2:1. Results have been as follows:

	£
Y/e 31.5.26	33,000
Y/e 31.5.27	51,000
Y/e 31.5.28	72,000

Required

Complete the following table showing the profit allocations for the partners for the years ending 31 May 2026, 2027 and 2028.

(Workings not provided in the assessment)

Sharing of profits

	Total	M	G	B
		£	£	£

BPP

Chapter summary

- A partnership is a group of self-employed individuals trading together.
- Calculate tax-adjusted profits for a partnership in the same way as you would calculate the tax-adjusted profits of a sole trader.
- Divide the tax-adjusted profits of a period of account between the partners in accordance with their profit-sharing arrangements during the period of account.
- If profit-sharing arrangements change during a period of account, time apportion profits to the periods before and after the change before allocating them to partners.

Activity answers

Activity 1: Partnership profit allocation

	Ron £	Steve £
Profit share	38,000	22,000

Workings (not provided in the assessment)

	Ron £	Steve £	Total £
Year ended 30 June 2027			
Salary	5,000	______	5,000
Balance (3:2)	33,000	22,000	55,000 (bal)
Assessments	38,000	22,000	60,000

Activity 2: Change in profit-sharing arrangements

	Ron £	Steve £
Profit share	50,500	39,500

Workings (not provided in the assessment)

	Ron £	Steve £	Total £
Year ended 30 June 2027			
1 July–31 December 2026			
Salary (6/12) × 5,000	2,500		2,500
Balance (3:2)	25,500	17,000	42,500
(6/12) × 90,000			45,000
1 January–30 June 2027			
(6/12) × 90,000			
Split 1:1	22,500	22,500	45,000
	50,500	39,500	90,000

Activity 3: Change in partnership personnel

(Workings not provided in the assessment)

Sharing of profits

	Total	M £	G £	B £
Y/e 31.5.26, ie £33,000				
(1:1)	33,000	16,500	16,500	______
Y/e 31.5.27, ie £51,000				
Up to 1.12.26 (1:1) 51,000 × 6/12	25,500	12,750	12,750	______
From 1.12.26 (2:1 each) 51,000 × 6/12	25,500	17,000		8,500
	51,000	29,750	12,750	8,500
Y/e 31.5.28, ie £72,000				
(2:1)	72,000	48,000		24,000

Test your learning

1 **The adjusted profit of a partnership is divided between the partners in accordance with the profit-sharing agreement in existence during what period?**

Tick ONE box.

	✓
The calendar year	
The tax year	
The period of account concerned	
The period agreed by the partners	

2 Dave and Joe are in partnership together and make a profit of £18,000 for the year to 31 March 2027. Up to 31 December 2026, they share profits and losses equally but thereafter, they share 3:2.

Required

Dave's taxable profits for 2026/27 are:

£ ☐

and Joe's taxable profits for 2026/27 are:

£ ☐

3 Holly and Jasmine are in partnership sharing profits equally after paying a salary of £5,000 to Holly and a salary of £80,000 to Jasmine. Taxable profits for the year to 31 March 2027 were £200,000.

Required

Using the proforma layout provided, show the taxable profits of each of the partners for the year.

	Total £	Holly £	Jasmine £
Salary			
Division of profits 1:1			

4 Barry and Steve have been in partnership for many years. Profits are shared three-quarters to Barry and one-quarter to Steve. For the year ended 31 March 2026, the partnership made a profit of £60,000 and for the year ended 31 March 2027, the profit was £80,000.

Required

The profit taxable on Steve for the year ended 31 March 2027 is:

Tick ONE box.

	✓
£60,000	
£15,000	
£45,000	
£20,000	

5 Abdul and Ghita have been in partnership for many years. On 1 September 2026, Sase joins the partnership and profits are shared between the partners in the ratio 2:2:1 with Sase receiving the smallest profit share. For the year to 31 August 2027, the partnership makes a profit of £120,000.

Required

Sase's share of the profit for the year to 31 August 2027 is £ [ ]

6 William, Ann and John have been in partnership for many years, sharing profits equally. Accounts have always been prepared to 31 October each year. On 31 December 2026, William left the partnership. Profits continued to be shared equally. Recent results were:

	£
Y/e 31 October 2025	21,000
Y/e 31 October 2026	33,000
Y/e 31 October 2027	36,000

Required

Using the proforma layout provided, show how the profits of each period will be divided between the partners.

	Total £	William £	Ann £	John £
Y/e 31.10.25				
Y/e 31.10.26				
Y/e 31.10.27				

9 Unincorporated trader losses

Syllabus learning outcomes

2.5	**Calculate trading income for sole traders and partners** Learners need to understand: 2.5.16 options available to sole traders and partners to relieve trading losses: • carry back • current year • carry forward 2.5.17 how to select the relief that gives the maximum tax benefit for losses
	Learners need to be able to: 2.5.21 identify how losses are allocated, according to: • specific instructions • achieve maximum tax benefit.
6.1	Understand administrative requirements of the UK's tax regime Learners need to understand: 6.1.5 time limits for loss relief claims • individual

Assessment context

Trading losses are likely to be assessed in task 9. There will likely be a question covering losses for unincorporated businesses, and one relating to losses for companies, so ensure you read the question carefully as the rules for companies are different to the rules for sole traders and partners.

Qualification context

You will not see these rules outside of this unit.

Business context

Using loss relief to generate a tax repayment is often a lifeline for struggling businesses.

Chapter overview

Unincorporated trader losses

Relieving trading losses (individuals)

Tax year of loss

- Normal CYB
- Trading profits = nil
- Choose what to do with loss of the tax year

Options

- Carry forward loss relief
  - C/f vs first available trading profits
  - automatic
- Current year and/or prior year
  - Vs total income
  - All or nothing claim (may waste personal allowance)
  - CY only, PY only, CY and PY in any order

Considerations

- Timing
- Rate of tax saved
- Waste personal allowance

Introduction

Not all businesses make profits every year. In this chapter, we will see how unincorporated businesses (ie sole traders and partnerships) can obtain tax relief for losses. We will look at losses for companies in chapter 13.

1 Trade losses

KEY TERM

> **Trading losses:** Losses incurred in the ordinary course of business that may be able to be offset against other income or profits, reducing the overall tax liability.

We have previously seen that the starting point for computing a business's trading results is to take the statement of profit or loss and adjust it for tax purposes. If this adjusted figure is negative, then there is a **trading loss,** rather than a taxable profit.

Note that the deduction of capital allowances can actually increase an adjusted loss, or even turn an adjusted profit into a trading loss.

If there is a trading loss, the **taxable trading figure in the income tax computation will be nil**; it is not the negative amount.

Note. Losses in a partnership are allocated to the partners in the same way as profits. Each partner will then decide on the best method of relief for their share of the loss.

Illustration 1: How it works

If a trader makes a loss of £5,000 in the year to 31 March 2027, the **2026/27 taxable** profits based on that period will be **£nil**.

There will be a trading loss in **2026/27** of £5,000 which can be relieved by using it to reduce the taxpayer's other taxable income.

The taxpayer has a choice as to how this loss is relieved, as follows:

- Carry forward of losses against future trading income
- Losses set against total income in the tax year of the loss (current year, CY)
- Losses set against total income of the previous tax year (prior year, PY)

There are also special loss relief rules which apply when a business is starting or ceasing to trade. These are not included in your syllabus.

2 Relief options for trading losses (individuals)

2.1 Losses set against profits of the same trade

If no claim is made against total income (see below) or some of the loss is left after such a claim, then the balance must be relieved against profits of the same trade.

The loss is relieved against the first available future profits of the same trade.

Setoff is automatic and compulsory.

Any unrelieved loss may be carried forward indefinitely.

2.2 Losses set against total income

The loss is available for setoff against total income of:

- The tax year in which the loss-making accounting period ends (**year of the loss**); and/or
- The tax year immediately preceding the year of the loss.

A taxpayer does not have to deduct a loss under either method if they do not wish to do so. If they do wish to make either of these deductions, they would need to make a claim to do so.

If a claim is made, the maximum possible loss must be set off in that year (ie personal allowances cannot be saved). The taxpayer can choose which year to use the loss first eg current year and then preceding year or vice versa. Any loss remaining must be carried forward for use against first available profits of the same trade.

Claims to offset the loss against total income must be made by 31 January, 22 months following the end of the tax year of the loss. For example, 31 January 2029 for losses in 2026/27.

The pro forma below shows where the trade loss offsets appear in an income tax computation.

	Non-savings £
Trading income	X
Carry forward relief against profits of the same trade	**(X)**
Savings income	X
Rental income	X
Total income	X
Current year and/ or prior year relief against total income	**(X)**
Net income	X
Personal allowance	(X)
Taxable income	X

Illustration 2: Loss relief

Ahmed, a sole trader, has the following taxable trading profits/(loss):

Tax year	£
2025/26	10,000
2026/27	(49,000)
2027/28	20,000

His only other income is rental income of £15,000 a year.

The loss of £49,000 in **2026/27** and could be deducted from:

- **Total income of £25,000** (trading income of £10,000 + rental income of £15,000) in 2025/26
- **Total income** (rental income) of £15,000 in **2026/27**

If both of these claims are made, the loss remaining unrelieved of £9,000 is automatically deducted from the **taxable trading profits** of £20,000 arising in **2027/28**.

Claiming to relieve the loss against total income of the current year and the prior year is optional. If the sole trader chooses not to make a claim to deduct the loss from total income, the loss is carried forward to deduct from taxable trading profits in future years.

The disadvantage of deducting a loss from total income in the year of the loss and/or in the preceding year is that **personal allowances may be wasted**. You will recall that every individual has a personal allowance that they can set against their net income. Income of up to the personal allowance is effectively tax-free income, so there is no benefit once the net income is reduced to an amount lower than the personal allowance.

Activity 1: Income tax trading loss options

Edward runs a gift card shop and his recent actual and budgeted trading results are as follows.

Year ended	£
31.3.2025 (2024/25)	5,000
31.3.2026 (2025/26)	(8,000)
31.3.2027 (2026/27)	20,000

He also receives £12,000 rental income per annum.

Required

Show if the following statements are true or false by ticking the correct box for each.

	True ✓	False ✓
Edward may offset the loss against total income in 2024/25 and then in 2023/24.		
Edward may offset the loss against total income in 2026/27.		
Edward may offset the loss against trading income only in 2024/25.		
Edward may offset the loss against the rental income in 2025/26.		

Activity 2: Utilisation of income tax losses

Pike commenced trading many years ago, making up accounts to 31 March each year. Pike's recent actual and budgeted results are as follows:

Year ended	£
31 March 2026	2,000
31 March 2027	(15,000)
31 March 2028	8,000
31 March 2029	4,000

He has received rental income as follows:

	£
2025/26	400
2026/27	1,000
2027/28	1,000
2028/29	1,000

Required

(a) Complete the following table showing Pike's total income for 2025/26 to 2028/29 assuming maximum and earliest claims against total income are made. Enter '0' in cells as appropriate.

	2025/26 £	2026/27 £	2027/28 £	2028/29 £
Trading income				
Loss carried forward				
Property income				
Total income				
CY loss relief				
PY loss relief				
Net income				

Workings (not provided in the assessment)

	Trading loss
Loss made in 2026/27	15,000

(b) Show if the following statement is true or false by ticking the correct box.

	True ✓	False ✓
Pike has used his loss in the most tax-efficient way possible		

3 Choosing loss relief

KEY TERM

Carry forward loss relief: Allows an individual to set a trading loss against the first available profits from the same trade in the future.

Current year loss relief: Allows an individual to set a trading loss against total income in the tax year of the loss.

Carry back loss relief: Allows an individual to set a trading loss against total income in the tax year prior to the tax year of the loss (no need to make a current year claim first).

3.1 Individuals

As we have seen above, several alternative loss reliefs may be available for an individual, including:

- Carry forward of losses
- Losses set against total income in the tax year of the loss
- Losses set against total income of the previous tax year

In making a choice, consider:

(a) The rate at which relief will be obtained.

We saw in Chapter 2 that individuals can pay income tax at the starting rate, the basic rate, the higher rate and the additional rate.

The most beneficial method is to try to offset losses against any income being taxed at the highest rate.

(b) How quickly relief will be obtained. Relief is obtained earlier, by carrying back the loss. It is therefore usually beneficial to set losses against income of the previous year and current year rather than to wait to carry forward loss relief.

(c) The extent to which personal allowances might be wasted.

3.2 Partnerships

Remember that for tax purposes a partnership is simply a group of sole traders. So, once any trade loss has been shared between the partners, each partner can use their share of the trade loss using whichever sole trade rules they would like. Each partner makes their own decision about what claims to make based on their own circumstances.

Chapter summary

- For an individual, a trading loss can be:
  - Carried forward to be deducted from the first available profits of the same trade
  - Deducted from total income in the tax year of the loss and/or in the preceding tax year
- An individual can choose the order in which to claim for current year loss relief and prior year loss relief.
- When selecting a loss relief, consider the rate at which relief is obtained, the timing of relief, and the effect on personal allowances.

Activity answers

Activity 1: Income tax trading loss options

The correct answers are:

	True ✓	False ✓
Edward may offset the loss against total income in 2024/25 and then in 2023/24.		✓
Edward may offset the loss against total income in 2026/27.		✓
Edward may offset the loss against trading income only in 2024/25.		✓
Edward may offset the loss against the rental income in 2025/26.	✓	

Notes.

1 The loss has been made in tax year 2025/26. It can, therefore, be used in 2025/26 and/or 2024/25, so the first option is false.

2 If Edward lets the loss carry forward to 2026/27, then it offsets automatically against trading income only, so the second option is false.

3 If Edward chooses to carry the loss back to 2024/25, it will offset against total income, not just trading income, so the third option is false.

4 If Edward makes a claim for 2025/26, it will offset against his total income. The only income he has is rental income so the fourth option is true.

Activity 2: Utilisation of income tax losses

(a)

	2025/26 £	2026/27 £	2027/28 £	2028/29 £
Trading income	2,000	0	8,000	4,000
Loss carried forward	0	0	(8,000)	(3,600)
	2,000	0	0	400
Property income	400	1,000	1,000	1,000
Total income	2,400	1,000	1,000	1,400
CY loss relief	0	(1,000)	0	0
PY loss relief	(2,400)	0	0	0
Net income	0	0	1,000	1,400

Workings (not provided in the assessment)

	Trading loss
Loss made in 2026/27	15,000
Carry back against total income in 2025/26	(2,400)
Use against total income in current year 2026/27	(1,000)
Carry forward against trading income in year 2027/28	(8,000)
Carry forward against trading income in year 2028/29 (balancing figure)	(3,600)
	0

(b) The correct answers are:

	True ✓	False ✓
Pike has used his loss in the most tax-efficient way possible		✓

Explanation

Pike's income is below the personal allowance in all years, so it is a waste to carry back the loss or use it in the year of the loss.

It is wasteful to use it in the future years as well but Pike has no control over this. The carry forward is automatic.

Note. The question told you to use the loss as soon as possible, so prior year relief should be claimed before current year.

Test your learning

1 Harold (a sole trader), who has been in business for many years, makes a trading loss of £20,000 in the tax year 2026/27.

Required

In which year(s) may the loss be relieved against total income, assuming relief is claimed as soon as possible? Tick ONE box.

	✓
2026/27 only	
2027/28 and/or 2026/27	
2025/26 only	
2026/27 and/or 2025/26	

2 Identify whether the following statement is true or false.

Required

For an individual, trading losses can only be carried forward for deduction in the six succeeding tax years.

	✓
True	
False	

3 **Where trade losses are carried forward by an individual, against what sort of income may they be relieved? Tick ONE box.**

	✓
Against non-savings income	
Against total income	
Against trading income arising in the same trade	
Against trading income arising in all trades carried on by the taxpayer	

4 Mallory (a sole trader), who has traded for many years, has the following recent tax-adjusted results:

Year ended 31 March 2026	Profit	£10,000
Year ended 31 March 2027	Loss	£(40,000)
Year ended 30 March 2028	Profit	£25,000

Mallory has other income of £9,000 each year.

Required

Explain how the loss in 2026/27 can be relieved.

5 CR Ltd has the following results for the two years to 31 March 2027:

	Year ended 31 March	
	2026	2027
	£	£
Trading profit (loss)	170,000	(320,000)
Interest	5,000	60,000
Qualifying charitable donation	5,000	5,000

Required

Calculate the amount of trading loss remaining to be carried forward at 1 April 2028 assuming that all possible earlier loss relief claims against total profits are made.

£ [ ]

6 JB Ltd had the following results in the three accounting periods to 31 March 2027:

	Year ended 30 September 2025	Six months to 31 March 2026	Year ended 31 March 2027
	£	£	£
Trading profit/(loss)	4,000	6,000	(10,000)
Qualifying charitable donation	1,000	3,000	1,500

Required

Identify the amount, if any, of the trading loss incurred in the year ended 31 March 2027 that may be relieved against total profits in the year ended 30 September 2025. Tick ONE box.

	✓
£Nil	
£2,000	
£4,000	
£3,000	

10 National insurance contributions

Learning outcomes

2.3	**Calculate income tax and National Insurance contributions (NICs) payable**
	Learners need to understand: 2.3.1 NICs for category A employees: • employee Class 1 • employer Class 1 • Class 1A 2.3.2 the circumstances in which the employment allowance can be claimed. 2.3.3 Class 4 NICs
	Learners need to be able to: 2.3.4 calculate NICs • employee Class 1 • employer Class 1 • Class 1A • Class 4

Assessment context

Task 3 in the AAT practice assessments tests the calculation of Class 1 Employee, Class 1 Employer and Class 1A (employer) National Insurance for 2 marks. Task 4 tests the calculation of Class 4 National Insurance contributions for 2 marks.

National Insurance contributions calculations are simple and straightforward and should earn you easy marks in the assessment. Under the old syllabus, the task covering National Insurance contributions calculations was identified by the Chief Assessor as the best performing task in the assessment overall, so it is vital you can prepare these calculations.

Qualification context

You will not see the information in this chapter outside of this unit.

Business context

National Insurance is a significant extra cost for an employer and an employee. An employer will have to consider the National Insurance cost when taking on new staff or offering increased salary or benefits to existing staff.

These taxes are also a significant extra cost for self-employed people.

Chapter overview

National insurance

Payable by partners and sole traders

- Class 4
- Trade profits ≤ £12,570 nil
- Trade profits £12,570 – £50,270 6%
- Trade profits > £50,270 2%

Payable by employers and employees

Class 1

- On cash earnings
- Exclude reimbursed expenses
- Include excessive mileage payments > 45p/mile
- Calculate weekly or monthly
- Annual calculation for directors

Employee

- Cost to employee
  - £1-£12,570 0%
  - £12,571-£50,270 8%
  - £50,271 and above 2%

Employer

- Cost to employer
  - £1-£5000 0%
  - £5001 and above 15%
  - Deduct employment allowance of £10,500 from total bill

Class 1A

- Payable by employer
- On benefits
- Rate 15%

Introduction

Paying National Insurance Contributions (NICs) builds up an individual's entitlement to certain state benefits, such as pensions.

In this chapter we cover the NICs payable by self-employed and employed individuals, and employers.

An employer will have to deduct **Class 1 Employee National Insurance** from their employees' cash earnings and pay this over to HMRC. This is a cost to the employee. In addition to this, employers will have to pay over **Class 1 Employer National Insurance** on the employees' cash earnings as well as **Class 1A National Insurance** on non-cash benefits received by the employee (for example use of a car owned by the company). Both of these represent an additional cost to the employer. National Insurance contributions are sometimes abbreviated to NIC.

1 Class 1 Employee National Insurance

KEY TERM

Employee's National Insurance Contributions (NIC): A UK tax incurred by employees on employment income, deducted at source by their employer. Alternative term: Class 1 Primary NIC.

1.1 What are earnings?

'Earnings' broadly comprise gross cash payments, excluding benefits which cannot be turned into cash by surrender (eg annual leave entitlement). **Certain payments are exempt.** In general, the income tax and NIC exemptions mirror one another so if a payment is exempt for income tax it is also exempt for National Insurance. We considered exempt payments in detail in Chapter 4; for example, if an employee works away from home their employer can pay them up to £5 a night to cover incidental expenses and these payments would not be chargeable to income tax or National Insurance.

An expense with a business purpose is not treated as earnings. For example, if an employee is reimbursed for business travel or for staying in a hotel on the employer's business this is not normally 'earnings'.

In general, vouchers are subject to Class 1 Employee and Employer NIC as they are deemed to be a cash equivalent. For exempt vouchers see Chapter 4.

1.2 Rates of contributions

The rates of contribution for 2026/27, and the income bands to which they apply, are provided in the assessment and set out in the *Reference material* section at the end of this Course Book.

Employees pay Class 1 employee's contributions at 8% of earnings between the employee's threshold of £12,570 and the upper earnings limit (UEL) of £50,270. They also pay additional Class 1 employee's contributions of 2% on earnings above the upper earnings limit.

Illustration 1: Class 1 Employee National Insurance

Sally works for Red plc. She is paid £5,000 per month. Show Sally's Class 1 employee contributions deducted by Red plc for 2026/27.

Annual salary £5,000 × 12 = £60,000

Employee contributions	£
£(50,270 – 12,570) = £37,700 × 8% (main)	3,016
£(60,000 – 50,270) = £9,730 × 2% (additional)	195
Total employee contributions	3,211

Activity 1: Class 1 Employee National Insurance

Tyrone is one of 3,000 employees of Taverner plc.

	£
Salary for 2026/27	52,500
Non-cash benefits	6,450

Required

What amount of national insurance does Tyrone suffer in the tax year?

£ [ ]

2 Class 1 Employer National Insurance

KEY TERM

Employer's National Insurance Contributions (NIC): A UK tax incurred by employers as a result of employing an employee. Alternative term: Class 1 Secondary NIC.

2.1 What are earnings?

We use the same figure we calculated for the employee calculation above.

2.2 Rates of contributions

The rates of contribution for 2026/27, and the income bands to which they apply, are provided in the assessment and set out in the *Reference material* section at the end of this Course Book.

Employers pay contributions of 15% on earnings above the employer's threshold of £5,000. There is no upper limit.

Illustration 2: Class 1 Employer National Insurance

Sally works for Red plc. She is paid £5,000 per month.

Show Sally's employer contributions paid by Red plc for 2026/27.

Annual salary £5,000 × 12 = £60,000

Employer's threshold £5,000

Red plc	£
Employer contributions	
£(60,000 – 5,000) = £55,000 × 15%	8,250

Activity 2: Class 1 Employer National Insurance

Tyrone is one of 3,000 employees of Taverner plc.

	£
Salary for 2026/27	52,500
Non-cash benefits	6,450

Required

What amount of Class 1 employer national insurance does Tyrone's employer pay in the tax year?

£ [ ]

3 The employment allowance

KEY TERM

Employment allowance: An amount that can be deducted from the employer's Class 1 Employer's liability.

An employer can make a claim to reduce its total Class 1 employer contributions by an **employment allowance equal to those contributions**, subject to a **maximum allowance of £10,500 per tax year.**

Some employers **are excluded employers** for the purposes of the employment allowance. These include those who employ **employees for personal, household or domestic work, public authorities** and employers who **carry out functions either wholly or mainly of a public nature** such as provision of National Health Service services. Companies where the director is the only employee are also excluded from the employment allowance.

Illustration 3: The employment allowance

Blue plc is a trading company which has two employees, one who earns £60,000 per year and the other who earns £40,000 per year. Each employee is paid in equal monthly amounts and so an annual computation of Class 1 can be made.

Required

Calculate the Class 1 employer contributions payable by Blue plc for 2026/27.

Solution

	£
Employee 1: £(60,000 – 5,000) = 55,000 × 15%	8,250
Employee 2: £(40,000 – 5,000) = 35,000 × 15%	5,250
	13,500
Less employment allowance (maximum)	(10,500)
Employer contributions 2026/27	3,000

Activity 3: The employment allowance

Stoney Heap Ltd is a trading company which has two employees, one earns £18,000 per year and the other earns £15,000 per year. Each employee is paid in equal monthly amounts.

Required

How much Class 1 employer contributions are payable by Stoney Heap Ltd for 2026/27?

£ ______

4 Class 1A National Insurance

KEY TERM

Class 1A NICs: A UK tax incurred by employers on the provision of assessable benefits.

4.1 What are benefits?

If an employee is provided with non-cash benefits such as the use of a car belonging to the employer then we must calculate a cash equivalent value so that income tax and National Insurance may be applied. The calculation of the cash equivalent value is addressed in Chapter 4.

> **Assessment focus point**
>
> In National Insurance questions you will probably be given the value of the benefit although you may be expected to apply the rules in Chapter 4 to calculate it.

4.2 Rates of contributions

The rates of contribution for 2026/27 are provided in the assessment and set out in the *Reference material* section of this Course Book.

We simply apply 15% to the cash value of the benefits.

Illustration 4: Class 1A National Insurance

Sally has the following benefits for income tax purposes.

	£
Company car	5,200
Living accommodation	10,000
Medical insurance	800

Required

Calculate the Class 1A NICs that the employer will have to pay.

Solution

Total benefits are £16,000 (£10,000 + £5,200 + £800)

Class 1A NICs:

£16,000 × 15% = £2,400

Activity 4: Class 1A National Insurance

Tyrone is one of 3,000 employees of Taverner plc.

	£
Salary for 2026/27	52,500
Non-cash benefits	6,450

Required

The Class 1A National Insurance payable by Taverner plc is

£ [ ]

5 Reimbursed expenses including business mileage

As noted above, reimbursement of genuine expenses incurred in doing your job are not subject to Class 1 National Insurance.

However, if the employer was paying for a private expense of the employee, it would be subject to National Insurance. For example, if the employer reimbursed the employee for specific business phone calls National Insurance would not apply. If the employer paid for all of the employee's calls Class 1 Employee and Employer would be applied to the cost of the private calls reimbursed.

An employee may use their own car on their employer's business and be reimbursed for the cost incurred. The employer may reimburse up to 55p a mile without any National Insurance implications. Any sums paid in excess of 55p would be subject to Class 1 Employee and Employer National Insurance. Note this is slightly different from the income tax treatment we saw in Chapter 4 where a lower rate applies after 10,000 miles have been driven in a tax year.

Illustration 5: Business mileage

Sophie uses her own car for business travel. During the tax year, Sophie drove 15,400 miles in the performance of her duties. Sophie's employer paid her a mileage allowance.

Required

How is the mileage allowance treated for National Insurance purposes assuming that the rate paid is:

(a) 40p a mile?

(b) 60p a mile?

Solution

(a)

	£
Mileage allowance received (15,400 × 40p)	6,160
Permitted payment (15,400 × 55p)	(8,470)
Excess over limit	0

As the payment is within the permitted amount there is no charge to National Insurance.

(b)

	£
Mileage allowance received (15,400 × 60p)	9,240

	£
Less tax-free amount (above)	(8,470)
	770

As the payment is above the permitted amount the excess of £770 will be chargeable to Class 1 National Insurance, Employee and Employer.

6 Tax planning

An employee may choose to receive non-cash benefits rather than a cash pay rise as cash earnings would be subject to Class 1 Employee whereas benefits would not be. The employer would probably be indifferent here between providing cash and benefits, as cash would be subject to Class 1 Employer whereas benefits would be subject to Class 1A, both at 15%.

7 NICs payable by the self-employed

Self-employed people (ie partners and sole traders) must pay Class 4 NICs.

Open book reference:

The information needed in order to calculate Class 4 NIC is clearly stated in section 7 of the reference material you have access to in the assessment.

7.1 Class 4 National Insurance Contributions

KEY TERM

Class 4 National Insurance Contributions (NIC): A UK tax incurred by self-employed individuals on their trading profits.

Class 4 contributions are based on the level of the individual's trading profits after loss relief for a tax year.

They are calculated as:

- 6% of 'profits' between the lower earnings limit (LEL) of £12,570 and the upper earnings limit (UEL) of £50,270
- 2% of 'profits' above the UEL of £50,270

Activity 5: National insurance contributions

Note. You should calculate the following to pounds and pence.

A trader has trading income of £14,000 for 2026/27.

Required

(a)

Their Class 4 NI contributions at 6% are:

£ [ ]

Mr Seye has trading income of £78,000 in 2026/27.

Required

(b)

His Class 4 NI contributions at 6% are:

£ [ ]

His Class 4 NI contributions at 2% are:

£ [ ]

Assessment focus point

Please refer to the reference material at the end of this Course Book to see which elements of this chapter will be available to you as a pop-up window in the live assessment.

Chapter summary

- Class 1 National Insurance is applied to an employee's cash earnings from employment. Vouchers are included but reimbursed business expenses are excluded.
- Class 1 Employee contributions are deducted from an employee's earnings. It is therefore a cost to the employee.
- Class 1 Employer contributions are paid in addition to an employee's earnings. It is therefore a cost to the employer.
- An employer is allowed to deduct the employment allowance from the Class 1 Employer's liability reducing the cost to them.
- Class 1A is payable by the employer on the cash equivalent value of non-cash benefits received by the employee.
- There is no Class 1 on the reimbursement of genuine business expenses but if the employer pays a private expense of the employee it will be subject to National Insurance. This includes excessive payments to an employee for the use of their own car.
- Self-employed traders pay:
  - Class 4 contributions based on the level of their profits.
- Main rate Class 4 NICs are 6% of profits between the UEL and LEL.
- Additional Class 4 NICs are 2% of profits above the UEL.

Activity answers

Activity 1: Class 1 Employee National Insurance

£ 3,061

Working

Tyrone suffers Class 1 Employee contributions on his cash earnings.

(50,270 – 12,570) × 8% =	3,016
(52,500 – 50,270) × 2% =	45
	3,061

Activity 2: Class 1 Employer National Insurance

£ 7,125

The Class 1 Employer National Insurance is

Working

Class 1 Employer contributions

(52,500 – 5,000) × 15% = 7,125

Activity 3: The employment allowance

£ 0

Working

	£
Employee 1: £(18,000 – 5,000) × 15%	1,950
Employee 2: £(15,000 – 5,000) × 15%	1,500
	3,450
Less employment allowance (maximum £10,500, restricted)	(3,450)
Employer contributions	0

Activity 4: Class 1A National Insurance

£ 968

Working

Class 1A

6,450 @ 15% = 968

Activity 5: National insurance contributions

(a) Their Class 4 NI contributions at 6% are:

£ 85.80

Working

Workings (not provided in the assessment)

		£
Class 4	(£14,000 – £12,570) × 6%	85.80

(b) His Class 4 NI contributions at 6% are:

£ 2,262.00

His Class 4 NI contributions at 2% are:

£ 554.60

Working

Workings (not provided in the assessment)

		£
Class 4 at 6%	(£50,270 – £12,570) × 6%	2,262.00
Class 4 at 2%	(£78,000 – £50,270) × 2%	554.60

Test your learning

1 Robert is one of 3,000 employees of George plc. He receives the following from his employer in tax year 2026/27:

	£
Salary	42,000
Reimbursed business expenses	3,000
Non-cash benefits	8,000

Required

(a) **What amount of Class 1 Employee National Insurance contributions does Robert's employer pay over on his behalf?**

£ [ ]

(b) **What amount of Class 1 Employer National Insurance contributions does Robert's employer pay in the tax year?**

£ [ ]

(c) **What amount of Class 1A National Insurance contributions does Robert's employer pay in the tax year?**

£ [ ]

2 Ursa Minor Beta plc is a trading company which has two employees, one earns £25,000 per year and the other who earns £60,000 per year. Each employee is paid in equal monthly amounts.

Required

The Class 1 Employer contributions payable by Ursa Minor Beta plc are

£ [ ]

3 **Toby uses his own car for business travel. During the tax year, Toby drove 18,500 miles in the performance of his duties. Toby's employer paid him a mileage allowance.**

If the mileage allowance is 35p a mile the amount subject to Class 1 National Insurance is £

[ ]

If the mileage allowance is 60p a mile the amount subject to Class 1 National Insurance is £

[ ]

4 Compute the following total sole traders' liabilities to NICs for 2026/27.

Note. You should calculate the following to pounds and pence.

Acker

Taxable trading profits £5,050

Required

(a)

Acker's total Class 4 contributions are £ [ ]

Bailey

Taxable trading profits £60,000

Required

(b)

Bailey's total Class 4 contributions are £ [ ]

Cartwright

Taxable trading profits £20,850

Required

(c)

Cartwright's total Class 4 contributions are £ [ ]

11 Chargeable gains

Learning outcomes

4	**Calculate capital gains tax payable by UK taxpayers**
4.1	**Calculate chargeable gains and allowable losses** Learners need to understand: 4.1.1 that individuals are taxed on their gains in a tax year
	4.1.2 the meaning of: • chargeable assets • chargeable disposals • chargeable persons • connected persons • gross sales proceeds • market value • net sales proceeds • allowable costs
	4.1.3 that exempt assets include: • cars • wasting chattels • gifts to charity • cash • stocks and shares held in an ISA • prizes/lottery wins/betting wins
	4.1.4 the situations where market value is used instead of sales proceeds 4.1.5 transfers between spouses 4.1.6 transfers to connected persons 4.1.7 part disposals 4.1.8 non-wasting chattel disposals 4.1.9 plant and machinery disposals
	Learners need to be able: 4.1.10 calculate chargeable gains and allowable losses for: • chargeable assets • part disposals • chattels

4.2	**Calculate capital gains tax payable**
	Learners need to understand: 4.2.1 the rates applicable to capital gains 4.2.2 current year losses 4.2.3 brought forward losses 4.2.4 the restriction for losses from disposals to connected persons 4.2.5 the annual exempt amount
	Learners need to be able to: 4.2.6 calculate chargeable gains and allowable losses: • offset current year losses efficiently • offset brought forward losses efficiently 4.2.7 deduct the annual exempt amount efficiently 4.2.8 calculate capital gains tax

Assessment context

Task 6 in the AAT practice assessments requires the calculation of chargeable gains for a number of different disposals testing a variety of the different rules in this chapter including those for chattels, part disposals, exempt assets, connected parties, and your understanding of the use of capital losses. 10 marks are available.

Qualification context

You will not see the information in this chapter outside of this unit.

Business context

People sell assets for a variety of reasons. It is important to realise when a charge to capital gains tax arises and when capital gains tax needs to be paid if a taxpayer is to avoid paying interest and penalties.

Chapter overview

Chargeable gains

Computing capital gains tax

Basis

- Disposals in tax year
- Chargeable person
  - Individuals
- Chargeable disposal
  - Sale
  - Gift
  - Insurance proceeds
  - Not on death
- Chargeable asset
  - Any asset not exempt

Calculation

- Proceeds
  - Usually: Proceeds – disposal costs
  - Connected parties: Market value – disposal costs
  - Spouses/Civil partners: Original cost + acquisition cost + enhancement
  - Gifts: Market value – disposal costs

LESS

- Cost
  - Cost + acquisition cost + enhancement

- Gains and/or
- Losses
  - CY use all
  - CF excess
  - BF use after deducting the AEA

- Deduct AEA of £3000
- Tax @ 18% (basic rate) or 24%
- Due date 31.1.28

Exempt assets

- Cars
- Gilts
- QCBs
- Some chattels
- Premium bonds
- ISAs

Further aspects of chargeable gains

Part disposal

Apply $\frac{A}{A+B}$ to cost

Connected parties

- Direct relatives
- Proceeds = MV
- Loss may only be offset versus same person

Chattels

- Wasting
  - < 50-year life exempt
- Non-wasting
  - > 50-year life
-

Cost \ Proceeds	> 6,000	≤ 6,000
> 6,000	Normal	Gross proceeds = 6,000
≤ 6,000	Restrict gain to 5/3 × (gross proceeds – 6,000)	Exempt

Introduction

Income is a regular receipt that is expected to recur. A gain is a one-off disposal of a capital item.

Individuals pay **income tax** on income and **capital gains tax** on capital gains.

1 When does a chargeable gain arise?

KEY TERM

Chargeable gain: When a chargeable asset is sold for more than its cost.

For a disposable to be taxable there must be a **chargeable disposal** of a **chargeable asset** by a **chargeable person**.

1.1 Chargeable person

KEY TERM

Chargeable person: An individual, partners in a partnership, or a company that disposes of a chargeable asset.

In this chapter we will be focussing on the taxation of individuals as **chargeable persons**.

1.2 Chargeable disposal

An individual is taxed on gains arising from chargeable disposals in the current tax year.

KEY TERM

Chargeable disposal: The sale, gift or transfer of an asset that triggers a capital gain.

Exempt disposal: A disposal on which no chargeable gain or allowable loss arises.

The following are the most important **chargeable disposals**:

- Sales of assets or parts of assets
- Gifts of assets or parts of assets
- The loss or destruction of an asset

A chargeable disposal occurs on the date of the contract (where there is one, whether written or oral), or the date of a conditional contract becoming unconditional.

Exempt disposals include:

- Transfers on death
- Gifts to charities

On death the heirs inherit assets as if they bought them at death for their then market values. There is no capital gain or allowable loss on death.

1.3 Chargeable assets

KEY TERM

Chargeable asset: All assets other than exempt assets.

Exempt assets: Assets that are not subject to UK capital gains tax.

The following assets are exempt:

- Motor vehicles suitable for private use
- **Wasting chattels** (greyhounds, racehorses) (see later)
- Investments held in an ISA
- Cash
- Prizes/lottery wins/betting wins

Assessment focus point

Make sure you identify an exempt asset, state that it is exempt in the exam and do not tax it.

2 Calculation of chargeable gains and allowable losses

Illustration 1: Basic capital gains computation

	£
Disposal consideration/gross sales proceeds (or market value)	X
Less incidental costs of disposal	(X)
Net sales proceeds	X
Less allowable costs (including acquisition cost)	(X)
Less enhancement expenditure	(X)
Capital gain/(capital loss)	X/(X)

We now look at each of the items in the above proforma in turn.

2.1 Disposal consideration

Usually this is proceeds received. Note, though, that a disposal is deemed to take place at **market value** when the disposal is:

- A gift
- Made for a consideration that cannot be valued
- Deliberately sold for a consideration of less than market value
- Made to a connected person (see later)

Note that if a taxpayer makes a sale to an unconnected person and strikes a bad bargain then the actual proceeds achieved will be used. Market value is only used for a sale between unconnected persons when the taxpayer deliberately chooses to sell at undervalue to give the buyer a benefit.

Where a chargeable asset is lost or destroyed the taxpayer may receive insurance money as compensation for their loss. In that case the loss/destruction is treated as a chargeable disposal, with the money received from the insurance company being the disposal proceeds.

2.2 Costs

The following costs are deducted in the above proforma:

(a) **Incidental costs of disposal**

These are the costs of selling an asset. They may include advertising costs, estate agents' fees, legal costs and valuation fees. These costs should be deducted separately from any other allowable costs.

(b) **Allowable costs**

These include:

(i) The original purchase price of the asset

(ii) Costs incurred in purchasing the asset (estate agents' fees, legal fees, etc)

(a) **Enhancement expenditure**

KEY TERM

Enhancement expenditure: Capital expenditure that enhances the value of the asset and is reflected in the state or nature of the asset at the time of disposal.

Illustration 2: Calculation of capital gain

Jack bought a holiday cottage for £25,000. He paid legal costs of £600 on the purchase.

Jack spent £8,000 building an extension to the cottage.

Jack sold the cottage for £60,000. He paid estate agents' fees of £1,200 and legal costs of £750.

Required

What is Jack's chargeable gain on sale?

Solution

Jack's chargeable gain on sale is £24,450

	£
Disposal consideration	60,000
Less incidental costs of disposal (1,200 + 750)	(1,950)
Net proceeds	58,050
Less allowable costs (25,000 + 600)	(25,600)
Less enhancement expenditure	(8,000)
Chargeable gain	24,450

Activity 1: Capital gain calculation

Mr Dunstable bought an asset for £12,700 in February 1986. He incurred legal fees of £500. He sold the asset for £35,500 incurring expenses of £1,500. While he owned the asset he improved it at a cost of £3,000.

Required

Complete the table showing Mr Dunstable's gain.

	£
Proceeds	
Less selling expenses	
Net proceeds	
Less cost	
Less legal fees on purchase	
Less enhancement	
Capital gain	

3 Computing taxable gains in a tax year

An individual pays capital gains tax (CGT) on any **taxable gains** arising in a **tax year** (6 April to 5 April).

All the chargeable gains made in the tax year are added together, and any capital losses made in the same tax year are deducted to give net gains (or losses) for the year. Next, we deduct the annual exempt amount. Finally, we are able to deduct any unrelieved capital losses brought forward from previous years to arrive at taxable gains, on which CGT will be applied.

Illustration 3: Year-end computation

	£
Current-year gains	X
Current-year losses (all)	(X)
Net capital gains	X
Annual exempt amount	(3,000)
Loss brought forward from earlier years	(X)
Taxable gains	X

Unused annual exempt amounts cannot be carried forward.

KEY TERM

Taxable gains: The chargeable gains of an individual for a tax year, after deducting allowable losses of the same tax year, the annual exempt amount and any unrelieved capital losses brought forward.

3.1 Annual exempt amount

KEY TERM

Annual exempt amount:

The amount of capital gains that an individual can make each tax year without paying Capital Gains Tax.

All individuals are entitled to an annual exempt amount. This means that in 2026/27 an individual can make gains of up to £3,000 and they will be tax free. As you can see above, it is deducted from the total net gains for the year before the deduction of capital losses brought forward.

3.2 Losses

KEY TERM

Allowable loss: When a chargeable asset is sold for less than its cost.

If losses have been made in the current year they must be offset against the gains of that year even if this means that some or all of the annual exempt amount is wasted.

If the losses in a year are greater than the gains, then the excess losses are carried forward.

When a capital loss is carried forward it is set against net gains in the next tax year AFTER the deduction of the annual exempt amount. This means the taxpayer does not lose the benefit of the annual exempt amount.

Any further loss remaining is carried forward.

Illustration 4: Capital losses

Tim has chargeable gains for 2026/27 of £32,000 and allowable losses of £30,000. As the losses are current year losses, they must be fully relieved against the gains to produce net gains of £2,000, despite the fact that net gains are below the annual exempt amount.

	£
Net chargeable gains in the year	32,000
Less losses in tax year	(30,000)
Net chargeable gains	2,000
Less annual exempt amount	(3,000)
Taxable gain	0

Hattie has chargeable gains of £12,500 for 2026/27 and allowable losses brought forward of £15,000. Hattie restricts her loss relief to £9,500 so as to take the taxable gain down to nil.

	£
Net chargeable gains	12,500
Less annual exempt amount	(3,000)
Less capital loss brought forward	(9,500)
Taxable gain	0

Activity 2: Current year losses

In 2026/27, Ted makes gains of £45,000 and £10,000. He also makes a loss of £52,500. Ted has no losses to bring forward from earlier years.

Required

Complete the following sentences:

Ted's net capital gain for 2026/27 before the annual exempt amount is £ [ ]

Ted has a loss to carry forward of £ [ ]

Activity 3: Prior year losses

Tara makes a gain on a property in 2026/27 of £12,800 (proceeds of £25,800 less cost of £13,000). She makes no other disposals in the tax year. Tara has losses brought forward from the previous year of £15,000.

Required

Tara's net capital gain for 2026/27 after the annual exempt amount is £ ____________

Tara has a loss to carry forward of £ ____________

4 Computing capital gains tax (CGT) payable

KEY TERM

Capital gains tax: A UK tax incurred by individuals on gains made on the disposal of capital assets that have increased in value.

An individual's taxable gains are chargeable to CGT at the rate of 18% or 24% depending on the individual's taxable income for 2026/27.

If the individual is a basic rate taxpayer, then CGT is payable at 18% on an amount of taxable gains up to the amount of the taxpayer's **unused** basic rate band and at 24% on the excess.

If the individual is a higher or additional rate taxpayer, then CGT is payable at 24% on all their taxable gains. Note the basic rate band covers taxable income and gains up to £37,700 (for 2026/27).

Note that a large gain may take a taxpayer out of the basic rate band and into the higher rate band. Don't forget that the bands will be extended by Gift Aid and/or personal pension scheme contributions.

Illustration 5: Calculating capital gains tax

Sally has taxable income (ie the amount after the deduction of the personal allowance) of £10,000 in 2026/27 and made taxable gains (ie gains after deduction of the annual exempt amount) of £20,000 in 2026/27.

Required

(a) Sally's CGT liability is:

Hector has taxable income of £50,000 in 2026/27 (ie he is a higher rate taxpayer).

He made taxable gains of £10,000 in 2026/27.

Required

(b) Hector's CGT liability is:

Isabel has taxable income of £33,200 in 2026/27 and made taxable gains of £25,000 in 2026/27.

Isabel has (£37,700 – £33,200) = £4,500 of her basic rate band unused.

Required

(c) Isabel's CGT liability is:

Solution

(a) £20,000 × 18% = £3,600

The taxable income uses £10,000 of the basic rate band, leaving £27,700 of the basic rate band unused, therefore all of the taxable gain is taxed at 18%.

(b) £10,000 × 24% = £2,400

All of Hector's basic rate band has been taken up by the taxable income, therefore the taxable gain is taxed at 24%.

(c) The CGT liability is therefore £5,730

	£
4,500 × 18%	810
20,500 × 24%	4,920
25,000	5,730

Activity 4: Computing capital gains tax payable

Mr Dunstable (see Activity 1) had a chargeable gain of £17,800 in 2026/27. He has taxable income of £31,200.

Required

What is Mr Dunstable's capital gains tax payable?

Mr Dunstable's capital gains tax payable is £ [ ]

5 Self-assessment for CGT

5.1 Administration

CGT is generally payable on 31 January following the end of the tax year.

Unlike income tax there are no requirements for payments on account.

On a disposal of UK residential property, a payment on account of the CGT must be made within 60 days of completion. The payment is an estimate of the CGT due in relation to the property disposal.

Administration is covered in more detail in chapter 14.

6 Special rules applying to specific disposals

Assessment focus point

The following rules need to be used in particular circumstances. Make sure you spot them in the assessment and apply them when required.

6.1 Part disposals

KEY TERM

Part disposal: When part of an asset is disposed of rather than the whole asset.

Sometimes part, rather than the whole, of an asset is disposed of. For instance, one-third of a piece of land may be sold. In this case, we need to be able to compute the chargeable gain or allowable loss arising on the part of the asset disposed of.

The problem is that, although we know what the disposal proceeds are for the part of the asset disposed of, we do not usually know what proportion of the 'cost' of the whole asset relates to that part. The solution to this is to **use the following fraction to determine the cost of the part disposed of.**

Formula to learn

The fraction is: (Cost x (A ÷ (A + B)))

A is the 'gross' proceeds (or market value) before deducting incidental costs of disposal.

B is the market value of the part of the asset that was not sold.

Illustration 6: Part disposal calculation

	£
Gross proceeds	X
Less selling costs	(X)
	X
Less:	
(Original cost of the whole asset × (A ÷ (A + B)))	(C)
Gain	X

Illustration 7: Part disposal

Mr Jones bought 4 acres of land for £270,000. He sold 1 acre of the land at auction for £200,000, before auction expenses of 15%. The market value of the 3 remaining acres is £460,000.

Required

The cost of the land being sold is:

Solution

(£270,000 x (£200,000 ÷ (£200,000 + £460,000))) = £81,818

	£
Disposal proceeds	200,000
Less incidental costs of sale (15% × £200,000)	(30,000)
Net proceeds	170,000
Less cost (see above)	(81,818)
Chargeable gain	88,182

Activity 5: Part disposal

Tom bought 10 acres of land for £20,000.

He sold 3 acres of land for £10,000 incurring disposal costs of £950 when the remaining 7 acres were worth £36,000.

Required

Complete the following sentences:

The chargeable gain on the disposal of the land is £ [ ]

The cost of the remaining land carried forward is £ [ ]

6.2 Chattels

KEY TERM

Chattels: Tangible moveable property. For example, a painting or an antique.

Wasting chattel: Chattels with apredictable life of 50 years or less, eg a racehorse or greyhound.

Wasting chattels are exempt from CGT so there are no chargeable gains and no allowable losses.

Non-wasting chattels are chargeable to CGT in the normal way, subject to the following exceptions/restrictions.

Illustration 8: Rule for computing gains/losses on non-wasting chattels

Cost	Proceeds		
≤ 6,000	≤ 6,000	Wholly exempt	• No need to calculate any gain
≤ 6,000	> 6,000	Any gain restricted to max of: $^{5}/_{3}$ × (Gross proceeds – £6,000)	• Calculate gain, compare to the maximum, take the lower figure

Cost	Proceeds		
> 6,000	≤ 6,000	Gross proceeds deemed to be £6,000	• Do normal calculation but always use £6,000 as gross proceeds figure
> 6,000	> 6,000	Wholly taxable	• Calculate a gain using the normal rules

Illustration 9: Proceeds > £6,000, Cost < £6,000

John purchased a painting for £3,000. On 1 January this year he sold the painting at auction.

If the gross sale proceeds are £4,000, the gain on sale will be exempt.

If the gross sale proceeds are £8,000 with costs of sale of 10%, the gain arising on the disposal of the painting will be calculated as follows:

	£
Gross proceeds	8,000
Less incidental costs of sale (10% × £8,000)	(800)
Net proceeds	7,200
Less cost	(3,000)
Chargeable gain	4,200
Gain cannot exceed $^{5}/_{3}$ × £(8,000 – 6,000)	3,333
Therefore, chargeable gain is £3,333.	

Illustration 10: Proceeds < £6,000, Cost > £6,000

Magee purchased an antique desk for £8,000. She sold the desk in an auction for £4,750 net of auctioneer's fees of 5% in November.

Magee obviously has a loss and therefore the allowable loss is calculated on deemed proceeds of £6,000. The costs of disposal can be deducted from the deemed proceeds of £6,000.

	£
Deemed disposal proceeds	6,000
Less incidental costs of disposal (£4,750 × 5/95)	(250)
	5,750
Less cost	(8,000)
Allowable loss	(2,250)

Activity 6: Chattels

Complete the following sentences:

Orlando Gibbons purchased a rare manuscript for £500. He sold it several years later for £9,000, before deducting the auctioneer's commission of £1,000.

Required

(a) The chargeable gain on the disposal is £ [ ]

(b) He also had an antique bought for £7,000 which he sold two years later for £3,000.

The loss on the disposal is £ [ ]

6.2.1 Plant and machinery

All plant and machinery is deemed to have a predictable life of less than 50 years, so these items are therefore wasting chattels. This is the case no matter what the actual life of the item of plant or machinery proves to be. Where the item has not been used in a business, any gain or loss is exempt from CGT (as seen above).

However, where the item has been used in a business, and capital allowances were or could have been claimed on it, any gain on disposal is chargeable. Losses, however are not allowable, as relief has already been given for the fall in value by way of capital allowances.

6.3 Transfers to connected persons

If a disposal by an individual is made to a connected person, **the disposal is deemed to take place at the market value of the asset.**

If an **allowable loss arises** on the disposal, it can **only be set against gains** arising in the same or future tax years from disposals **to the same connected person**, and the loss can only be set off if they are still connected with the person making the loss.

KEY TERM

Market value: The price which an asset might reasonably be expected to sell for in the open market.

KEY TERM

Connected person: An individual is connected with the following persons for the purposes of capital gains tax:

(a) Their spouse or civil partner

(b) Their relatives*

(c) Relatives of their spouse or civil partner.

*Relatives are:

- Brothers or sisters
- Ancestors (eg parents, grandparents)
- Lineal descendants (eg children, grandchildren)
- Spouses and civil partners of any of the above relatives

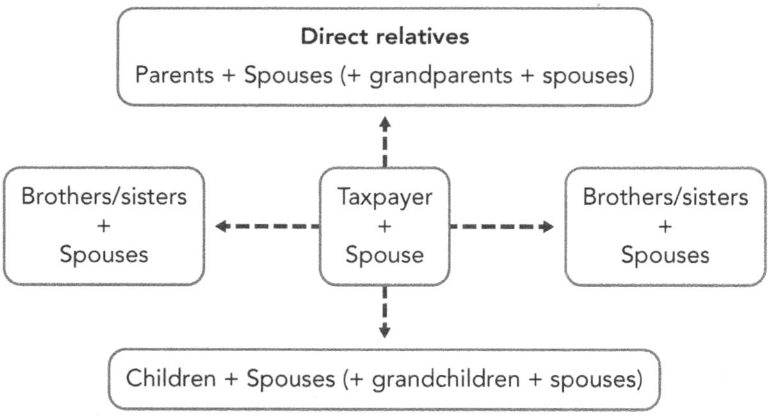

6.4 Transfers between spouses/civil partners

Spouses/civil partners are taxed as two separate people. Each individual has an annual exempt amount, and allowable losses of one individual cannot be set against gains of the other.

Disposals between spouses/civil partners do not give rise to chargeable gains or allowable losses. The disposal is said to be on a **'no gain/no loss'** basis. The acquiring spouse/civil partner takes the base cost of the disposing spouse/civil partner.

Activity 7: Transfers between spouses/civil partners

William sold an asset to his wife Kate in the current tax year for £32,000 when its market value was £45,000. William acquired the asset for £14,000 in June 2006.

Required

Calculate the chargeable gain on this transfer. Tick one box.

	✓
Nil	
£18,000	
£31,000	
£13,000	

7 Tax planning

Consider:

(a) Delaying sale of an asset until after the end of the tax year, this would give you a whole extra year until you had to pay the tax and allow you to use next year's annual exempt amount (if you have already used this year's).

(b) Spouses and civil partners may transfer assets at no gain no loss. This effectively transfers the asset over at its original cost so that the gain will be the same whichever party sells it. It therefore makes sense to ensure an asset is sold by the spouse/civil partner who:

- (i) Pays tax at a lower rate
- (ii) Has an unused annual exemption
- (iii) Has capital losses

Chapter summary

- A chargeable gain arises when there is a chargeable disposal of a chargeable asset by a chargeable person.
- Enhancement expenditure can be deducted in computing a chargeable gain if it is reflected in the state and nature of the asset at the time of disposal.
- Taxable gains are net chargeable gains for a tax year (ie minus allowable losses of the current tax year and any unrelieved capital losses brought forward) minus the annual exempt amount.
- Losses brought forward are deducted AFTER deduction of the annual exempt amount.
- The rates of CGT are 18% and 24%, but the lower rate of 18% only applies if and to the extent that the individual has any unused basic rate band.
- CGT is payable by 31 January following the end of the tax year, or within 60 days if it is a disposal of UK residential property
- On the part disposal of an asset the formula A/(A + B) must be applied to work out the cost attributable to the part disposed of.
- Wasting chattels are exempt assets (eg racehorses and greyhounds).
- If a non-wasting chattel is sold for gross proceeds of £6,000 or less and was bought for £6,000 or less then any gain arising is exempt.
- If gross proceeds exceed £6,000 on the sale of a non-wasting chattel but the cost is less than £6,000, any gain arising on the disposal of the asset is limited to 5/3 × (Gross proceeds – £6,000).
- If the gross proceeds are less than £6,000 on the sale of a non-wasting chattel but it was bought for more than £6,000 any loss otherwise arising is restricted by deeming the gross proceeds to be £6,000.
- Plant and machinery used in a business on which capital allowances were or could have been claimed is chargeable if sold at a gain. If sold at a loss, the loss is not an allowable capital loss.
- A disposal to a connected person takes place at market value.
- For individuals, connected people are broadly brothers, sisters, lineal ancestors and descendants and their spouses/civil partners plus similar relations of a spouse/civil partner.
- Losses on disposals to connected people can only be set against gains on disposals to the same connected person.
- Disposals between spouses/civil partners take place on a no gain/no loss basis.

Activity answers

Activity 1: Capital gain calculation

	£
Proceeds	35,500
Less selling expenses	(1,500)
Net proceeds	34,000
Less cost	(12,700)
Less legal fees on purchase	(500)
Less enhancement	(3,000)
Capital gain	17,800

Activity 2: Current year losses

Ted's net capital gain for 2026/27 before the annual exempt amount is £ 2,500

Ted has a loss to carry forward of £ nil

Working

	£
Gains 45,000 + 10,000	55,000
Less loss	(52,500)
Net capital gains	2,500
Less annual exempt amount	(3,000)
Taxable gains	Nil
The balance of the annual exempt amount is wasted.	

Activity 3: Prior year losses

Tara's net capital gain for 2026/27 after the annual exempt amount is £ 9,800

Tara has a loss to carry forward of £ 5,200

Working

	£
Gain of 2026/27	12,800
Less annual exempt amount	(3,000)
Net gain	9,800
Less capital loss brought forward	(9,800)

	£
Taxable gains	Nil
Losses to c/f £(15,000 – 9,800)	5,200

Activity 4: Computing capital gains tax payable

Mr Dunstable's capital gains tax payable is £ 3,162

Working

	£
Capital gain	17,800
Less annual exempt amount	(3,000)
Taxable gain	14,800
Basic rate band	37,700
Taxable income	(31,200)
Basic rate band remaining	6,500

	£
Capital gains tax payable	
6,500 × 18%	1,170
8,300 × 24%	1,992
14,800	3,162

Activity 5: Part disposal

The chargeable gain on the disposal of the land is £ 4,702

The cost of the remaining land carried forward is £ 15,652

Working

	£
Gross proceeds	10,000
Less disposal costs	(950)
Net proceeds	9,050
(£20,000 x (£10,000 ÷ (£10,000 + £36,000)))	(4,348)
Chargeable gain	4,702
Cost of remaining land for future CGT calculations: = 20,000 – 4,348	15,652

Activity 6: Chattels

(a) The chargeable gain on the disposal is £ 5,000

Working

Non-wasting chattel: cost ≤ £6,000, proceeds > £6,000	£
Proceeds	9,000
Less commission	(1,000)
Net proceeds	8,000
Less cost	(500)
Normal chargeable gain	**7,500**
$^5/_3$ (Gross proceeds – 6,000)	
$^5/_3$ (9,000 – 6,000) = **5,000**	
The chargeable gain is therefore the **lower of**: (1) The normal capital gain of £7,500 and (2) The 5/3 gain calculation, which gives rise to a gain of £5,000. Therefore, the chargeable gain is £5,000.	

(b) He also had an antique bought for £7,000 which he sold two years later for £3,000.

The loss on the disposal is £ 1,000

Working

Non-wasting chattel: cost > £6,000, proceeds ≤ £6,000	£
Proceeds (deemed)	6,000
Less cost	(7,000)
Allowable loss	(1,000)

Activity 7: Transfers between spouses/civil partners

The correct answer is:

	✓
Nil	✓
£18,000	
£31,000	
£13,000	

The chargeable gain on transfer is:

The transfer takes place at no gain/no loss and Kate assumes the base cost of £14,000 as her cost.

£18,000 is a chargeable gain based on actual proceeds. £31,000 is a chargeable gain based on market value. £13,000 is the difference between market value and actual proceeds.

Test your learning

1 **Tick to show if the following disposals would be chargeable or exempt for CGT.**

	Chargeable ✓	Exempt ✓
A gift of an antique necklace		
The sale of a building		
Sale of a racehorse		

2 Janet bought a plot of land for £80,000. She spent £10,000 on drainage. She sold the land for £200,000.

Required

Using the proforma layout provided, compute the gain on sale.

	£
Proceeds of sale	
Less cost	
Less enhancement expenditure	
Chargeable gain	

3 Philip has chargeable gains of £171,000 and allowable losses of £5,300 in 2026/27. Losses brought forward at 6 April 2026 amount to £10,000.

Required

The amount liable to CGT in 2026/27 is:

£ ______

The losses carried forward are:

£ ______

4 Martha is a higher rate taxpayer who made chargeable gains (before the annual exempt amount) of £21,800 in October 2026.

Required

Martha's CGT liability for 2026/27 is:

£ ______

5 **The payment date for capital gains tax in relation to the sale of a painting for 2026/27 is (insert date XX/XX/XXXX):**

______

6 Richard sells 4 acres of land (out of a plot of 10 acres) for £38,000. Costs of disposal amount to £3,000. The 10-acre plot cost £41,500. The market value of the 6 acres remaining is £48,000.

Required

The chargeable gain/allowable loss arising is:

Tick ONE box.

	✓
£16,663	
£17,500	
£19,663	
£18,337	

7 Mustafa bought a non-wasting chattel for £3,500.

Required

The gain arising if he sells it for:

(a) **£5,800 after deducting selling expenses of £180 is:**

£ [ ]

(b) **£8,200 after deducting selling expenses of £220 is:**

£ [ ]

8 Decide whether the following statement is true or false.

Required

A loss arising on a disposal to a connected person can be set against any gains arising in the same tax year or in subsequent tax years.

	✓
True	
False	

9 Decide whether the following statement is true or false.

Required

No gain or loss arises on a disposal to a spouse/civil partner.

	✓
True	
False	

10

Complete the table by ticking the appropriate box for each scenario.

	Actual proceeds used ✓	Deemed proceeds (market value) used ✓	No gain or loss basis ✓
Paul sells an asset to his civil partner Joe for £3,600.			
Grandmother gives an asset to her grandchild worth £1,000.			
Sarah sells an asset worth £20,000 to her best friend Cathy for £12,000. Sarah knows the asset is worth £20,000.			

12 Corporation tax

Learning outcomes

5	**Prepare tax computations for trading companies**
5.1	**Calculate taxable total profits (TTP)**
	Learners need to understand: 5.1.1 the meaning of an accounting period for corporation tax purposes: • when an accounting period begins • when an accounting period ends
	5.1.2 the allocation of components of TTP when a financial accounting period exceeds 12 months
	5.1.3 trading income: • that the accruals basis is used for allocation • allowable and disallowable expenditure • trade interest payable
	5.1.4 interest income: • that the accruals basis is used for allocation • the meaning of loan relationships • non-trade interest payable • non-trade interest receivable
	5.1.5 property income: • that the accruals basis is used for allocation • allowable and disallowable expenditure
	5.1.6 chargeable gains: • that the date of disposal is used for allocation • identification of net sales proceeds • identification of allowable costs
	5.1.7 qualifying charitable donations (QCDs): • that the date of payment is used for allocation

	5.1.8 trading losses: • current year • current year and carry back • carry forward
	5.1.9 property losses: • current period then carry forward
	5.1.10 capital losses: • current period then carry forward
	5.1.11 how to select the relief that gives the maximum tax benefit for losses
	Learners need to be able to: 5.1.12 adjust accounting profit for tax purposes
	5.1.14 calculate: • trading income • interest income • property income • chargeable gains • TTP
	5.1.15 allocate components of TTP in a long accounting period
	5.1.16 identify how losses are allocated according to: • specific instructions • maximum tax benefit
5.2	**Calculate corporation tax payable**
	Learners need to understand: 5.2.1 that corporation tax is calculated for an accounting period
	5.2.2 how the calculation of corporation tax is impacted by: • the tax year(s) in which the accounting period falls • the size of the company • the length of the accounting period • the number of associated companies
	Learners need to be able to: 5.2.3 calculate corporation tax payable
6.1	**The administrative requirements of UK tax law** Learners need to understand: 6.1.5 time limits for loss relief claims • company

Assessment context

In the assessment, task 2 is about trading income, and you may be required to deal with trading income of a company (or a sole trader or partnership). Task 7 is about tax computations for companies for 8 marks. You may be required you to calculate taxable total profits (TTP) and calculate corporation tax.

Qualification context

You will not see this topic outside of this assessment.

Business context

Companies need to know how much corporation tax they need to pay.

Chapter overview

Computing corporation tax

Taxable total profits (TTP)

AP ≤ 12m

- Accruals
  - Trading income
  - Property income
  - Investment income
- Actual
  - Chargeable gains
  - QCDs
- Ignore dividends

One computation based on AP

AP > 12m

- Time apportion
  - Trading income
- Accruals
  - Property income
  - Investment income
- Actual
  - Capital allowances
  - Chargeable gains
  - QCDs

- 2 CT/CA computations
  - 1st 12m
  - β

Computing corporation tax payable

Basic calculation

- TTP x rate

Rate

- For a 12 month AP and no associates:
  - 19% if TTP is less than £50,000 for a 12 month AP
  - 25% if TTP is more than £250,000
- 25% less marginal relief if between the upper and lower limits
- Reduce limits if short AP (× n/12) or company has associates

Losses

Trading losses

- Options
  - Carry forward
    - Trade losses ore carried forward and can be offset against total profits of a later accounting period if a claim is made
  - Current year
    - Offset against total profits (before qualifying charitable donations)
    - Optional
    - All or nothing
  - Carry back
    - Offset against total profits (before qualifying charitable donations)
    - Optional
    - All or nothing
    - Must do CY first
    - Previous 12 months
    - Extended to 36 months for terminal loss
- Considerations
  - Timing
  - Waste of charitable payments

Capital losses

- Offset automatically against capital gains
- Excess carry forward into future years

Property losses

- Current year - auto v total profits (before)
- Carry forward - claim v total profits

Introduction

In this chapter, we will look at the different types of income earned by a company, how this income is included in the tax calculation and how to calculate corporation tax.

1 Taxable total profits (TTP)

KEY TERM

Corporation tax: A UK tax incurred by companies on their taxable total profits.

Taxable total profits (TTP): The total amount of profit on which a company must pay Corporation Tax, after all allowable deductions and reliefs have been applied.

Period of account: The period for which the company prepares its accounts.

Financial year: Runs from 1 April to the following 31 March and is identified by the calendar year in which it begins.

Qualifying charitable donations: Charitable gifts on which tax relief is given.

A company prepares a calculation of its taxable total profits by listing all its taxable profits and summing them together to get total profits. Qualifying charitable donations are then deducted to get TTP. See an example proforma in Illustration 1 below. Each category of income and deduction will be considered in more detail later in this chapter.

The computation will usually be prepared for the company's period of account although there are special rules that apply where a company prepares a set of accounts for a period of more than 12 months (see later in this chapter).

Illustration 1: Corporation tax computation for the X months to <date>

	£
Trading income	X
Investment income (NTL-R) (Interest income)	X
Property income	X
Chargeable gains	X
Total profits	X
Less qualifying charitable donations (QCDs)	(X)
Taxable total profits	X

1.1 Trading income

Trading income for a company is, broadly, computed in the same way that trading income for a sole trader is computed (see Chapter 5).

As a reminder, there are some important differences:

(a) Companies always use the accruals basis

(b) Companies are entitled to an additional type of capital allowance referred to as full expensing. This detail was covered in the earlier capital allowance chapter.

(c) There are never any private use adjustments for a company when either adjusting the accounting profit or calculating capital allowances.

(d) Companies deal with a long period of account (accounts that have been made up for more than 12 months) in a different way to individuals or partnerships.

Note. Bad debts may be referred to as impairment losses in the financial statements of a company.

1.2 Investment income (NTL-R)

KEY TERM

> **Loan relationships:** Loan relationship rules determine how companies are taxed on their interest paid and interest received. These rules look at whether the loans are trade-related or non-trade-related loans.

In a corporation tax computation, interest/investment income and expenses are often referred to as loan relationship income and expenses. The taxation treatment of the interest income/expense will depend on whether the loan relationship exists for trade/non-trade reasons.

Virtually **all interest receivable** by companies will be **non-trading loan relationship (NTL-R) income**. It is taxed as **investment income/NTL-R income** on the **accrual** basis. You may also see the income being referred to as a NTL-R credit. As the company will account for interest income on an accruals basis in its accounts, this interest income would be deducted in the adjustment to profits to remove it from the trade profit figure and would then be taxed as investment income.

Interest payable is deductible, but where it is deductible depends on the nature of the loan:

- If the loan is for a **trading purpose, the interest is deductible when computing the company's trading income.** Common examples of trading interest payable include interest on loans to buy plant and machinery or trading stock or bank overdraft interest. This tax treatment means that if the interest payable is showing as an expense in the statement of profit or loss, **no** adjustment is needed for tax purposes.
- If the loan is for a **non-trading purpose**, the interest is **deductible from investment income** (which is essentially all the company's interest income receivable) **to give a net 'investment income' figure to be used in computing taxable total profits.** Common examples of non-trading interest expense would be interest on loans used to buy investments such as shares or properties to rent out. The non-trading interest expense may be referred to as a NTL-R debit and it is the NTL-R credits and debits which are pooled to give the net 'investment income' figure in TTP. In some cases, there may be a net deficit of non-trading interest paid over non-trading interest received (or 'loss'), but the treatment of such a deficit (or loss) is not in your syllabus.

1.3 Property income

A company with property business income must **pool the rents and expenses on all its properties, to give a single profit or loss**. Property business income is taxed on an **accruals basis** for companies.

Property income is calculated in the same way as business income, in other words, expenses need to be incurred wholly and exclusively for business purposes, revenue expenses are allowed (not capital expenses). Loan interest on a loan taken out to purchase a property is not deductible from the property income, but is deductible from non-trade loan relationships as seen above.

1.4 Chargeable gains

Companies do not pay capital gains tax. Instead, their **net chargeable gains** (current period gains less current period and brought forward capital losses) **are brought into the computation of taxable total profits.**

The calculation of chargeable gains and losses for companies is the same as for individuals (see chapter 11). The key difference is that companies do not receive an annual exempt amount. The calculation of gains on the disposal of assets which were acquired before January 2018 is not on your syllabus

1.5 Qualifying charitable donations (QCDs)

Qualifying charitable donations are charitable gifts on which tax relief is given; however, they cannot be deducted as a trading expense. If a qualifying charitable donation has been deducted in computing the accounting profit, the amount deducted must be added back in computing

trading profits (adjustment of profits), but the amount actually paid during the period can then be deducted from the total profits when computing taxable total profits.

Activity 1: Calculating taxable total profits

Abel Ltd, a UK trading company with no associated companies, produced the following results for the year ended 31 March 2027.

Income	£
Adjusted trading profits	2,440,000
Property income	150,000
Bank deposit interest accrued	40,000
Chargeable gains: 25 September 2026	350,000
28 December 2026	70,000
(There were capital losses of £80,000 brought forward at 1 April 2026)	
Loan interest paid (loan was used to buy investments)	10,000
Qualifying charitable payment	70,000

Required

Complete the following table calculating taxable total profits for the year ended 31 March 2027.

Corporation tax computation y/e 31 March 2027

	£
Trading profits	
Property income	
NTL-R income (Investment income)	
Chargeable gains	
Total profits	
Less qualifying charitable payment	
Taxable total profits	

2 Long periods of account

2.1 Accounting periods exceeding 12 months

KEY TERM

Period of account: The period for which a company prepares its accounts.

Accounting period: The period for which corporation tax is charged.

A company's accounting period is usually the same as its period of account. However, **an accounting period cannot be longer than 12 months**. This means that **if a period of account exceeds 12 months, it must be divided into two accounting periods of:**

- The first 12 months
- The remaining balance of months

It is necessary to prepare separate computations of taxable total profits for each accounting period.

Splitting income and expenditure

Income and expenditure are split between the two computations using the following rules:

- Trading income (before deducting capital allowances) is apportioned on a time basis.
- Capital allowances and balancing charges are calculated separately for each accounting period. The annual investment allowance (AIA) and writing-down allowances (WDAs) will need to be apportioned for the short period.
- Property income is apportioned over the period the property is actually rented out, ie on an accrual basis.
- Investment income (NTL-R income) is apportioned on an accrual basis.
- Qualifying charitable donations are allocated to the accounting period in which they are paid.
- Chargeable gains by reference to the date the asset is sold.

Assessment focus point

Dealing with long periods of account for corporation tax has historically been identified as a weak area by the Chief Assessor. Make sure you know the rules for how to split the long set of accounts and its results into two accounting periods. The AAT have stated that if there is no information given in a question about capital allowances that you should simply assume that the trading profit figure given should be time apportioned. Likewise, if no clear information is given about how interest income accrues, you should consider that it accrues evenly. The practice of applying these rules to tasks is also essential for you to be successful.

Activity 2: Calculating taxable total profits – long period of account

B plc prepares accounts for a 16-month period to 31 December 2027. The results for the period include the following:

	£
Adjusted trading profit before capital allowances	3,600,000
Bank interest receivable (accrued evenly over the period)	32,000
Chargeable gain (sale of asset on 13.10.27)	40,000
Qualifying charitable donation paid (annually on 31 July)	20,000

The tax written-down value of plant and machinery qualifying for capital allowances at 1 September 2026 was £37,500. The only capital transaction during the 16-month period was the purchase of a new van for £6,876 on 15 November 2027.

Required

Complete the following table, calculating taxable total profit for the two accounting periods that comprise the long period of account.

Long period of account

	£	£
Adjusted trading profits (12:4)		

BPP

	£	£
Less capital allowances (W1)		
Trading profits		
NTL-R income (Investment income) (12:4)		
Chargeable gain		
Total profits		
Less qualifying charitable donation		
TTP		

3 Losses

Where a company generates a loss, it is important to know what relief is available. In your assessment, you need to be able to deal with:

(a) Trade losses
   (i) Current year
   (ii) Current year and carry back
   (iii) Carry forward

(b) Property losses

(c) Capital losses

3.1 Trading losses

We have previously seen that the starting point for computing a company's trading results is to take the statement of profit or loss and adjust it for tax purposes. If this adjusted figure is negative then there is a trading loss, rather than a trading profit

Note that the deduction of capital allowances can actually increase an adjusted loss, or even turn an adjusted profit into a trading loss.

If there is a trading loss in an accounting period, the trading profit to include in the taxable total profits for that accounting period will be nil.

You need to be aware of the following three methods by which a company may obtain relief for its trading losses:

(a) Current year

(b) Current year and carry back

(c) Carry forward

You will also need to be aware of the impact that losses can have on qualifying charitable donations. This is included within the examples and tasks below.

We will look at each of the three methods of obtaining loss relief. These are similar to the rules for individuals but there are some significant differences.

3.1.1 Carry forward of trading losses

Trading losses are carried forward in a flexible manner. Unused trading losses are carried forward and a claim can be made to offset some or all of the loss against total profits of future accounting periods. There is no requirement to allocate the loss against the first available profits and the claim specifies the amount of loss to be offset.

Illustration 2: Carry forward loss relief

P Ltd has the following results for the three years to 31 March 2027:

	Year ended 31 March		
	2025	2026	2027
	£	£	£
Trading profit/(loss)	(8,000)	3,000	6,000
NTL-R income	0	4,000	2,000

Carry forward loss relief would be relieved as follows, assuming that the company wants to use the carried forward losses as soon as possible and a claim is made:

	Year ended 31 March		
	2025	2026	2027
	£	£	£
Trading profit	0	3,000	6,000
NTL-R income	–	4,000	2,000
Total profits	0	7,000	8,000
Less carry forward loss relief	–	(7,000)	(1,000)
Taxable total profits	0	0	7,000

Activity 3: Carry forward loss relief

Strontium Ltd has the following actual and budgeted results for the three years to 31 March 2027.

	Year ended 31 March		
	2025	2026	2027
	£	£	£
Trading profit/(loss)	(20,000)	5,000	6,000
Property income	–	2,000	2,000

Required

Assuming Strontium Ltd carries the loss forward and claims to utilise as much loss as possible, the loss carried forward at 31 March 2027 is:

£ [ ]

3.1.2 Current year and carry back relief

A company may make a claim for a trading loss to be offset against its total profits in the current year and the preceding year. The claim must be made within two years of the end of the loss-making period.

Current year loss relief

Carrying the loss forward has a cash flow disadvantage for the company due to it only reducing future tax bills. The company may therefore prefer to consider using the loss to make a current year loss claim.

The trade loss may be relieved against total profits (including gains) before qualifying charitable donations in the period in which the loss arose.

The loss relief claim is 'all or nothing', so any qualifying charitable donations that become unrelieved are lost.

Carry back loss relief

Trading losses can be carried back against total profits (including gains) before qualifying charitable donations of the preceding 12 months.

The carry back claim may only be made **after** a current year claim (note that this is different to the rules for individuals).

This claim is also 'all or nothing' and any qualifying charitable donations which become unrelieved are lost.

Any loss remaining unrelieved after current period and **carry back loss relief** claims **must be carried forward** and offset according to the rules explained above.

A company is permitted to carry back the loss for 12 months. If the loss is carried back to an accounting period that partly falls outside the permitted carry back period, then the total income before qualifying charitable donations of this period must be time apportioned to determine how much of the profits may be relieved.

Activity 4: Current year and carry back relief

Kayo Ltd has the following actual and budgeted results.

	Year ended 31 March		
	2025	2026	2027
	£	£	£
Trading income	20,000	10,000	(100,000)
Capital gains	50,000	50,000	50,000

Required

Show if the following statements are true or false by ticking the correct box for each.

	True ✓	False ✓
Kayo Ltd may claim to offset £60,000 of the loss against total profits in y/e 31.3.2026.		
If Kayo Ltd makes the maximum permissible claims, it will have £90,000 loss to carry forward at 31.3.2027.		
Kayo Ltd may claim to offset the loss against total profits in y/e 31.3.2026 and then against total profits in y/e 31.3.2027.		
Kayo Ltd may claim to offset the loss against total profits in y/e 31.3.2027 and carry the remaining loss forward to the y/e 31.3.2028.		

Activity 5: Comprehensive example

Janet plc has the following actual and budgeted results.

	Y/e 30.9.2024 £	P/e 31.3.2025 £	Y/e 31.3.2026 £	Y/e 31.3.2027 £
Trading income	20,000	30,000	(155,000)	15,000
NTL-R income	10,000	10,000	10,000	10,000
Qualifying charitable payments	(5,000)	(5,000)	(5,000)	(5,000)

Required

Complete the following table, assuming the company will make the maximum permissible claims. Use the picklist for narrative entries. Insert '0' as appropriate.

Show all qualifying charitable donations, even if the company does not actually claim relief for them.

	Y/e 30.9.2024 £	P/e 31.3.2025 £	Y/e 31.3.2026 £	Y/e 31.3.2027 £
Trading profits				
NTL-R income				
Total profits				
▼				
▼				
▼				
▼				
Taxable total profits				

Picklist

- Current year relief
- Losses carried forward
- Prior year relief
- Qualifying charitable donation

3.1.3 Choosing loss relief

KEY TERM

Carry forward loss relief: The trade loss is carried forward and can be offset with a claim against a future period's total profits.

Current year loss relief: Allows a company to set a trading loss against total profits before deducting qualifying charitable donations in the loss-making accounting period.

Carry back loss relief: Allows a company to set a trading loss against total profits (before deducting qualifying charitable donations) in the 12 months preceding the period of the loss (after it has made a claim against current year total profits first).

Companies

There are several alternative loss reliefs available for a company, including:

- Carry forward of losses
- Losses set against current period total profits
- Losses set against total profits from earlier years

3.2 Capital losses for companies

These can only be set against capital gains. The order of relief here is:

(a) First, against current period gains

(b) Second, any surplus losses are relieved against gains in future accounting periods

Note. Capital losses cannot be carried back to preceding years.

We have seen that capital gains form part of a company's taxable total profits (TTP) chargeable to corporation tax.

Any capital losses would be offset automatically against gains before considering how to allocate the trading loss.

3.3 Property losses

Where a company generates an overall loss in relation to its UK property business, there are two ways that relief may be obtained:

(a) Current year relief

(b) Carry forward relief

3.3.1 Current year relief

Property business losses are automatically offset against the company's total profits in the same accounting period. There is no option to disclaim the relief. The loss is offset before any relief for trading losses is given. As the loss is offset against total profits (in other words, before QCDs), relief for QCDs may be wasted.

3.3.2 Carry forward relief

Any remaining loss is carried forward. A company can claim for all or part of the loss to be treated as a property loss in the next accounting period, in other words, offset against total profits.

3.4 Choosing loss relief

In making a choice consider:

(a) The rate at which relief can be obtained. Companies can pay tax at between 19% and 25%. Offsetting losses against profit that is taxed at 25% will generate a higher tax saving than if they were offset against profits taxed at 19%. Moreover, profits in the marginal relief band between £50,000 and £250,000 have a marginal rate of tax of 26.5% (see section below regarding the calculation of corporation tax).

(b) How quickly relief will be obtained: loss relief against total profits using a current year and carry back claim is quicker than carry forward loss relief.

(c) The extent to which relief for qualifying charitable donations might be wasted.

Assessment focus point

Candidates often struggle with loss relief questions, so make sure you go over this chapter thoroughly before attempting further questions to ensure you are well prepared for the assessment. It is not enough just to read the questions and answers - you need to prepare the computations yourself to fully understand them.

4 Computing the corporation tax liability

The corporation tax liability is calculated for an accounting period. Each accounting period has a **taxable total profit (TTP)** which is multiplied by the applicable corporation tax rate to get the corporation tax liability.

The tax rate applied depends on the level of the company's TTP in the accounting period.

If a single company has a 12-month accounting period and its TTP is **£250,000** (the upper limit) or more, the TTP is taxed at **25%**. This is the main rate.

If it has TTP of less than **£50,000** (the lower limit), the corporation tax rate is **19%**. This is the small profits rate.

If it has TTP between £50,000 and £250,000 we will calculate its corporation tax liability by multiplying its TTP by 25% and then reducing the liability by deducting marginal relief.

Corporation tax at 25%	X
Less marginal relief 3/200 × (Upper limit – TTP)	(X)
Corporation tax payable	X

The upper limit of £250,000 and the lower limit of £50,000 are reduced if the company has:

- Associated companies ('associates');
- A short accounting period (<12 months); or
- Both.

See later for how we adjust the upper and lower limits. In the next few examples these reductions do not need to be made to the limits because they feature 12-month accounting periods and have no associates.

Open book reference: Corporation tax rates

The corporation tax rates and limits are provided to you in section 17 of your reference material in the exam.

Activity 6: Corporation tax payable (main rate)

B plc is a single company.

	£
Trading profits	1,500,000
Chargeable gain	50,000
Qualifying charitable donations	30,000

Required

How much corporation tax is payable by B plc?

£ [ ]

Activity 7: Corporation tax payable (small profits rate)

C Ltd has taxable total profits in the year ended 31 March 2027 of £35,000 in the accounting period. C Ltd has no associated companies.

Required

How much corporation tax is payable by C Ltd?

£ [ ]

Illustration 3: Corporation tax payable (marginal relief)

In the year ended 31 March 2027, Chapman Ltd had the following results.

	£
Trading income	90,000
Chargeable gain	40,000

Chapman Ltd has no associated companies in the accounting period.

Required

What is Chapman Ltd's corporation tax payable for the year ended 31 March 2027?

Solution

Chapman Ltd's taxable total profits (TTP) are £130,000 for the year.

	£
Trading income	90,000
Chargeable gain	40,000
TTP	130,000

As its TTP is greater than £50,000 but smaller than £250,000, Chapman Ltd is a marginal relief company and its corporation tax payable is calculated as TTP multiplied by 25% less marginal relief.

Marginal relief is equal to:

3/200 × (Upper limit less TTP)

	£
Corporation tax at 25%	32,500
Less 3/200 × (£250,000 - £130,000)	(1,800)
Corporation tax payable	30,700

Activity 8: Corporation tax payable

In the year ended 31 March 2027, Ulvaeus Ltd has trading income of £239,000 and property income of £6,000. It made a qualifying charitable donation of £10,000 in the accounting period. Ulvaeus Ltd has no associated companies.

Required

Calculate the following items for Ulvaeus Ltd for the year ended 31 March 2027.

Taxable total profits: £ ____________

Corporation tax payable: £ ____________

4.1 Associated companies and short accounting periods

The upper and lower limits of £250,000 and £50,000 are reduced if:

- The company has associated companies; and/or
- It has a short accounting period (of less than 12 months).

Assessment focus point

You do not need to know the definition of associated companies in your assessment, you will be told how many associates there are.

4.1.1 Short accounting periods

If a company has an accounting period of less than 12 months the upper and lower limits are reduced by multiplying them by n/12, n being the number of months in the accounting period.

Illustration 4: Corporation tax payable and associated companies

In the year ended 31 March 2027, RMC Ltd has TTP of £45,000.

RMC Ltd has two associated companies.

Required

Calculate the corporation tax payable by RMC Ltd for the year ended 31 March 2027.

Solution

RMC Ltd has taxable total profits of £45,000.

There are three associated companies, including RMC Ltd.

The upper limit is £250,000/3 = £83,333

The lower limit is £50,000/3 = £16,667

RMC Ltd is therefore a marginal relief company and the corporation tax payable by RMC Ltd is:

	£
TTP × 25%	11,250
Less 3/200 × (£83,333 - £45,000)	(575)
Corporation tax payable	10,675

Activity 9: Associated companies and a short accounting period

Osterdahl Ltd has prepared its accounts for the nine-month period ended 31 March 2027.

It has one associated company in the accounting period.

Required

Calculate the upper and lower limits for Osterdahl in the period to 31 March 2027.

Upper limit: £ ______

Lower limit: £ ______

Chapter summary

- Adjustment of profit for companies is similar to that for individuals but companies are entitled to the full expensing for capital allowances and there is no private use adjustment.
- Loan relationships are interest paid and received. Non-trading loan relationship income and expenses are pooled together as investment income. Trade-related loan relationships are included in trading profits.
- To compute taxable total profits, aggregate all sources of income (eg trading, investment, property) and chargeable gains. Deduct qualifying charitable donations.
- An accounting period cannot exceed 12 months in length.
- A long period of account must be split into two accounting periods: a period of 12 months and then a period covering the balance of the period of account.
- A financial year runs from 1 April in one year to 31 March the following year and is identified by the calendar year in which it begins.
- The taxable total profits will be charged to corporation tax at 19%, 25% or 25% less marginal relief depending on the company's profits, the number of associated companies it has and how long its accounting period is.
- For a company, a trading loss can be:
  - Carried forward and set against future total profits if a claim is made
  - Deducted from total profits (before QCDs) in the accounting period of the loss
  - Deducted from total profits (before QCDs) in the 12 months preceding the period of the loss (after a current period offset)
  - Carried back 36 months on a LIFO basis against total profits if a terminal loss
- For a company, a claim for current year loss relief must be made before a loss is carried back.
- Company capital losses can be set against current year gains and then carried forward to set against gains in the future.
- Property losses are automatically offset in the current year against total profits. Remaining losses are carried forward, and a claim can be made to offset them against total profits.
- When selecting a loss relief, consider the rate at which relief is obtained, the timing of relief, and the effect on personal allowances or QCDs.

Activity answers

Activity 1: Calculating taxable total profits

Corporation tax computation y/e 31 March 2027

	£
Trading profits	2,440,000
Property income	150,000
NTL-R income (Investment income) (40,000 - 10,000)	30,000
Chargeable gains (350,000 + 70,000 – 80,000)	340,000
Total profits	2,960,000
Less qualifying charitable payment	(70,000)
Taxable total profits	2,890,000

Activity 2: Calculating taxable total profits – long period of account

Long period of account

	12 months to 31.8.27 £	4 months to 31.12.27 £
Adjusted trading profits (12:4)	2,700,000	900,000
Less capital allowances (W1)	(5,250)	(8,381)
Trading profits	2,694,750	891,619
NTL-R income (Investment income) (12:4)	24,000	8,000
Chargeable gain	–	40,000
Total profits	2,718,750	939,619
Less qualifying charitable donation	(20,000)	–
TTP	2,698,750	939,619

Working

(not provided in assessment)

	FYA Full expensing	General pool	Allowances
1.9.26 to 31.8.27 (12m)			
TWDV @ 1.9.26		37,500	
WDA (14%)		(5,250)	5,250

	FYA Full expensing	General pool	Allowances
		32,250	
1.9.27 to 31.12.27 (4m)			
Addition	6,876		
AIA	(6,876)		6,876
WDA (14%) × 4/12		(1,505)	1,505
		30,745	
			8,381

Activity 3: Carry forward loss relief

£ 5,000

The loss carried forward at 31 March 2027 is

Working

(not provided in the assessment)

	Year ended 31 March 2025 £	2026 £	2027 £
Trading profit	–	5,000	6,000
Property income	–	2,000	2,000
Total profits	–	7,000	8,000
Less trade loss carried forward		(7,000)	(8,000)
TTP	–	–	–

Loss memorandum			£
Y/e 31 March 2025			20,000
Loss relief y/e 31 March 2026			(7,000)
			13,000
Loss relief y/e 31 March 2027			(8,000)
c/f			5,000

Activity 4: Current year and carry back relief

The correct answers are:

	True ✓	False ✓
Kayo Ltd may claim to offset £60,000 of the loss against total profits in y/e 31.3.2026.		✓
If Kayo Ltd makes the maximum permissible claims, it will have £90,000 loss to carry forward at 31.3.2027.		✓
Kayo Ltd may claim to offset the loss against total profits in y/e 31.3.2026 and then against total profits in y/e 31.3.2027.		✓
Kayo Ltd may claim to offset the loss against total profits in y/e 31.3.2027 and carry the remaining loss forward to the y/e 31.3.2028.	✓	

Workings

1 ***(not provided in assessment)***

The loss arises in year ended 31 March 2027, so this is the current year.

We cannot carry back to the prior year of 31 March 2026 unless we have made a current year claim in y/e 31.3.2027 first, so the first statement is false because only £50,000 of the loss would remain after a current year claim.

If the company makes the maximum permissible claims, it will offset in the current year of 31.3.2027, then carry back to y/e 31.3.2026, setting losses against total profits including gains (see below). It will have insufficient losses to reduce the y/e 31.3.2026 income to nil so there will be no losses to carry forward. The second statement is, therefore, false.

If we wish to offset in y/e 31.3.2026 and y/e 31.3.2027, we must offset y/e 31.3.2027 before y/e 31.3.2026, so the third statement is false.

We can choose to offset the loss in y/e 31.3.2027 only, so the fourth statement is true. Once we have offset in y/e 31.3.2027, we could choose to make a further claim to offset in y/e 31.3.2026 or to carry it forward into future accounting periods.

	Year ended 31 March		
	2025	2026	2027
	£	£	£
Trading income	20,000	10,000	–
Capital gains	50,000	50,000	50,000
Total profits	70,000	60,000	50,000
Loss relief	–	(ii)(50,000)	(i)(50,000)
TTP	70,000	10,000	–

2 ***(not provided in assessment)***

Loss memorandum			£
Y/e 31.3.2027			100,000
Less relief y/e 31.3.2027 (optional claim)			(50,000)(i)

Loss memorandum			£
Less relief y/e 31.3.2026 (additional optional claim after y/e 31.3.2027 claim)			(50,000)(ii)
			Nil

Activity 5: Comprehensive example

	Y/e 30.9.2024 £	P/e 31.3.2025 £	Y/e 31.3.2026 £	Y/e 31.3.2027 £
Trading profits	20,000	30,000	0	15,000
NTL-R income	10,000	10,000	10,000	10,000
Total profits	30,000	40,000	10,000	25,000
Current year relief	0	0	(10,000)(i)	0
Prior year relief	(15,000)(iii)	(40,000)(ii)	0	0
Losses carried forward	0	0	0	(25,000)
	15,000	0	0	0
Qualifying charitable donation	(5,000)	(5,000)	(5,000)	(5,000)
Taxable total profits	10,000	0	0	0

Working

(not provided in assessment)

Loss memo				£
Y/e 31.3.2026				155,000
Current – y/e 31.3.2026			(i)	(10,000)
Carry back – 6m P/E 31.3.2025			(ii)	(40,000)
– Y/e 30.9.2024 – max claim 6/12 × 30,000			(iii)	(15,000)
				90,000
C/fwd y/e 31.3.2027			(iv)	(25,000)
C/fwd				65,000

Tutorial note. Full relief has been claimed in the y/e 31.3.2027 because the question stated that maximum reliefs must be taken as early as possible. However, it would be possible in this scenario to restrict the relief in y/e 31.3.2027 to £20,000 in keep the relief from the qualifying charitable donation and carry the remaining loss of £5,000 for offset in y/e 31.3.2028.

Activity 6: Corporation tax payable (main rate)

£ 380,000

Working

(not provided in assessment)

	£
Trading profits	1,500,000
Chargeable gain	50,000
Qualifying charitable donations	(30,000)
Taxable total profits	1,520,000
TTP is higher than £250,000 Corporation tax due is TTP × 25% £1,520,000 × 25%	£380,000

Activity 7: Corporation tax payable (small profits rate)

£ 6,650

C Ltd has TTP of £35,000, which is less than the lower limit of £50,000 so the applicable rate of corporation tax is 19%. The corporation tax payable is therefore 19% x £35,000, ie £6,650.

Activity 8: Corporation tax payable

Taxable total profits: £ 235,000

Corporation tax payable: £ 58,525

Taxable total profits = £239,000 + £6,000 - £10,000 = £235,000

The corporation tax payable is £58,525

	£
TTP × 25%	58,750
Less 3/200 × (£250,000 - £235,000)	(225)
	58,525

Activity 9: Associated companies and a short accounting period

Upper limit: £ 93,750

Lower limit: £ 18,750

Two associates are in the group structure including Osterdahl Ltd. The limits must first be divided by the number of associates and then by n/12.

Upper limit is £250,000/2 × 9/12 = £93,750.

Lower limit is £50,000/2 × 9/12 = £18,750.

Test your learning

1 Indicate whether the following statements are true or false.

	True ✓	False ✓
A company with a nine-month period of account will calculate capital allowances for nine months and deduct them from adjusted trading profits.		
A company with an 18-month period of account will calculate capital allowances for 18 months and deduct them from adjusted trading profits, and then prorate the answer between the appropriate accounting periods.		
A company with an 18-month period of account will calculate capital allowances for the first 12 months, then capital allowances for the remaining 6 months, and deduct them from the relevant prorated trading profits allocated to each accounting period.		

2 A company has accrued interest payable of £4,000 (gross) for the year ended 31 March 2027.

The interest is payable on a loan taken out to buy some machinery for use in the company's trade.

Required

Identify how this will be treated in the corporation tax computation. Tick ONE box.

	✓
Added to trading income	
Added to net non-trading interest ie a NTL-R credit	
Deducted from trading income	
Deducted from net non-trading interest ie a NTL-R debit	

3 On 30 June 2026, Edelweiss Ltd makes a donation to a registered charity of £385. The donation is a qualifying charitable donation.

Required

The amount of deduction available in respect of the charitable donation when calculating taxable total profits is:

£ [ ]

4 X Ltd had been making up accounts to 31 May for several years. Early in 2026, the directors decided to make accounts to 31 August 2026 (instead of 31 May 2026) and annually thereafter to 31 August.

Required

Tick the box which correctly shows the two chargeable accounting periods for CT purposes for X Ltd.

	✓
1 June 2025 – 31 March 2026 and 1 April 2026 – 31 August 2026	
1 June 2025 – 31 May 2026 and 1 June 2026 – 31 August 2026	
1 June 2025 – 31 December 2025 and 1 January 2026 – 31 August 2026	
1 June 2025 – 31 August 2025 and 1 September 2025– 31 August 2026	

5 C Ltd prepares accounts for the 16 months to 30 April 2027. The results are as follows:

	£
Trading profits	320,000
Bank interest received (accrued evenly over period)	1,600
Chargeable gain (made 1 January 2027)	20,000
Qualifying charitable donation (paid 31 December 2026)	15,000

Required

Using the proforma layout provided, calculate the taxable total profits for the accounting periods based on the above results. Input 0 if your answer is zero.

	Year ended 31.12.26 £	4 months ended 30.4.27 £
Trading profits		
NTL-R income (Investment)		
Chargeable gain		
Total profits		
Qualifying charitable donation		
Taxable total profits		

6 P Ltd had taxable total profits of £155,000 for its six-month accounting period to 31 March 2027.

Required

Its corporation tax liability for the period will be:

£ [ ]

7 J Ltd had taxable total profits of £40,000 in the year ended 31 March 2027.

J Ltd has one associated company, called K Ltd and has no other shareholdings.

Required

The corporation tax liability for the year is:

£ [ ]

8 Decide whether the following statement is true or false.

Financial Year 2026 (FY26) begins on 1 April 2026 and ends on 31 March 2027.

Required

Tick ONE box.

	✓
True	
False	

9 J plc bought a plot of land in July 2016 for £80,000. It spent £10,000 on drainage in April 2019 and sold the land for £200,000 in August 2026.

Required

Using the proforma layout provided, compute the gain on sale.

	£
Proceeds of sale	
Less cost	
Less enhancement expenditure	
Chargeable gain	

13 Administration

Learning outcomes

6	**Understand administrative requirements of the UK's tax regime**
6.1	**The administrative requirements of UK tax law**
	Learners need to understand: 6.1.1 the threshold for Making Tax Digital (MTD) for Income Tax Self-Assessment (ITSA)
	6.1.2 filing deadlines: • Income tax self-assessment • Corporation tax self-assessment • reporting capital gains on residential property • reporting capital gains on other assets
	6.1.3 tax payment dates: • Income tax (including payments on account) • Corporation tax (small and/or large companies) • Capital gains tax (residential and/or other property)
	6.1.4 time limits for notifying chargeability to tax: • Income tax • Corporation tax
	6.1.6 the enquiry window
	6.1.7 the time period within which amendments to a tax return can be made
	6.1.8 the records that need to be maintained: • format • time period
	Learners need to be able to: 6.1.9 calculate amounts of tax due on each date: • payments on account for individuals • balancing payments for individuals • instalment payments for large companies
6.2	**Penalties for non-compliance**

	Learners need to understand: 6.2.1 penalties for: • late filing • late payment • failing to notify chargeability • errors in tax returns • not providing records in an enquiry • not retaining proper records
	6.2.2 when interest is payable
	6.2.3 the meaning of: • careless errors • deliberate errors • deliberate and concealed errors • unprompted disclosure • prompted disclosure
	Learners need to be able to: 6.2.4 calculate penalties for non-compliance

Assessment context

There are a lot of very specific rules, dates and percentages in this chapter that could be tested in the assessment.

Task 8 in your assessment is about the administration of the UK tax system. This task is worth 12 marks, so this chapter is very important. Make sure you learn the detail and know when you can use the reference material.

Qualification context

You will not see the information in this chapter outside of this unit.

Business context

It is vital for a tax adviser to ensure that their client's tax affairs are dealt with in a timely fashion and all information is properly submitted to HMRC. Serious financial penalties will arise if these deadlines are missed.

Chapter overview

Administration for individuals

Records

Retain
- Employed +1 year
- Self-employed/property income +5 years

From 31.1 following tax year [or retain until enquiries over] Max £3,000 penalty

Notification

- 5.10 following tax year

Payment

- IT + Class 4 NIC POAs 31.1, 31.7 Balance due 31.1 following the tax year
- CGT 31.1 following tax year, unless residential property = within 60 days of completion

Submission

Due date
- Paper 31.10
- Online 31.1

Following tax year

Enquiries
- Within 1 year of filing
- Amend/appeal <30 days after end of enquiry

Capital gains
- Normally reported on self-assessment tax return
- For UK residential property - report within 60 days

Making tax digital

- Keep digital records
- Quarterly updates:

Period	Update filing deadline
6 April to 5 July	7 August
6 April to 5 October	7 November
6 April to 5 January	7 February
6 April to 5 April	7 May

- MTD return due 31.1

Enquires

HMRC can start within 12 months of receipt of return

Penalties

Errors

	Max	Unprompted	Prompted
Careless	30%	0%	15%
Deliberate not concealed	70%	20%	35%
Deliberate concealed	100%	30%	50%

Late submission (non MTD)

- <3m £100
- >3m but <6m £10 per day (max 90 days)
- >6m 5% of tax due (min £300)
- >12m Additional 5% or greater if deliberate (min £300)

Late submission under MTD

- 1 point per late filing (no penalty points for late quarterly updates for 2026/27)
- No penalty applies until penalty point threshold reached
- £200 penalty on reaching penalty threshold (4 points for quarterly updates)
- Further £200 penalty for each subsequent late submission, but no additional points given
- Points expire 2 years from the end of month of the failure, provided penalty point threshold not reached
- If threshold reached, points total is reset to zero if:
  - No late submissions for a period of compliance (12m for quarterly updates)
  - All returns due in past 24m have been submitted

Late payment (non MTD)

- Penalties on final payment
  - >1 month late 5%
  - >6 months late additional 5%
  - >12 months late additional 5%

Late payment under MTD

Paid	Penalty
By day 15	No penalty
16 days - 30 days	3% of tax owed at day 15, or no penalty if first year of MTD
From day 31	3% of tax owed at day 15 plus 3% of the tax owed at day 30 Plus, annual rate of 10% per year on the outstanding amount, charged daily from day 31 until the tax is paid, or up to 2 years

Interest on POAs and final payment

Administration for companies

Tax returns and records

Notification
- Co becomes chargeable → 3m
- Co doesn't receive notice to deliver → 12m from AP end

Late notification → same penalties for individuals

Filing
- Deadline
  - Later of
    - 12m from POA end
    - 3m from notice to deliver
- Penalties
  - <3m £200
  - >3m £400
  - >6m 10% of tax due
  - >12m 20% of tax due

Enquiries
- Deadlines
  - Filed
    - Early or on time 12m from filing date
    - Late 12m from quarter end
- Conduct
  - HMRC may request documents
  - £300 penalty + £60 daily until produced
- Conclusion
  - HMRC amend return
  - 30 days for Co to appeal

Records
- Deadline
  - Retain later of
    - 6 yrs from AP end
    - Date enquiries completed
    - Date after which enquiries may not commence
- Penalties
  - £3,000 for each period

Payment of tax and interest

Large companies augmented profits ≥ £1,500,000
- Due dates
  - Day 14 of
    - M7
    - M10
    - M13
    - M16

    } From AP start
  - Penalties for deliberately incorrect instalments

Others
- 9 months and 1 day following AP end

Introduction

There are a number of strict deadlines that a taxpayer will need to meet. In this chapter, we look at those deadlines and the penalties that occur if those deadlines are not met.

1 Individuals

An individual's tax return comprises a tax form, together with supplementary pages for particular sources of income and capital gains if required. We will look at self-assessment of income tax in this section. Administration for companies is covered in the next section.

1.1 Notice of chargeability

If you have income that needs to be reported on a self-assessment tax return, you have to notify HM Revenue & Customs (HMRC) by 5 October following the tax year in which the income was received.

Penalties for late notification of chargeability to tax are behaviour based and are calculated as a percentage of the potential lost revenue. This is the amount of tax outstanding as a result of the failure to notify. The maximum penalty is:

- 100% where the behaviour is deliberate and concealed
- 70% where the behaviour is deliberate but not concealed; and
- 30% in any other case.

Open book reference: Notice of chargeability

The deadlines for notification of chargeability are provided in section 10 of your reference material.

1.2 Filing returns

KEY TERM

Filing due date: The date by which a return must be filed.

Open book reference: Filing due date

The filing due date is provided in section 10 of your reference material.

Filing due date for **paper** returns	Filing due date for **online** returns
31/10/2027	31/1/2028
HMRC will calculate tax	Automatic electronic calculation of tax

Where a notice to make a return is issued after 31 July following the tax year, a period of three months is allowed for the filing of a paper return.

Where a notice to make a return is issued after 31 October following the tax year, a period of three months is allowed for the online filing of that return.

An individual may ask HMRC to do the calculation of tax due if a paper return is filed. Where an online return is filed, the tax computation is made automatically.

Note that filing requirements differ for individuals within Making Tax Digital (MTD) for Income Tax (see below).

Assessment focus point

In your assessment, take care if a task asks you to identify a date. The Chief Assessor has noted that some students are not careful enough in their application of the rules set out in the reference data. In addition, the Chief Assessor also notes that frequent errors are made when students calculate the period (in whole months) between two dates, meaning that the answer given is then wrong. Make sure you slow down to correctly calculate the length of time between two dates to help you apply your rules for penalties.

Illustration 1: Filing income tax returns

Advise the following clients (who do not use MTD) of the latest filing date for their personal tax return for 2026/27 if notice to file the return is received on the following dates, and the return is:

(a) Paper

(b) Online

Notice to file tax return issued by HMRC:

Norma	on 6 April 2027
Melanie	on 10 August 2027
Olga	on 12 December 2027

The latest filing dates are:

	Paper	Online
Norma	31 October 2027	31 January 2028
Melanie	9 November 2027	31 January 2028
Olga	11 March 2028	11 March 2028

1.2.1 Penalties for late filing

Open book reference: Late filing penalties

Penalties for late filing are shown in section 10 of your reference material.

Penalties for late filing (taxpayer does not use Making Tax Digital)

The penalties for filing a late tax return are:

Return outstanding	Penalty
0 - 3 months	£100
3 - 6 months	Daily penalty of £10 per day (max 90 days)
6 - 12 months*	5% of the tax due (min £300)
12 months+*	(a) A further 5% of the tax due if not deliberate (b) A further 70% of the tax due where withholding of information is deliberate and not concealed (c) A further 100% of the tax due where withholding of information is deliberate and concealed

*These tax-based penalties are subject to a minimum of £300

Penalties may be reduced for prompted and unprompted disclosures and cooperation with investigation.

1.3 Making Tax Digital for Income Tax

KEY TERM

> **Making Tax Digital for Income Tax:** The requirement for sole traders and landlords to keep digital records, submit quarterly updates and file a year-end tax return with HMRC.

Making Tax Digital for Income Tax (MTD IT) is a new way for sole traders and landlords to report their income and expenses to HMRC.

Under MTD for Income Tax, individuals will be required to:

- Create and store digital records
- Send quarterly updates to HMRC
- File their MTD year-end tax return

MTD IT will apply to sole traders and landlords whose gross qualifying income exceeds the relevant threshold. Qualifying income is broadly their combined income from trading and property before expenses.

- Sole traders and landlords with qualifying income above £50,000 must join MTD IT from 6 April 2026.
- Those with qualifying income over £30,000 will have to join from 6 April 2027.
- Those with qualifying income over £20,000 will have to join from April 2028.

A taxpayer must join MTD IT when their gross qualifying income shown on the previous tax year's submitted tax return exceeds the relevant threshold. For example, if a taxpayer's 2024/25 tax return reports qualifying income of more than £50,000, then they will have to join MTD IT from 6 April 2026.

Once in MTD IT, a taxpayer must remain in MTD until they have three consecutive years below the mandation threshold.

1.3.1 Digital records

Individuals will be required to keep digital records of the amount, category and date of income and expenses relating to their self-employment and/or property business in a software product or spreadsheet that works with MTD IT.

1.3.2 Quarterly updates

From the digital records, the taxpayer will have to submit a summary of their business income and expenses to HMRC every quarter using compatible software. A list of compatible software is available on HMRC's website.

The quarterly updates are cumulative, running from the start of the tax year: The quarters are the same for all businesses.

	Period	Update filing deadline
Quarterly update 1	6 April to 5 July	7 August
Quarterly update 2	6 April to 5 October	7 November
Quarterly update 3	6 April to 5 January	7 February
Quarterly update 4	6 April to 5 April	7 May (the following tax year)

Alternatively, a business can elect to apply calendar quarters instead (amended to 1 April to 30 June/30 September/31 December/31 March) but the filing deadlines remain the same.

1.3.3 MTD year-end tax return (Final declaration)

After the final quarterly update has been submitted, the taxpayer must complete an MTD year-end tax return. This is similar to the self-assessment return but will be pre-populated with the income and expenses already submitted through the quarterly updates. Any necessary adjustments can then be made.

The return is due by the normal Self-Assessment deadline of 31 January following the end of the tax year.

Open book reference: Making Tax Digital

The mandation threshold and filing deadlines for MTD are provided in section 19 of your reference material.

1.3.4 Penalties for late filing under Making Tax Digital

A new points-based penalty regime applies to taxpayers using MTD IT from 2026/27.

- A penalty point is given each time a quarterly update or MTD year-end tax return is submitted late
- No financial penalty applies until the penalty point threshold is reached = 4 points for quarterly updates
- Once the penalty threshold is reached, a £200 penalty is charged
- A further £200 penalty for each subsequent late submission, but no additional points are given

Individual penalty points expire two years from the end of the month of the failure, provided the taxpayer remains below the points threshold.

Once the threshold has been reached, the points no longer expire after two years. To reset points to zero, the taxpayer must:

(a) Complete a period of compliance where they there are no further late submissions; and

(b) Have submitted all returns due in the previous 24 months.

The period of compliance is 12 months for quarterly updates

As 2026/27 is a transition year, no late filing penalties will apply for quarterly updates during that year. However, taxpayers must submit all their quarterly updates before they can submit their MTD year-end tax return.

1.4 Reporting capital gains

Most gains are reported via the individual's self-assessment tax return. As detailed above, the return is due on 31 January following the end of the tax year for online returns.

1.4.1 Reporting gains on UK residential property

Individuals who dispose of UK residential property must report this to HMRC within 60 days following the date of completion.

1.5 Payment of tax

1.5.1 Income tax

KEY TERM

Payment on account: An amount paid on account of income tax.

Open book reference: Payment dates

Payment dates are provided in section 19 of your reference material.

A taxpayer must usually make three payments of tax:

Date	Payment
31 January in the tax year	First payment on account
31 July after the tax year	Second payment on account
31 January after the tax year	Final payment to settle any remaining liability

Each payment on account (POA) is equal to 50% of the tax payable under self-assessment (ie not deducted at source) for the previous year.

If HMRC is late in requesting a tax return, then the final payment date is extended to three months following the 'notice to deliver' date (provided the taxpayer has notified chargeability on time).

POAs may be reduced if the taxpayer expects this year's liability to be lower than last year's. Interest will be charged if POAs are reduced and the final tax is greater than expected.

POAs are not required if the income tax payable for the previous year is less than £1,000 or if more than 80% of last year's liability was deducted at source.

Illustration 2: Payments on account

Jeremy's tax liability for 2025/26 totalled £12,000. None of the tax was deducted at source.

Each payment on account for 2026/27 would therefore be £6,000 (50% × £12,000)

1.5.2 Capital gains tax

Capital gains tax is normally due on 31 January following the tax year. Capital gains tax is never paid by instalments (payments on account).

Capital gains tax due on the disposal of residential property must be reported and paid within 60 days of completion.

Open book reference: CGT payment date

Capital gains tax due dates are provided in section 19 of your reference material.

Activity 1: Payments on account and balancing payments

Vorus's tax for 2025/26 was as follows:

	£
Income tax liability	7,000
PAYE (tax deducted at source from employment income)	4,000
Capital gains tax	5,000

His tax for 2026/27 is as follows:

	£
Income tax liability	8,000
PAYE (tax deducted at source from employment income)	2,500
Capital gains tax	1,000

Required

How is his tax liability for 2026/27 settled?

	£

1.5.3 Penalties for late payment

Open book reference: Late payment penalties

Penalties for late payment of tax are provided in section 19 of your reference material.

Penalties for late payment (taxpayer does not use Making Tax Digital)

Penalties for late payment of tax will be imposed in respect of balancing payments of income tax.

A penalty is chargeable where tax is paid after the penalty date. **The penalty date is 30 days after the due date for tax.** Therefore, no penalty arises if the tax is paid within 30 days of the due date.

Paid	Penalty
Less than 30 days	0%
30 days – 6 months	5% of unpaid tax at that date
6 months – 12 months	Further 5% of unpaid tax at that date (10%)
12 months +	Further 5% of unpaid tax at that date (15%)

Penalties for late payment under Making Tax Digital

Penalties for late payment of tax for those within MTD will be imposed in respect of balancing payments of income tax.

Paid	Penalty
By day 15	No penalty is payable
16 days - 30 days	3% of tax owed at day 15, or no penalty if in first year of MTD
From day 31	3% of tax owed at day 15 plus 3% of the tax owed at day 30 Plus, an annual rate of 10% per year on the outstanding amount, charged daily from day 31 until the tax is paid, or up to two years.

Penalties for late payment of tax **apply to balancing payments** of income tax only. They **do not apply to late payments on account**.

1.5.4 Interest

KEY TERM

Interest: Charged on late payments on account and on late balancing payments.

Interest is chargeable on late payments on account and late balancing payments. In both cases, interest runs from the due date until the day before the actual date of payment.

- POAs:
  - From 31 January during tax year
  - From 31 July following end of tax year
- Final payment:
  - From 31 January following end of tax year

If a taxpayer claims to reduce their payments on account and there is still a final payment to be made, interest is normally charged on the payments on account as if each of those payments had been the lower of:

(a) The reduced amount, plus 50% of the final income tax payable

(b) The amount which would have been payable had no claim for reduction been made

1.6 Compliance checks and enquiries

KEY TERM

Enquiry window: The period during which HMRC is legally allowed to open an enquiry into a submitted tax return.

Usually, under self-assessment, HMRC will accept taxpayers' figures.

However, HMRC has the power to conduct a compliance check.

Some returns are selected for a compliance check at random, others for a particular reason – for example, if HMRC believes that there has been an underpayment of tax due to the taxpayer's failure to comply with tax legislation.

There are two types of compliance check:

- Pre-return check using information powers
- Enquiries into submitted returns

Examples of when a pre-return check may be carried out in practice include:

- To assist with clearances or ruling requests
- Where a previous check has identified poor record keeping
- To check that computer systems will produce the information needed to support a return
- To find out about planning or avoidance schemes

- Where fraud is suspected

HMRC must give notice of intention to conduct an enquiry not later than 12 months after submission of the return.

HMRC has only one opportunity to open a formal enquiry and a tax return cannot be subject to a formal enquiry more than once.

In the course of the enquiries, the taxpayer may be required to produce documents, accounts or other information. There is a penalty of £300 for failing to produce these documents, with an additional £60 penalty charged each day the failure continues. The taxpayer can appeal to the Tax Tribunal against this.

HMRC must issue a closure notice when the enquiries are complete, state the conclusions and amend the self-assessment accordingly. If the taxpayer is not satisfied with the amendment, they may, within 30 days, appeal to the Tax Tribunal.

If the enquiry is complex or where there is avoidance or a large amount of tax at risk, then HMRC may issue a partial closure notice. This is issued ahead of a final closure notice and allows the taxpayer certainty on discrete matters without having to wait for the full enquiry to be resolved.

Open book reference: Enquiries

The deadline for HMRC to open an enquiry, and the penalty for failure to produce enquiry documents are provided in section 19 of your reference materials.

Assessment focus point

Please refer to the reference material at the end of this Course Book to see which elements of this chapter will be available to you as a pop-up window in the live assessment.

1.7 Amending a tax return

Tax returns may be amended by the individual, or corrected by HMRC after their submission.

An individual may make an amendment to their tax return within 12 months of the filing deadline. The filing deadline is usually 31 January following the tax year to which the return relates.

HMRC may make amendments to correct obvious errors and omissions within 9 months of the date of submission of the return.

1.8 Retention of records

Where a self assessment return is required, the individual must keep sufficient records to support the entries on the return.

Where the taxpayer is self-employed or has property income, the following records should be kept:

- Amount and description of all receipts and expenses
- Details of all purchases and sales of goods

Records may be kept in any form. Original documents may be kept as copies unless HMRC specify otherwise.

Under Making Tax Digital, most businesses will be required to keep records digitally using software.

Open book reference: Retention of records

The record retention periods are detailed in your reference material in section 19.

All records must be retained until the latest of:

- One year following 31 January after the end of the tax year (eg 31 January 2029 for tax year 2026/27)
- Five years following 31 January after the end of the tax year (eg 31 January 2033 for tax year 2026/27) for taxpayers who are self-employed or have property income. Note. All records must be retained for this time, not just property and self-employment records.
- Time at which enquiries can no longer be opened
- Time at which enquiries are concluded

The maximum penalty for failure to keep records is £3,000 per tax year.

2 Companies

2.1 Notification of chargeability

A company must notify HM Revenue & Customs (HMRC) when it first comes within the scope of corporation tax. This will usually be when it starts trading.

The notice must be made within three months of the date when it first became chargeable.

If notice of chargeability is not given the same penalties apply as for individuals covered in the earlier chapter.

Open book reference: Notify of chargeability

The deadline to notify HMRC of chargeability is provided in section 18 of your reference material.

2.2 Filing company tax returns

All companies and organisations must submit their Company Tax Return (Form CT600) online, except in exceptional circumstances. Additionally, tax computations and (with very few exceptions) the accounts that form part of the Company Tax Return must be submitted in 'Inline eXtensible Business Reporting Language' (iXBRL) format.

Assessment focus point

If your assessment asks for a specific date to be determined from a calendar, you must remember that precision is essential. The Chief Assessor has noted that students do not always take sufficient care in this style of task. In addition, take care in identifying the length of time between two dates to identify a penalty due.

2.2.1 Filing date

KEY TERM

Filing due date: The date by which a tax return must be filed.

Complete accounts, computations and a tax return for each of the company's accounting periods is due on or before the filing due date. This is normally the later of:

(a) 12 months after the end of the period of account concerned

(b) 3 months from the date on which the notice requiring the return was made

An obligation to file a return arises only when the company receives a notice requiring a return.

Open book reference: Filing date

The filing due date is provided in section 18 of your reference materials.

Illustration 3: Filing date

Size Ltd prepares accounts for the 12 months to 30 September 2026. A notice requiring a CT600 return for the year ended 30 September 2026 was issued on 1 June 2027. The date by which Size Ltd must file its Company Tax Return for the year to 30 September 2026 is 30 September 2027, being the later of: 30 September 2027 (12 months from end of period of account) and 1 September 2027 (3 months after notice to deliver).

If a period of account is more than 12 months long, there will be two accounting periods based on the period of account. The first accounting period is 12 months long; the second is for the remainder of the period of account (PA).

A tax return must be filed for each accounting period. The tax returns for both accounting periods must be filed within 12 months of the end of the period of account.

Illustration 4: Long period of account

Octo Ltd prepares accounts for the 18 months to 30 June 2026.

The two accounting periods relating to this period of account are year ended 31 December 2025 and six months to 30 June 2026.

The date by which Octo Ltd must file its Company Tax Returns based on this period of account, assuming a notice requiring the returns was issued shortly after the end of the period of account, is 30 June 2027.

2.2.2 Penalties for late filing

Companies are subject to the following late filing penalties:

Return outstanding	Penalty
<3 months late	£200 (£100 for returns due before 1 April 2026)
>3 months late	£400 (£200 for returns due before 1 April 2026)
>6 months late	10% of tax unpaid at 6m late date
>12 months late	20% of tax unpaid at 6m late date

Open book reference: Penalties for late filing

Penalties for late filing are provided in section 9 of your reference materials.

2.3 Payment of tax and interest

All tax must be paid electronically.

2.3.1 Non-large companies

Corporation tax is due for payment nine months and one day after the end of the accounting period for a company with annual taxable total profits (TTP) of no more than £1,500,000 for a 12-month accounting period.

Illustration 5: Corporation tax due date

K Ltd makes up accounts to 31 March 2027. Its profits do not exceed £1,500,000 and it has no dividend income. The corporation tax for the year to 31 March 2027 is £30,000.

The corporation tax is due on 1 January 2028.

2.3.2 Large companies

KEY TERM

Large companies: Companies with annual profits that exceed £1,500,000 for a 12-month accounting period.

Large companies, which have annual profits of more than £1,500,000 (adjusted by the length of the period), are required to pay their estimated tax liability in four quarterly instalments, due on the 14th day of the 7th, 10th, 13th and 16th month after the start of the accounting period.

Assessment focus point

You will not be expected to deal with very large companies with annual augmented profits over £20 million.

Open book reference: Payment date

Corporation tax payment dates for both large and non-large companies are provided in section 18 of your reference material.

Illustration 6: Payment in instalments

A company which prepares accounts to 31 December 2026 will pay instalments as follows:

Instalment	Due date
1	14 July 2026
2	14 October 2026
3	14 January 2027
4	14 April 2027

Activity 2: Payment of corporation tax

A plc has taxable total profits (TTP) of £2.1m in the year to 31 March 2027.

Required

Show how the corporation tax in respect of the year to 31 March 2027 will be paid.

	£

	£

You will note that tax must be paid before the end of the accounting period on profits that have not yet been earned.

(a) At each quarter end, the directors will have to estimate how much the total tax bill will be for the year.

(b) They then calculate the proportion of this tax due to date (eg by the time of the second instalment 2/4, ie 1/2 of the tax is due).

(c) They will then pay over the difference compared to what they have paid to date.

2.3.3 Interest to HMRC

Interest arises on late-paid instalments (from the due date to the actual payment date).

2.3.4 Interest from HMRC

Interest on overpaid instalments will run from the date that the tax was originally paid to the repayment date (note that interest on overpaid tax cannot run any earlier than from the due date of the first instalment).

Interest on tax paid late is a deductible expense and interest on overpaid tax is taxable. This will be added to, or subtracted from, interest income.

2.3.5 Long period of account

A long period of account gives rise to two accounting periods. Each accounting period will have its own due date(s).

Illustration 7: Long period of account

Z Ltd is not a large company for the purposes of corporation tax payment dates. It has a 15-month period to 30 September 2026.

Z Ltd will have two chargeable accounting periods:

- 12 months to 30 June 2026
- 3 months to 30 September 2026

Z Ltd will therefore have two payment dates:

- 1 April 2027
- 1 July 2027

Assessment focus point

Much of this information is included in the reference material which is available to you as a pop-up window in the live assessment.

2.3.6 Penalties for late payment of corporation tax

In most situations, there is no penalty for late payment of corporation tax.

2.4 Compliance checks and enquiries

As with an individual, HMRC may conduct a compliance check into a company's tax return.

An enquiry is a compliance check into a return that has already been filed.

HMRC must give written notice of an enquiry within 12 months of the actual filing date.

Only one enquiry may be made in respect of any one return.

HMRC may request documents.

- There is a £300 penalty if the company does not provide them.
- HMRC may then charge £60 a day until these are produced.

An enquiry ends when HMRC gives notice that it has been completed.

- HMRC will amend the return.
- The company may appeal the amendments to the Tax Tribunal within 30 days.

In the same way that we saw for individuals, HMRC can issue a partial closure notice over certain matters where the enquiry is complex.

Open book reference: Enquiry

Enquiry deadlines and penalties are provided in section 9 of your reference materials.

Illustration 8: Enquiries

Green Ltd prepares accounts for the 12 months to 30 April 2026. The Company Tax Return for the year was filed on 31 March 2027.

The date by which HMRC may commence an enquiry into the return based on these accounts is:

31 March 2028 (12 months from the actual filing date).

2.5 Record keeping

Companies must keep records until the latest of:

(a) Six years from the end of the accounting period

(b) The date any enquiries (compliance checks) are completed

(c) The date after which enquiries may not be commenced

All business records and accounts, including contracts and receipts, must be kept.

Failure to keep records can lead to a penalty of up to £3,000 for each accounting period affected.

Open book reference: Record retention

Record retention periods and penalties are provided in section 9 of your reference materials.

3 Penalties for errors

Open book reference: Penalties for incorrect returns

The penalties for errors (incorrect returns) are provided in your reference material in section 20.

If a taxpayer makes an error in their tax return, they can amend it within 12 months of the filing date. They can also make a claim for overpayment relief within four years of the end of the tax year.

A penalty may be imposed where a taxpayer makes an inaccurate return if they have:

(a) **Been careless** because they have not taken reasonable care in making the return or they discover the error later but do not take reasonable steps to inform HMRC

(b) **Made a deliberate error** but do not make arrangements to conceal it

(c) **Made a deliberate error and has attempted to conceal it**, eg by submitting false evidence in support of an inaccurate figure

If there is more than one error, HMRC may charge more than one penalty.

Penalties may be reduced if the errors are brought to HMRC's attention by the taxpayer.

This could be **unprompted**, where the taxpayer admits the error before HMRC has any knowledge of irregularity, or **prompted**, when the taxpayer suspects the error has been, or is about to be, discovered.

KEY TERM

Errors: Errors are classified into three categories based on the behaviour of the taxpayer:

(a) Careless: an error caused by a failure to take reasonable care.

(b) Deliberate: an error where the taxpayer knowingly provides inaccurate information or withholds relevant information.

(c) Deliberate and concealed: a deliberate error (see above) where the taxpayer also takes steps to hide the inaccuracy from HMRC.

Disclosures - prompted and unprompted: When a taxpayer discloses an error to HMRC, those disclosures are classified into two categories:

(a) Unprompted disclosure: when a taxpayer tells HMRC about an error before they have any reason to believe HMRC has discovered or is about to discover the issue

(b) Prompted disclosure: when a taxpayer tells HMRC about an error after HMRC has initiated contact, such as writing to inform the taxpayer of a compliance check or investigation.

Potential lost revenue (PLR): The tax that would have been lost if the error had gone undetected.

Penalties are as follows (provided in your reference materials):

Type of error	Maximum penalty	Minimum penalty with unprompted disclosure	Minimum penalty with prompted disclosure
Genuine mistake	No penalty	No penalty	No penalty
Careless	30%	0%	15%
Deliberate but not concealed	70%	20%	35%
Deliberate and concealed	100%	30%	50%

The scale of the reduction will vary depending upon the help the taxpayer has given HMRC in respect of:

- Advising about the error, making full disclosure, and explaining how it was made
- Assisting HMRC to enable it to quantify the error
- Allowing access to records

A penalty for a careless error may be suspended by HMRC to allow the taxpayer to take action to ensure that the error does not occur again (eg where the error has arisen from failure to keep proper records).

HMRC will impose conditions which the taxpayer has to satisfy, eg establishing proper record-keeping systems.

The penalty will be cancelled if the conditions imposed by HMRC are complied with by the taxpayer within a period of up to two years.

A taxpayer may appeal against:

- The penalty being charged
- The amount of the penalty
- A decision by HMRC not to suspend a penalty
- Conditions set by HMRC in relation to the suspension of a penalty

Activity 3: Penalties

Kelly deliberately omitted an invoice from her trading income in her 2025/26 tax return but did not destroy the evidence. She later disclosed this error, before she had reason to believe HMRC might investigate the matter.

Required

Complete the following sentence:

Kelly's penalty can be reduced from [ ] % of the potential lost revenue (for a deliberate, but not concealed error) to [ ] %, with the unprompted disclosure of her error.

BPP

Chapter summary

- Taxpayers must notify HMRC by 5 October following the end of the tax year if a tax return is needed.
- A tax return must be filed by 31 January following a tax year, provided it is filed online. Paper returns must be filed by 31 October following the tax year.
- Making Tax Digital (MTD) requires taxpayers to keep digital records and submit quarterly updates, followed by a year-end tax return (Final declaration) due by 31 January after the tax year.
- Capital gains are normally reported on a self-assessment tax return. However, for disposals of UK residential property, these must be reported within 60 days of the date of completion.
- A fixed penalty of £100 applies if a return is filed late; followed by a potential daily penalty of £10 if the return is filed between three and six months late.
- A tax-geared penalty will also apply if a return is filed more than 6 months late, with a further penalty if this is over 12 months late.
- Late submissions under MTD are subject to a points-based penalty system, where missed deadlines accumulate points and, once a threshold is reached, £200 penalties apply for each further default, with separate penalties for late payment of tax.
- Payments on account of income tax are required on 31 January in the tax year and on 31 July following the tax year.
- Balancing payments of income tax are due on 31 January following the tax year.
- Capital gains tax is normally due by 31 January following the end of the tax year. However, CGT in relation to UK residential property disposals is due within 60 days of the date of completion.
- Late payment penalties apply to balancing payments of income tax. They do not apply to late payments on account.
- Interest is chargeable on late payment of both payments on account and balancing payments.
- HMRC can enquire into a return within one year of receipt of the return. There is a penalty of £300 for failing to produce documents requested in an enquiry which increases by £60 per day that the failure continues.
- A taxpayer can amend a tax return within 12 months of filing date or make a claim for overpayment relief within 4 years of the end of the tax year.
- Individual taxpayers must keep records until the later of:
  (1) One year after 31 January following the tax year
  (2) Five years after 31 January following the tax year if in business or with property income
- A company must usually file its CT600 online return within 12 months of the end of the period of account concerned.
- Fixed penalties arise if the return is up to six months late. If the return is over six months late, there may be a tax-geared penalty.
- Large companies must pay their CT liability in four instalments, starting in the seventh month of the accounting period. The final instalment is due in the fourth month following the end of the accounting period.
- Other companies must pay their corporation tax liability nine months and one day after the end of an accounting period.
- Companies must normally keep records until six years after the end of the accounting period concerned.
- HMRC can enquire into a return. Notice of an enquiry must usually be given within 12 months of the actual filing date.
- A penalty may be imposed if the taxpayer makes an error in their tax return based on the potential lost revenue as a result of the error.

Activity answers

Activity 1: Payments on account and balancing payments

	£
2025/26 income tax payable 7,000 – 4,000 =	3,000
The payments on account for 2026/27 are therefore:	
31.1.27 50% × 3,000	1,500
31.7.27 50% × 3,000	1,500
The final payment is therefore:	
Income tax liability	8,000
Less PAYE	(2,500)
Less payments on account (2 × 1,500)	(3,000)
	2,500
Capital gains tax liability	1,000
31.1.28 Final payment	3,500

Activity 2: Payment of corporation tax

	£
Corporation tax due	
2,100,000 × 25%	525,000
Due by instalments on the 14th day of month 7, 10, 13 and 16, counting from the start of the period – ie 1 April 2026.	
14 October 2026	131,250
14 January 2027	131,250
14 April 2027	131,250
14 July 2027	131,250

Activity 3: Penalties

Kelly's penalty can be reduced from 70 % of the potential lost revenue (for a deliberate, but not concealed error) to 20 %, with the unprompted disclosure of her error.

Test your learning

1

The due filing date for an income tax return for 2026/27, assuming the taxpayer will submit the return online is: [ ]

2 **Select the correct answers to the four questions from the four picklists provided.**

The 2026/27 payments on account will be calculated as (1) ▼ of the income tax payable for (1) ▼ and will be due on (3) ▼ and (4) ▼

Picklist 1

- 100%
- 2025/26
- 25%
- 50%

Picklist 2

- 2024/25
- 2025/26
- 2026/27

Picklist 3

- 1 January 2027
- 31 January 2026
- 31 January 2027
- 31 January 2027

Picklist 4

- 31 December 2027
- 31 January 2028
- 31 July 2027

3 A notice requiring a tax return for 2026/27 is issued in April 2027 and the return is filed online in May 2028. All income tax was paid in May 2028. No payments on account were due.

Required

Explain what charges will be made on the taxpayer.

4 Susie filed her 2025/26 tax return online on 28 January 2027.

Required

By what date must HMRC give notice that it is going to enquire into the return? Tick ONE box.

	✓
31 January 2028	
31 March 2028	
6 April 2028	
28 January 2028	

5 Jamie paid income tax of £12,000 for 2025/26. In 2026/27, his tax payable was £16,000.

Required

Jamie's 2026/27 payments on account will each be

£ [ ] and will be due on (insert date as XX/XX/XX)

[ ]

and

[ ]

Jamie's balancing payment will be

£ [ ] and will be due on (insert date as XX/XX/XX)

[ ].

6 Tim should have made two payments on account of his 2026/27 income tax payable of £5,000 each. He actually made both of these payments on 31 August 2027.

Required

State the amount of any penalties for late payment.

£ [ ]

7 **By what date must a taxpayer generally submit a tax return for 2026/27 if it is filed as a paper return?**

	✓
30 September 2027	
31 October 2027	
31 December 2027	
31 January 2028	

8 **On which dates are payment on accounts due for 2026/27?**

	✓
31 January 2028 and 31 July 2028	
31 January 2027 and 31 July 2027	
31 October 2027 and 31 January 2028	
31 July 2027 and 31 January 2028	

9 Lola accidentally fails to include an invoice of £17,000 on her 2026/27 tax return. She pays basic rate tax at 20%, and has not yet disclosed this error.

Required

Identify the maximum penalty that could be imposed on her. Tick ONE box.

	✓
£5,100	
£3,400	
£1,020	
£2,380	

1 A company has been preparing accounts to 30 June for many years. It submitted its CT600 return for the year to 30 June 2025 on 1 June 2026.

Required

By what date must HMRC give notice that it is going to commence an enquiry into the return?

[ ]

2 A company filed its CT600 return for the year to 31 December 2025 on 28 February 2027.

Required

What is the maximum penalty in respect of the late filing of the return for the year to 31 December 2025?

£ [ ]

3 Girton Ltd has augmented profits of £150,000 in the year ended 31 December 2026.

Required

When will its first payment of corporation tax be due?

	✓
14 July 2026	
1 October 2027	
31 December 2027	
1 January 2028	

4 Eaton Ltd has augmented profits of £2,400,000 for both its years ended 31 December 2025 and 31 December 2026.

Required

The final payment of the corporation tax liability for the year ended 31 December 2026 will be due on:

	✓
14 July 2026	
14 April 2027	
1 October 2027	
31 December 2027	

5 M Ltd, a large company, has an estimated corporation tax liability of £240,000 in respect of its accounting year to 31 March 2027.

Required

What will be the amount of each of the company's quarterly instalments?

£ [ ]

14 Tax planning

Learning outcomes

7	**Understand tax planning opportunities**

7.1	**Personal tax planning opportunities**
	Learners need to understand:
	7.1.1 why an individual may wish to undertake tax planning:
	• make use of:
	  - tax exemptions
	  - allowances
	• avoid higher rates of taxes
	• avoid abatement of the personal allowance
	• avoid the high income child benefit charge
	• minimise the combined income tax liability for a couple

	7.1.2 opportunities that individuals may have to minimise their tax liability: • choice of employment benefits • pension contributions • charity donations • use of ISAs • choice of investment types • marriage allowance • transfer of assets between spouses/civil partners • choosing which partner purchases income generating assets/joint ownership • choosing which partner in a relationship makes charity donations/pension contributions
	Learners need to be able to: 7.1.3 identify tax planning opportunities
	7.1.4 calculate tax for different tax planning options
	7.1.5 calculate after tax income for different tax planning options
	7.1.6 calculate tax savings from tax planning opportunities

7.2	**Business tax planning opportunities** Learners need to understand: 7.2.1 how the choice of business structure may affect: • tax due • after tax income
	7.2.2 how the choice of extraction of profits from a company may affect: • tax due • after tax income
	7.2.3 tax planning opportunities for couples: • employment at a reasonable wage • shareholders • partners
	Learners need to be able to: 7.2.4 identify tax planning opportunities
	7.2.5 calculate tax for different tax planning options
	7.2.6 calculate after tax income for different tax planning options
	7.2.7 calculate tax savings from tax planning opportunities

Assessment context

Task 9 in your assessment will include some of the tax planning ideas covered within this chapter. In the AAT's practice assessments, the tax planning tasks totalled 6 marks.

Qualification context

You will not see the information in this chapter outside of this unit.

Business context

The information included within this chapter is very useful if you are advising a client about opportunities to minimise their tax liabilities. People often don't realise that different business structures have very different tax consequences.

Chapter overview

Tax planning for businesses

Personal tax planning

- Plan tax efficient remuneration via benefits, pension contributions, payroll giving
- Make personal pension contributions and gift aid donations
- Invest in ISAs
- Transfer of assets between spouses and civil partners
- Make use of marriage allowance

Choice of business structure

Considerations

- Sole trader/partnership
  - More private, fewer regulations
  - Pays income tax, Class 4 NIC
  - Two payments on account, 31 July, 31 January
  - Taxed before any profits extracted
- Company
  - Separate legal entity, more rules and regulations
  - Pays corporation tax, Class 1 NICs on any employee salaries
  - Due 9 months and 1 day after end of accounting period
  - Profit extraction has tax consequences

Extraction of profit

- Salary
  - Salary and class 1 employer's NIC due thereon are tax deductible for the company
  - Individual pays income tax and employee's NIC on salary
- Dividend
  - Not tax deductible for company and no NICs
  - Individual pays income tax at lower rates and no NICs

Spouse or civil partner planning

- Income tax planning
  - Ensure use of both personal allowances
  - Ensure further income is received by spouse paying lower rates of tax
- Capital gains tax planning
  - Assets pass at nil gain nil loss
  - Ensure both annual exempt amounts utilised
  - Further gains to be taxed on spouse paying lower rate of tax
  - Ability to claim reliefs

Introduction

In this chapter we look at tax planning for individuals and businesses. Tax planning involves using tax reliefs for the purpose for which they were intended. For example, claiming tax relief on capital investment, savings in a tax-exempt ISA, or saving for retirement by making pension contributions. These are all legitimate forms of tax planning as they are not contrived or artificial transactions.

We will start by considering personal tax planning opportunities such as choice of employment benefits, pension contribution, charity donations, use of ISAs and so on. In your assessment you may be required to calculate an individual's after tax income, or the tax saved if the taxpayer were to implement the tax planning idea.

We will move on to look at one of the most basic decisions that needs to be made when setting up in business – choice of business structure. As well as practical and legal considerations, the tax consequences of different structures are different. We will consider the choice of setting up the business as an unincorporated business (ie as a sole trader or partnership) or as an incorporated business (ie a company).

Next, we need to consider how we extract profits from the new business and what tax consequences this may have.

Finally, we will consider some spouse/ civil partner tax planning ideas.

1 Personal tax planning

We will consider a number of different tax planning opportunities for individuals in the following sections. The methods that are used for tax planning could involve:

(a) Making use of tax exemptions or allowances, for example the tax exemption for interest received from an ISA, or ensuring that both spouses or civil partners make use of their personal allowance.

(b) Avoid higher rates of tax, for example by making charitable donations under the gift aid scheme, or personal pension contributions to extend the tax bands

(c) Avoid abatement of the personal allowance by making charitable donations or personal pension contributions to reduce adjusted net income.

(d) Avoid the high income child benefit charge by keeping both partners' adjusted net income below £60,000. Consider transferring income producing assets between partners, or making charitable donations of pension contributions.

(e) Minimise the combined income tax liability for a couple

1.1 Opportunities for personal tax planning

1.1.1 Employment benefits

There are a number of ways an employee can legally reduce their taxable income from employment:

(a) Select exempt benefits over taxable benefits

(b) Select benefits with a lower cash equivalent over benefits with a higher cash equivalent

(c) Ensure that any contribution towards the private use of an employer's car is for the use itself as this would be deductible rather than for the private fuel which would not be deductible

(d) Pay into a company pension scheme

(e) Make payments to charity under the payroll giving scheme

(f) Claim all allowable deductions, for example any travel costs of attending meetings at 'temporary workplaces'

(g) Seek rewards in benefits rather than in cash as there will be no National Insurance cost to the employee on benefits (note that the employer would have to pay National Insurance here) (see Chapter 10)

BPP

1.1.2 Pension contributions and charitable donations

Payments into personal pension schemes and donations to charity under the Gift Aid scheme are advantageous from a tax perspective because:

(a) They are made net of tax, so for every £8 cash given/invested, the charity/pension receives £10.

(b) The taxpayer's income tax bands are extended by the gross contribution (£10 in the above illustration). This means that more income is taxed at a lower rate. Also, this may preserve the personal savings allowance at the higher rate of £1,000 if the taxpayer stays within the extended basic rate band. Note that if the individual is already a basic rate taxpayer then there will be no additional advantage here.

(c) The gross donation is deducted from the taxpayer's adjusted net income. Adjusted net income is used:

  (i) To determine the level of abatement of the personal allowance

  (ii) To determine how much high income child benefit charge is levied

1.1.3 ISAs and other investment types

Taxpayers could invest in products that yield exempt income such as ISAs or premium bonds.

1.1.4 Opportunities for spouses and civil partners

Where a couple are married or in a civil partnership, they are treated separately for tax purposes. Each will pay income tax based on their own income with their own personal allowance.

However, income generating assets, such as shares or rental property, can usually be passed between themselves with no tax consequences (referred to as nil gain nil loss transfers) allowing the couple to reduce their combined income tax by:

- Ensuring both partners are fully utilising their personal allowance
- Moving income generating assets from a partner paying higher or additional rate tax to a partner paying basic rate tax.

Passing capital assets between spouses/civil partners also allows for capital gains tax planning. Where assets are to be sold realising chargeable gains, ownership should be arranged in such a way that allows each spouse to fully utilise their own annual exempt amount and then for any further gains to be realised by the spouse paying the lower rate of capital gains tax. Consideration could also be given as to whether only one spouse might be able to claim business asset disposal relief.

Marriage allowance

As we saw in chapter 2, the marriage allowance permits the lower-earner of married couples or civil partners to transfer part of their personal allowance to the other party. Remember that both individuals must be either basic rate or non-taxpayers. The receiving spouse or civil partner obtains relief as a tax reducer at 20% of the amount transferred.

Transfer of assets between spouses/civil partners

Where one individual pays tax at a higher rate than the other, it is beneficial to transfer income-producing assets between spouses and civil partners so that the income is taxed at a lower rate.

Even if both people in a marriage/civil partnership pay tax at the same rate they should consider transferring assets between each other to ensure they get the maximum benefit from the savings allowance and the dividend allowance. For example, if each person is paying tax at the higher rate, they will each receive a personal savings allowance of £500. If one party owns all the invested cash and is in receipt of £1,000 of interest, then £500 of it will be above the allowance and will be taxable. If half of the cash is transferred to the other party, then they will both be in receipt of £500 which will be covered by their personal savings allowance and together they will not pay tax on the interest.

From a capital gains tax perspective, spouses and civil partners can transfer assets at no gain no loss. This effectively transfers the asset over at its original cost so that the gain will be the same whichever party sells it. It therefore makes sense to ensure an asset is sold by the spouse/civil partner who:

(a) Pays tax at a lower rate
(b) Has an unused annual exemption
(c) Has a capital loss

Choosing which partner purchases income generating assets/joint ownership

If possible, married couples and civil partners should consider whether cash balances yielding interest and shares yielding dividends could be held by the partner paying the lower rate of tax to avoid having unused personal allowances.

Choosing which partner in a relationship makes charity donations/pension contributions

As seen above, there are a number of tax advantages to making charitable donations and pension contributions. It would make sense for the partner who pays tax at the higher rate to make these donations or contributions.

Activity 1: Spouse/civil partner tax planning

Kemi and Isla who live in England, have been married for many years and have two young children. Kemi works full time on a salary of £70,000 and receives dividends of £5,000 each year and is a higher rate taxpayer. Isla is a full-time student and will not have any income for the next tax year.

The couple are considering investing in shares and thus earning dividend income.

Required

Advise the couple as to who should buy the shares in order to minimise their overall tax bill.

1.2 Calculating tax savings and after tax income

In your assessment, you may be required to calculate the tax savings from tax planning opportunities, or after tax income for different tax planning options.

KEY TERM

Tax saving: Is the difference between the tax payable with or without implementing the tax planning opportunity.

After tax income: Is the income received by the individual after tax and national insurance contributions.

Illustration 1: After tax income

Craig lives in England and his only source of income is his salary of £40,000.

Required

What is Craig's after tax income for 2026/27?

£ [ ]

Solution

£ 32,320

Income tax

	£
Salary	40,000

BPP

	£
Less: personal allowance	(12,570)
Taxable	27,430
27,430 × 20%	5,486

National insurance contributions

Class 1 employee NIC: (40,000 - 12,570) × 8% = £2,194

After tax income

	£
Income	40,000
Less: income tax	(5,486)
Less: NIC	(2,194)
After-tax income	32,320

Where an individual is extracting profits from a company, and you are asked about after tax income, you must consider the corporation tax paid by the company as well as the income tax and national insurance contributions payable by the individual.

If profits are extracted from the company by way of a dividend:

- There is no corporation tax deduction for the company for the payment of the dividend
- There is no NIC payable on dividends
- The individual will benefit from the dividend allowance for income tax purposes

If profits are extracted from the company by way of a salary or bonus:

- The company will get a corporation tax deduction for the salary/bonus and associated employer's Class 1 NIC
- The individual will pay Class 1 Employee NIC

Illustration 2: Ana

Ana, who lives in England, owns 100% of the shares in her company Frozen Ltd. The company makes a profit of £40,000.

Required

(a) What would be the maximum dividend that Ana could extract from the company?

£ [ ]

(b) How much would Ana keep after paying tax on the dividend?

£ [ ]

Solution

(a) £ 32,400

There is no corporation tax deduction for dividends paid, so the maximum dividend payable is based on the company's profits after corporation tax. The company pays tax at 19%.

	£
Taxable profits	40,000
Less: corporation tax at 19%	(7,600)
Profits available for distribution as a dividend	32,400

(b) £ 30,322

	£
Dividend	32,400
Less: PA	(12,570)
Taxable	19,830

	£
500 × 0%	0
(19,830 - 500) × 10.75%	2,078
Income tax payable	2,078

Therefore, the after tax dividend is (£32,400 – £2,078) = £30,322

Comparing the after-tax income in the illustration Ana with the illustration Craig above, we can see that with a profit level of £40,000 it is more tax-efficient to run the business as a sole trader than a company (if all of the profits are extracted as a dividend).

Illustration 3: Srinija

Srinija, who lives in England, is the 100% shareholder of Cake Ltd. Cake Ltd made a trading profit of £50,000 for the year ended 31 March 2027. Srinija will extract these profits by way of a salary of £5,000, and the balance of the profits as a dividend.

Required

(a) What is the maximum dividend that Srinija can extract?

(b) What is Srinija's after tax income?

Solution

(a)

	£
Company profits	50,000
Less: salaries paid	(5,000)
Less: employer's Class 1 NIC (below threshold)	(0)
Taxable profits	45,000

	£
Corporation tax @ 19%	(8,550)
Distributable profits	36,450

The maximum dividend that Srinija can extract is the distributable profits of £36,450.

(b)

	Non savings	Dividend
	£	£
Salary	5,000	
Dividend		36,450
Less: PA	(5,000)	(7,570)
Taxable	0	28,880

	£
500 × 0%	0
(28,880 - 500) × 10.75%	3,051
Income tax	3,051

No employee's Class 1 NIC as below threshold

	£
Salary	5,000
Dividend	36,450
Less: income tax	(3,051)
Less: employee NIC	(0)
After-tax income	38,399

2 Business tax planning

In your assessment, in task 9, you may be asked about tax planning involving a business. You may need to identify tax planning opportunities, calculate tax, tax savings, or after tax income. One of the first things to consider for a business is how to structure the business.

2.1 Choice of business structure

KEY TERM

Business structure: How the business is set up. It can be an unincorporated business, such as a sole trader or partnership, or incorporated such as a company.

When starting a business, an individual must decide whether to set up as an unincorporated business (ie a sole trader or partnership) or as an incorporated business (ie a company). This choice has very different practical, legal and tax considerations.

The table below sets out the key differences in an individual's choice of business structure:

	Sole trader/Partnership	Company
Liability	The individual and the business are the same entity. The individual is personally liable for the liabilities of the business.	The company is a separate legal entity from the owners, with the individual owning shares in the company. The individual's assets are protected by limited liability.
Accounts, Regulations and Privacy	An unincorporated business has fewer rules and regulations with which to comply and does not need to file accounts at Companies House. This gives more privacy.	A company is subject to more rules and regulations including the Companies Act. There is a requirement to file accounts at Companies House, so results are public.
Tax on profits	Trading profits (adjusted for tax) subject to income tax at non-savings rates (20/40/45%) dependent on levels of taxable income. The personal allowance may be available. Class 4 NICs will also be due. Class 4 NIC 6% on trading profits between £12,570 and £50,270 and 2% above.	The company pays corporation tax on trading profits (adjusted for tax) at between 19% and 25%. Class 1 NICs will be due on cash earnings of any employees and are deductible for the company. The company suffers Class 1 employer NIC at 15% on earnings over £5,000. A £10,500 employment allowance is available to offset the first £10,500 of employer's NIC due (although this is not available to companies with a single director and no other employees). The employee will pay Class 1 employee's NIC at 8% on cash earnings between £12,570 and £50,270 and 2% above.
Tax payments	Two payments on account 31 January 2027 and 31 July 2027.	Probably a small company, therefore tax is due nine months and one day after end of the accounting period.
Extraction of profits	The sole trader extracts profits as drawings or owner's 'salary'. Income tax is paid on trade profits before any drawings or owner's salary is deducted so how the profits are extracted, or how much, has no tax consequences.	Profits need to be extracted from the company to the individual, usually by way of either director's salary or dividends (or a combination). The different tax consequences are covered in the next section.

Activity 2: Sole trader versus company

Select whether the following statements are true or false:

	True ✓	False ✓
A sole trader business is a separate legal entity from its owner.		

	True ✓	False ✓
Profits can be extracted from a sole trade business with no tax consequences.		
Sole traders who live in England pay income tax on their trade profits at 20%.		
Companies pay their tax in two payments on account.		
A sole trader will pay Class 4 NICs.		
A company pays Class 1 Employee's NIC on any cash earnings in excess of £5,000 at 15%.		

2.2 Extraction of profit

KEY TERM

Extraction of profits: The ways owners take money out of their business, such as salary, benefits, dividends and drawings.

The profits of an unincorporated business before deduction of any drawings or owners' salaries are taxed to income tax on the sole trader or partner. They can therefore extract profit by way of drawings or owner's salary and with no tax consequences.

In contrast, if the business is set up as a company, the owner will be a separate entity to the company, and they will need to consider how to extract their profits from the company. The most common methods of profit extraction are for the owner to take a salary or dividend. These have very different tax consequences for both the individual and the company which are summarised below:

Method	Company	Individual
Salary	Class 1 employer's NIC will be due on any cash salary in excess of £5,000 at 15%. The company has a £10,500 employment allowance which can be deducted from the first Employer's NIC due (although this is not available to companies with a single director and no other employees). The salary and the Class 1 Employer's NIC are deductible from trading profits thus reducing TTP and saving corporation tax.	Income tax will be due on any salary in excess of the personal allowance at 20%, 40% or 45% dependent on the individual's other income. Class 1 Employee's NIC will be due at 8% on any cash salary in excess of £12,570 up to £50,270. If the cash salary exceeds £50,270 there is 2% NIC on the excess.
Dividends	Not tax deductible for the company. No NICs.	Income tax will be due on any dividends in excess of the personal and dividend allowance at 10.75%, 35.75% or 39.35% depending on the individual's other income. No NICs.

Illustration 4: Extraction of profit 1

Inga, who lives in England, is the sole shareholder and director of Labrador Ltd. The company doesn't have any other employees. During the year ended 31 December 2027, Labrador Ltd makes tax adjusted trading profits of £20,000 and has no other income or gains.

Inga has other cash earnings from the company of £18,000 and dividend income of £2,000 making her a basic rate taxpayer.

Required

Calculate the maximum dividend that Inga can take this year and the post-tax cash that she would receive.

Solution

	£
Labrador Ltd's TTP	20,000
Less corporation tax @ 19%	(3,800)
Profits available to distribute as a dividend = dividend	16,200
As a basic rate taxpayer, Inga will suffer 10.75% income tax on this dividend with no NIC. (10.75% × £16,200)	(1,742)
After-tax dividend kept by Inga	14,458

If Inga instead chose to extract all of her profits as a salary, calculate how much post-tax cash she would receive.

	£
Labrador Ltd's TTP	20,000
Employer's NIC will be due at 15% on any salary that Inga chooses to take from the company. So, the TTP figures represents 115% of the salary. Employer's NIC on salary to withdraw (15/115 × £20,000) (Note)	(2,609)
Salary for Inga to withdraw (100/115 × £20,000)	17,391
This salary will be taxed on Inga, a basic rate taxpayer, at a rate of 20% income tax and 8% employee's NICs. Thus 28% tax will be suffered (28% × £17,391)	(4,869)
After tax salary kept by Inga	12,522

Note. As Inga is the sole director and employee of the company, there is no employment allowance available.

Activity 3: Extraction of profit 2

Dash, who lives in England, is the sole shareholder of Pringle Ltd. During the year ended 31 December 2027, Pringle Ltd makes tax adjusted trading profits of £75,000 and has no other income or gains.

Dash has other employment income of £60,000 and dividend income of £6,000 making her a higher rate taxpayer.

Required

(a) **If Dash extracts the maximum possible dividend, how much income will she receive after tax.**

	£	£

(b) **If Dash instead chose to extract all of her profits as a salary, calculate how much post-tax cash she would receive.**

	£

Activity 4: Carlos

Carlos lives in England and is the 100% shareholder of his company Plants Ltd. There are no other employees. Plants Ltd has trading profits of £350,000 in the year ended 31 March 2027. Carlos takes a salary of £80,000.

Carlos also receives dividends from investments of £700 each year.

Required

(a) **What are Plants Ltd's available profits to be distributed to Carlos?**

(b) **What is the maximum possible dividend that Carlos can take in the year ended 31 March 2027?**

(c) **What is the maximum possible additional salary that Carlos can take in the year ended 31 March 2027?**

Chapter summary

- Tax planning for individuals may involve:
  - Making use of tax exemptions and allowances
  - Avoiding higher rates of tax or abatement of the personal allowance
  - Avoiding the high income child benefit charge
  - Minimising the overall tax liability of a couple
- The badges of trade give guidance as to whether a trade is being carried on.
- A new business can be set up as a sole trade/ partnership or a company
  - There is no legal distinction between the owner and an unincorporated business
  - A company is a separate legal entity from its shareholders
  - Unincorporated business have to comply with fewer rules and regulations than companies
  - Sole traders/partners pay income tax and Class 4 NICs on trade profits whereas companies pay corporation tax
  - Sole traders/partners pay their tax in two payments on account whereas a company usually pays corporation tax 9 months and 1 day after the end of its accounting period
  - A sole trader can extract their profit with no tax consequences. For a company extraction of profit has tax consequences
- Extraction of profit from a company
  - A salary creates Class 1 Employer's NIC for the company. The salary and employer's NIC are tax deductible reducing the company's corporation tax
  - The individual pays income tax and employee's NIC on the salary
  - Dividends are not tax deductible for the company and there are no NICs for wither the company or the shareholder
  - The individual pays income tax only on the dividend income
- Married couples/ civil partners should plan to use both individuals' personal allowances (for income tax) and annual exempt amounts (for capital gains tax). Any income/ gains should then arise on the individual paying tax at the lowest rate. Assets can pass between spouses/ civil partners at nil gain nil loss.

Activity answers

Activity 1: Spouse/civil partner tax planning

Kemi will pay income tax at 35.75% on any dividend income received.

In contrast, as Isla has no other taxable income, a full personal allowance is available to utilise against any dividend income. Isla can receive £13,070 of dividends income tax free due to the personal and dividend allowance. Any dividend income in excess of the personal and dividend allowance will be taxed at 10.75%.

Consequently, the couple's income tax liability will be minimised if the shares are owned by Isla.

Activity 2: Sole trader versus company

The correct answers are:

	True ✓	False ✓
A sole trader business is a separate legal entity from its owner. **Explanation:** It is a company that is a separate legal entity from its owner.		✓
Profits can be extracted from a sole trade business with no tax consequences. **Explanation:** How much profit and how the sole trader/partner extracts it from the business makes no difference to their tax bill because profits are taxed to income tax before any extraction.	✓	
Sole traders who live in England pay income tax on their trade profits at 20%. **Explanation:** The rate of income tax paid by a sole trader depends on their level of trade profits and their other income. It could be 20%, 40% or 45%.		✓
Companies pay their tax in two payments on account. **Explanation:** Sole traders make payments on account of their income tax and Class 4 NICs. Companies usually make one payment of corporation tax, 9 months and 1 day after the end of the accounting period unless their augmented profits are above £1,500,000.		✓
A sole trader will pay Class 4 NICs.	✓	
A company pays Class 1 Employee's NIC on any cash earnings in excess of £5,000 at 15%. **Explanation:** Companies pay Class 1 Employer's rather than Class 1 Employee's NIC. The threshold and rate are, however, correct.		✓

Activity 3: Extraction of profit 2

(a)

	£	£
Pringle Ltd's TTP		75,000
Less corporation tax @ 25%	18,750	
Less 3/200 x (£250,000 - £75,000)	(2,625)	
		(16,125)
Profits available to distribute as a dividend = dividend		58,875
As a higher rate taxpayer Dash will pay income tax at 35.75% on the dividend with no NIC (£58,875 × 35.75%)		(21,048)
After tax dividend kept by Dash		37,827

(b)

	£
Pringle Ltd's TTP	75,000
Employer's NIC will be due at 15% on any salary that Dash chooses to take from the company. So, the TTP figures represents 115% of the salary. Employer's NIC on salary to withdraw (15/115 × £75,000)	(9,783)
Salary for Dash to withdraw (100/115 × £75,000)	65,217
This salary will be taxed on Dash, a higher rate tax payer at a rate of 40% income tax and 2% employee's NICs. Thus 42% tax will be suffered (42% × £65,217)	(27,391)
After tax salary kept by Dash	37,826

Activity 4: Carlos

(a)

	£
Company profits	350,000
Salary to Carlos	(80,000)
Class 1 Employer's NIC on salary (80,000 - 5,000) × 15% = 11,250 (employment allowance not available as only one director-employee)	(11,250)
Taxable profit	258,750
Corporation tax @ 25%	(64,688)
Profits available for distribution	194,062

(b) Carlos can take the full distributable profits of £194,062 as a dividend.

(c) The company cannot distribute the full £194,062 as additional salary as they need to pay employer's Class 1 NIC on the salary at 15%.

The company will obtain a corporation tax deduction for the additional salary and associated Class 1 Employer's NIC.

Therefore, the taxable profit of £258,750 represents 115% of the salary that can be withdrawn.

Maximum additional salary to withdraw = £258,750 × 100/115 = £225,000.

Test your learning

1 **Tick to show whether each statement about sole traders and companies is true or false.**

	True ✓	False ✓
A company must comply with fewer rules and regulations than a sole trader.		
A sole trader can extract profits from the business with no direct tax consequence.		
Class 1 Employee's NIC is paid at 15% on any cash salary paid to an employee.		
A company pays its tax in two payments on account (31 July and 31 January).		

2 **Tick to show whether each statement about extraction of profits from a company is true or false.**

	True ✓	False ✓
There are fewer NICs due when profits are extracted by way of dividend rather than salary.		
A dividend payment will reduce the company's corporation tax liability.		
When a company pays a salary, the salary and the employer's NIC thereon is tax deductible for the company.		
Where profits are extracted as a dividend by a taxpayer who lives in England, the individual will pay income tax at 20%/40%/45%.		
A basic rate taxpayer who lives in England will suffer a combined total of 28% tax on any salary they receive.		
A higher rate taxpayer who lives in England will suffer a combined total of 52% tax on any salary they receive.		

Test your learning answers

Chapter 1

1 The correct answer is:

	✓
True	
False	✓

Tax evasion can lead to fines/imprisonment.

2 The correct answer is:

	✓
True	
False	✓

Most taxpayers are employees who have their tax deducted at source under PAYE so they do not need to complete a tax return.

3 The correct answer is:

	✓
The Chancellor of the Exchequer	
Companies House	
HM Revenue & Customs	✓
Members of Parliament	

4 The correct answers are:

	✓
Acts of Parliament	✓
HMRC statements of practice	
Statutory instruments	✓
Extra statutory concessions	

5 The correct answer is:

	✓
HMRC	
Nearest police station	
National Crime Agency	✓
Tax tribunal	

6 The correct answer is:

	✓
Tax planning	✓
Tax avoidance	
Tax evasion	
Not possible to say until decided by a judge	

7 The correct answer is:

	✓
True	
False	✓

The purpose of taxing cars with higher CO2 emissions is to encourage or discourage certain types of activity - in this case driving a less polluting car.

8 The correct answer is:

	✓
True	
False	✓

The GAAR is designed to penalise abusive tax arrangements. The arrangement described is legitimate tax planning.

Chapter 2

1 The correct answers are:

	Non-savings income ✓	Savings income ✓	Dividends ✓
Employment income	✓		
Dividends			✓
Property income	✓		
Bank interest		✓	
Pension income	✓		
Interest on government stock		✓	

2

	Amount received £	Amount in tax return £
Building society interest	240	240
Interest on an individual savings account	40	0
Dividends	160	160
Interest from government gilts	350	350

3

	Non-savings income £	Dividend income £	Total £
Employment income	30,000		30,000
Dividends		300	300
Net income	30,000	300	30,300
Less personal allowance	(12,570)		(12,570)
Taxable income	17,430	300	17,730

Premium bond winnings are exempt from income tax.

4

	Non-savings income £	Savings income £	Total £
Property income	3,000		3,000
Building society interest		9,000	9,000
Net income	3,000	9,000	12,000
Less personal allowance	(3,000)	(9,000)	(12,000)
Taxable income	Nil	Nil	Nil

The personal allowance is deducted first from non-savings income and then from savings income. The full personal allowance was available but not used as taxable income was less than £12,570.

5 The prize is exempt from income tax.

	Non-savings income £	Savings income £	Dividend income £	Total £
Employment income	112,200			112,200
Building society interest		5,000		5,000
Dividends			4,000	4,000
Net income	112,200	5,000	4,000	121,200
Less personal allowance (W)	(1,970)			(1,970)
Taxable income	110,230	5,000	4,000	119,230

Working

	£
Net income	121,200
Less income limit	(100,000)
Excess	21,200
Personal allowance	12,570
Less half excess	(10,600)
Adjusted personal allowance	1,970

6 The correct answer is:

0%, 20%, 40% and 45%	
40% and 45%	
20% only	
20%, 40% and 45%	✓

7 £ 1,409

Albert is a basic rate taxpayer so has a personal savings allowance of £1,000. The dividend allowance is always £500.

Working

	Non-savings income £	Savings income £	Dividend income £	Total £
Net income	17,520	2,000	3,000	22,520
Less personal allowance	(12,570)	–	–	(12,570)
Taxable income	4,950	2,000	3,000	9,950

	£
Tax on non-savings income	
4,950 × 20%	990
Tax on savings income	
1,000 × 0%	0
1,000 × 20%	200
Tax on dividend income	
500 × 0%	0
2,500 × 10.75%	269
Tax liability	1,459

8 £ 69,811

Working

	Non-savings income £	Savings income £	Dividend income £	Total £
Employment income	140,000			140,000
Interest		20,000		20,000
Dividends			30,000	30,000
Net income	140,000	20,000	30,000	190,000
Less personal allowance	(Nil)			(Nil)
Taxable income	140,000	20,000	30,000	190,000

The personal allowance and personal savings allowance are nil because the net income is so high.

	£
Tax on non-savings income	
37,700 × 20%	7,540
87,440 × 40%	34,976

	£
125,140 14,860 x 45% 140,000	6,687
Tax on savings income	
20,000 × 45%	9,000
Tax on dividend income	
500 × 0%	0
29,500 × 39.35%	11,608
30,000 190,000	
Income tax liability	69,811

9 Basic rate tax relief is obtained by paying Gift Aid donations net of 20% tax. Further tax relief is given to higher and additional rate taxpayers by extending the basic and higher rate bands by the gross amount of the Gift Aid donation.

10

	Non-savings income	Savings income	Dividend income	Total
	£	£	£	£
Business profits	39,600			39,600
Building society interest		2,000		2,000
Dividends			12,000	12,000
Net income	39,600	2,000	12,000	53,600
Less personal allowance	(12,570)			(12,570)
Taxable income	27,030	2,000	12,000	41,030

Tax on non-savings income	£
£27,030 × 20%	5,406
Tax on savings income	
£500 × 0%	0
£1,500 × 20%	300
Tax on dividend income	
£500 × 0% £10,170 × 10.75%	0 1,093
£1,330 × 35.75% (£12,000 – £500 – £10,170)	475

Income tax liability/payable	7,274

Note. Gross Gift Aid payment = £1,600 × 100/80 = £2,000. Basic rate extends to £39,700.

Adjusted net income = £53,600 – £2,000 = £51,600 > £50,270 so £500 personal savings allowance available.

11 The correct answer is:

£37,700	
£52,700	
£56,450	✓
£62,700	

Working

£15,000 × 100/80 = £18,750 + £37,700

£37,700 is the basic rate band without the adjustment for gift aid. £52,700 is the basic rate band plus the **net** gift aid payment. £62,700 grosses up the gift aid payment by 100/60.

12 The correct answer is:

	✓
50% each	✓
60% taxed on Emma, 40% taxed on Gabi	
100% on Emma	
100% on Gabi	

In the absence of an election, the joint income will be split 50% each.

13 The correct answer is:

	✓
His personal allowance will be reduced by £1,260	
His personal allowance will be increased by £1,260	
His income tax liability will be reduced by £252	✓
A marriage allowance claim is not possible	

If Sophie makes a marriage allowance claim, her personal allowance will be reduced by £1,260. This has no negative impact on Sophie as her income is below the level of this reduced personal allowance. Joe obtains a reduction in his income tax liability of 20% of the transferred amount, ie £252.

14 £ 2,048

	£
Net income	79,000

	£
Less: gross personal pension contributions (£400 x 12 x 100/80)	(6,000)
Adjusted net income	73,000
Less: threshold	(60,000)
Excess	13,000

13,000 / 200 × 1% = 65%

Therefore, child benefit tax charge is 65% × £3,150 = £2,048

15

	Non-savings	Savings	Dividends
	£	£	£
Salary	80,000		
Bank interest		10,000	
Dividends			5,000
Less: personal allowance	(12,570)		
Taxable income	67,430	10,000	5,000

Tax

	£
Non-savings:	
Starter rate: £3,967 × 19%	754
Basic rate: (£16,956 - £3,968) × 20%	2,598
Intermediate rate: (£31,092 - £16,957) × 21%	2,968
Higher rate: (£62,430 - £31,093) × 42%	13,162
Advanced rate: (£67,430 - £62,431) × 45%	2,250
Savings:	
£500 (savings allowance) × 0%	0
£9,500 × 40%	3,800
Dividends:	
£500 (dividend allowance) × 0%	0
£4,500 × 35.75%	1,609
Income tax liability	27,14

Working

Chapter 3

1 £ 1,800

Rent received 1 December 2026 and 1 March 2027 = $^2/_4$ × £3,600

2 £ 5,200

Working

Gross rental income less than £150,000, so cash basis used. Insurance premium paid in 2026/27 = payment on 1 October 2026

3 £ 6,667

Cash basis used by default, so taxed on rent received less expenses paid.

Working

	£
Rental income – first tenants (£4,000 × $^8/_{12}$)	2,667
Rental income – second tenants	5,000
Less expenses	(1,000)
Taxable rental income	6,667

4 To minimise their tax liability the property should be held in Ben's name

Polly is paying tax at 45%, Ben is paying tax at 20% so if the asset is held by Polly she will pay tax of £12,000 × 45% = £5,400 whereas if the asset is held by Ben he will pay tax of £12,000 × 20% = £2,400 saving them together £3,000.

5 The correct answer is:

	✓
Carried back one year and offset against property income only	
Offset against net income in the current year	
Carried forward for one year only and offset against property income	
Carried forward indefinitely and offset against property income only	✓

6 The correct answer is:

	✓
£8,000	
£5,000	✓
£500	
Nil	

Where gross rents are more than £7,500 a claim must be made for rent a room relief to apply. Without a claim, the taxable amount is simply gross rent less allowable expenses.

7 £42,650

	£
Rental income	50,000
Mortgage interest (Note 1)	0
Motor expenses (Working)	(6,000)
New sofas (Note 2)	0
Replacement curtains	(750)
Brought forward loss	(600)
Taxable property income	42,650

Note 1: mortgage interest is not given relief by way of a deduction from the property income. Instead relief is given in the income tax computation as a tax reducer at 20%.

Note 2: relief is only available for replacement items, not the original cost of domestic items.

Working: (10,000 miles @ 55p) + (2,000 @ 25p) = £6,000

Chapter 4

1 Someone is regarded as self-employed if they have a contract for services, whereas if they have a contract of service, they will be regarded as an employee.

2 Expenses are allowable if they are incurred wholly, exclusively and necessarily in the performance of the duties of employment.

3 £ (1,600)

Working

	£
Amount received: 8,000 × 35p	2,800
Less statutory limit: 8,000 × 55p	(4,400)
Deductible amount	(1,600)

4 The correct answer is:

True	
False	✓

There is no reduction in the taxable fuel benefit unless the employer is fully reimbursed for private fuel.

5 The correct answer is:

True	
False	✓

Only if total loans do not exceed £10,000 at any time in the tax year are they ignored.

6 £ 2,400

Working

Percentage = 10% (from tax tables)

Benefit 10% × £24,000 =£2,400

7 £ 33,396

	£
Car benefit (W)	23,760
Fuel benefit (£29,200 × 33%)	9,636
Telephone benefit (exempt – one mobile phone)	Nil
Total benefit	33,396

Working

CO_2 emissions = 135 g/km (rounded down)

Above baseline: 135 – 75 = 60 g/km

Divide 60 by 5 = 12%

Percentage = 12% + 21% = 33%

£72,000 × 33% = £23,760

8 The correct answers are:

Item	Taxable ✓	Exempt ✓
Write off loan of £8,000 (only loan provided)	✓	
Payments by employer of £500 per month into registered pension scheme		✓
Provision of one mobile phone		✓
Provision of a company car for both business and private use	✓	
Removal costs of £5,000 paid to an employee relocating to another branch		✓

Chapter 5

1 The correct answers are:

	✓
Legal fees incurred on the acquisition of a factory to be used for trade purposes	
Heating for factory	✓
Legal fees incurred on pursuing trade receivables	✓
Acquiring a machine to be used in the factory	

Legal fees on the acquisition of a factory are capital expenditure and so not allowable. Heating is a revenue expense and so allowable. Legal fees incurred on pursuing trade receivables are allowable as they relate to a revenue source. Acquiring a machine is a capital expense and so not allowable (although capital allowances will be available for this expenditure).

2 £ 700

The cost of staff entertaining is allowable. Gifts of food to customers are never allowable. The entertaining of customers is never allowable.

3 The correct answers are:

	Allowable ✓	Disallowable ✓
Parking fines incurred by the owner of the business		✓
Parking fines incurred by an employee while on the employer's business	✓	
Parking fines incurred by the director of a company while on company business		✓
Legal costs incurred in relation to acquiring a 10-year lease of property for the first time		✓
Legal costs incurred in relation to the renewal of a lease for 20 years	✓	
Gifts of calendars to customers, costing £4 each and displaying an advertisement for the company	✓	
Gifts of bottles of whisky to customers, costing £12 each		✓

4 The correct answer is:

	✓
£80 must be deducted from the accounts profit	
£80 must be added back to the accounts profit	
£96 must be deducted from the accounts profit	
£96 must be added back to the accounts profit	✓

The normal selling price of £80 + (20% × £80) = £96 must be added to the accounts profit.

5 £ 360

80% × £450 is disallowable for tax purposes.

6

	Taxable trading profits
Zack As trading receipts do not exceed £1,000 the trading allowance means trade profits will be nil.	0
Mythili As trading profits do not exceed £1,000 the trading allowance means trade profits will be nil. However, Mythili should elect for the trading allowance not to apply and instead deduct allowable costs, thus giving rise to a trading loss.	(100)
Rohan As trading profits exceed £1,000 the normal adjustment to profits will apply, meaning Rohan will be taxed on £700 of trade profits. However, as the allowable expenses are less than £1,000, Rohan should elect to instead deduct the trading allowance, which will give lower trade profits of £500.	500
Arthur As Arthur's trading receipts exceed £1,000 the normal adjustment to profits will apply, giving trading profits of £400. It would not be preferable to elect to deduct the trading allowance instead.	400

	£
Profit for the year in accounts	38,000
Add entertaining expenses	2,000
Add depreciation	4,000
	44,000
Less capital allowances	(3,500)
Taxable trading profit	40,500

Chapter 6

1 £ 2,000

A maximum of the original cost is deducted from the pool.

2 £ 173,308

Working

Year ended 30 September 2027

	AIA	General pool	Allowances
B/f		22,500	
Addition qualifying for AIA			
Addition 1.12.26	171,250		
AIA (max. £1,000,000)	(171,250)		171,250
Disposal 1.8.27			
Proceeds		(7,800)	
		14,700	
WDA @ 14%		(2,058)	2,058
C/f		12,642	
Allowances			173,308

3 £ 6,260

6 months ended 31 December 2026

	FYA (Cars)	General pool	Allowances
Addition (Car - no AIA, no full expensing)		18,000	
WDA @ 14% × 6/12		(1,260)	1,260
		16,740	
Addition	5,000		
FYA @ 100%	(5,000)		5,000
C/f		16,740	
			6,260

Note. The AIA and WDAs are time apportioned in a short period. FYAs are not. AIAs and FYAs are not available on a car with CO_2 emissions of 45g/km.

4 The correct answer is:

	✓
True	
False	✓

There is no AIA or WDA in the final period so a **balancing allowance** arises as follows:

	£
B/f	12,500
Addition	20,000
Proceeds	(18,300)

	£
	14,200
Balancing allowance	**(14,200)**

5 £ 1,080

Year ended 30 April 2026

	Private use asset @ 60%	Allowances
Addition	30,000	
WDA @ 6%	(1,800) × 60%	**1,080**
C/f	28,200	

6 **(a)** If Barry sells all the plant and machinery for £10,000 then he will have a balancing charge of £ 1,200 .

Workings

TWDV b/f	7,200
Addition	1,600
	8,800
Disposal	(10,000)
	(1,200)
Balancing charge	1,200

(b) If Barry sells his plant for £6,000 then he will have a balancing allowance of £ 2,800 .

Workings

TWDV b/f	7,200
Addition	1,600
	8,800
Disposal	(6,000)
	2,800
Balancing allowance	(2,800)

7 £ 684

Working

Cars are not entitled to the AIA.	
The car will be treated as a special rate item and will be entitled to 6% WDA.	
The WDA will be prorated by 9/12 as it is a 9-month accounting period.	
The WDA claimed will be restricted to 80% due to the private use.	
WDA = £19,000 × 6% × 9/12 × 80% =	£684

8 £ 40,500

£1,800,000 × 3% × 9/12 = £40,500

The qualifying cost for SBAs excludes acquisition fees. The SBA must be time-apportioned in the year of acquisition from the date the building is brought into use.

9 The correct answers are:

	True ✓	False ✓
If the contract for the factory is signed in 2026 and the factory brought into use in that year, an SBA will be available for the year ended 31 December 2026.	✓	
If the factory is constructed by 1 March 2026 and brought into use in A Ltd's trade on 1 July 2026 then an SBA of £24,000 is available as SBAs are claimed in full in year of construction/ purchase. **Explanation:** The SBA will only be available from 1 July 2026 and so must be time apportioned.		✓
The eligible cost qualifying for the SBA is £1,000,000. **Explanation:** Land does not qualify for an SBA.		✓

10

	AIA (max £1m x 3/12 = £250,000)	FYA	100% Full expensing	General pool	Special rate pool	Private use asset	Total allowances
TWDV brought forward at 1/7/2026				123,000			
Zero emission car		41,000					
Machinery	160,000						
Managing director's car				38,000			
Plant	90,000		46,000				

	AIA (max £1m x 3/12 = £250,000)	FYA	100% Full expensing	General pool	Special rate pool	Private use asset	Total allowances
FYA @ 100%		(41,000)					41,000
Full expensing			(46,000)				46,000
AIA	(250,000)						250,000
Disposal				(15,000)			
				146,000			
WDA @ 14% × 3/12				(5,110)			5,110
C/fwd/ total				140,890			342,110

Where the AIA and the full expensing FYA are both available for an addition of new plant and machinery, it is preferable to use the AIA first and then use full expensing for the balance.

If Nailsea Ltd were a sole trader, the full expensing FYA would not be available. Instead, the first £250,000 of expenditure on new plant and machinery would be eligible for the 100% AIA and the remainder would only attract 14% writing down allowances, thus giving lower total allowances.

In addition, consideration would need to be given to the managing director's car. If this was a car provided to the sole trader, a private use adjustment would arise meaning the business could only claim 90% of the allowance. If, however, the car was provided to an employee of the business then the full allowance can be claimed (as for if Nailsea Ltd is a company).

Chapter 7

1 1 September 2026 to 5 April 2027 = £64,000

2 6 April 2026 to 5 April 2027

(2/12 × 34,000) + (10/12 × 50,000) = £47,333

3 6 April 2027 to 31 July 2027

4/14 × 34,000 = £9,714

4

Tax year	Basis period	Taxable profits £
2026/27	1 February 2027 to 5 April 2027	4,000
2027/28	6 April 2027 to 5 April 2028	24,000

On commencement, he will be assessed from the date of commencement to the following 5 April.

1 February 2027 to 5 April 2027 = 2/17 × £34,000 = £4,000

In 2027/28, he will be assessed on the period arising during the tax year, ie from 6 April 2027 to 5 April 2028.

12/17 × £34,000 = £24,000

5 2026/27: 1 December 2026 to 5 April 2027 = 4/7 × £70,000 = £40,000

2027/28: 6 April 2027 to 5 April 2028 = (3/7 × £70,000) + (9/12 × £60,000) = £75,000

Chapter 8

1 The correct answer is:

	✓
The calendar year	
The tax year	
The period of account concerned	✓
The period agreed by the partners	

2 Dave's taxable profits for 2026/27 are:

£ 9,450

and Joe's taxable profits for 2026/27 are:

£ 8,550

Working

	Total £	Dave £	Joe £
1.4.26–31.12.26 (9/12) 1:1	13,500	6,750	6,750
1.1.27–31.3.27 (3/12) 3:2	4,500	2,700	1,800
	18,000	**9,450**	**8,550**

3

	Total £	Holly £	Jasmine £
Salary	85,000	5,000	80,000
Division of profits 1:1	115,000	57,500	57,500
	200,000	62,500	137,500

4 The correct answer is:

	✓
£60,000	
£15,000	
£45,000	
£20,000	✓

Year ended 31 March 2027

Taxable profits on Steve are £20,000 (1/4 × £80,000).

5 Sase's share of the profit for the year to 31 August 2027 is £ 24,000

Sase's profit share in the year to 31 August 2027 is 1/5 × £120,000 = £24,000.

6

	Total £	William £	Ann £	John £
Y/e 31.10.25	21,000	7,000	7,000	7,000
Y/e 31.10.26	33,000	11,000	11,000	11,000
Y/e 31.10.27				
1.11.26–31.12.26 (2/12)	6,000	2,000	2,000	2,000
1.1.27–31.10.27 (10/12)	30,000	0	15,000	15,000
	36,000	2,000	17,000	17,000

Chapter 9

1 The correct answer is:

	✓
2026/27 only	
2027/28 and/or 2026/27	
2025/26 only	
2026/27 and/or 2025/26	✓

The tax year of the loss is 2026/27. Claims against total income are for this year and/or 2025/26 (ie a current year claim and a carry back).

2 The correct answer is:

	✓
True	
False	✓

Trading losses can be carried forward indefinitely.

3 The correct answer is:

	✓
Against non-savings income	
Against total income	
Against trading income arising in the same trade	✓
Against trading income arising in all trades carried on by the taxpayer	

4 A loss incurred in 2026/27 can be:

(1) Deducted from total income of £9,000 in 2026/27 and/or from total income of £19,000 in 2025/26; and/or

(2) Carried forward to be deducted from taxable trading profits of £25,000 in 2027/28 and then in later years.

5 £ (85,000)

The amount of trading loss remaining to be carried forward at 1 April 2028 (assuming that all possible earlier loss relief claims against total profits are made) is:

(£320,000 – £60,000 – £175,000)

		Year ended 31 March	
		2026	2027
		£	£
Trading profit		170,000	0
Interest		5,000	60,000
Total profits		175,000	60,000
Less:	Current period loss relief	0	(60,000)
	Carry back loss relief	(175,000)	0
Less: Qualifying charitable donation		0	0
		0	0
Unrelieved qualifying charitable donations		5,000	5,000

6 The correct answer is:

	✓
£Nil	
£2,000	✓
£4,000	
£3,000	

		Year ended 30.9.2025 £	Six months 31.3.2026 £	Year ended 31.3.2027 £
Trading profit		4,000	6,000	0
Less:	Current period loss relief	0	0	0
	Carry back loss relief	(2,000)	(6,000)	0
	Qualifying charitable donation	(1,000)	–	–
Taxable total profits		1,000	–	–

The maximum relief for year ended 30.9.2025 is £4,000 × (6/12).

Chapter 10

1 **(a)** £ 2,354

(b) £ 5,550

(c) £ 1,200

Working

Class 1 Employee

Robert suffers Class 1 employee contributions on his cash earnings.

There is no National Insurance on his reimbursed expenses.

(42,000 – 12,570) × 8% = 2,354

Class 1 Employer

(42,000 – 5,000) × 15% = 5,550

Class 1A

8,000 @ 15% = 1,200

2 £ 750

	£
Employee 1: £(25,000 – 5,000) = 20,000 × 15%	3,000
Employee 2: £(60,000 – 5,000) = 55,000 × 15%	8,250
	11,250
Less employment allowance (maximum)	(10,500)
Employer contributions	750

3 If the mileage allowance is 35p a mile the amount subject to Class 1 National Insurance is £ nil

If the mileage allowance is 60p a mile the amount subject to Class 1 National Insurance is £ 925

Working

If the mileage allowance is 35p

	£
Mileage allowance received (18,500 × 35p)	6,475
Permitted payment (18,500 × 55p)	(10,175)
Excess over limit	0

As the payment is within the permitted amount there is no charge to National Insurance.

If the mileage allowance is 60p

	£
Mileage allowance received (18,500 × 60p)	11,100
Less tax-free amount (above)	(10,175)
Excess over limit	925
As the payment is above the permitted amount the excess of £925 will be chargeable to Class 1 National Insurance, employee and employer.	

4 **(a)** Acker's total Class 4 contributions are £ 0.00

No Class 4 NICs due, as profits below annual lower earnings limit of £12,570

(b) Bailey's total Class 4 contributions are £ 2,456.60

		£
Class 4 NICs	(£50,270 – £12,570) × 6%	2,262.00
	(£60,000 – £50,270) × 2%	194.60
Total NICs		**2,456.60**

(c) Cartwright's total Class 4 contributions are £ 496.80

Class 4 NICs (£20,850 – £12,570) × 6% = £496.80

Chapter 11

1 The correct answers are:

	Chargeable ✓	Exempt ✓
A gift of an antique necklace	✓	
The sale of a building	✓	
Sale of a racehorse		✓

2

	£
Proceeds of sale	200,000
Less cost	(80,000)
Less enhancement expenditure	(10,000)
Chargeable gain	110,000

3 The amount liable to CGT in 2026/27 is:

£ 152,700

The losses carried forward are:

£ 0

	£
Gains	171,000
Less current year losses	(5,300)
	165,700
Less annual exempt amount	(3,000)
	162,700
Less capital losses b/f	(10,000)
Taxable gains	152,700

4 £ 4,512

	£
Chargeable gains	21,800
Less annual exempt amount	(3,000)
Taxable gains	18,800
CGT on £18,800 @ 24%	4,512

5 31/01/2028

6 The correct answer is:

	✓
£16,663	✓
£17,500	
£19,663	
£18,337	

	£
Proceeds	38,000
Less costs of disposal	(3,000)
	35,000
Less (£41,000 × (£38,000 ÷ (£38,000 + £48,000)))	(18,337)
Chargeable gain	16,663

£17,500 is the cost from the part disposal calculation using the net proceeds. £19,663 ignores costs of disposal. £18,337 is the cost from the part-disposal calculation.

7 (a) £ Nil

There is no gain as the chattel cost and gross proceeds are both less than £6,000.

(b) £ 4,033

	£
Gross proceeds	8,420
Less selling expenses	(220)
Net proceeds	8,200
Less cost	(3,500)
Normal chargeable gain	4,700

Gain cannot exceed $^5/_3$ (8,420 – 6,000) = £4,033

Therefore, gain is £4,033

8 The correct answer is:

	✓
True	
False	✓

A loss on a disposal to a connected person can be set only against gains arising on disposals to the same connected person.

9 The correct answer is:

	✓
True	✓
False	

10 The correct answers are:

	Actual proceeds used ✓	Deemed proceeds (market value) used ✓	No gain or loss basis ✓
Paul sells an asset to his civil partner Joe for £3,600.			✓
Grandmother gives an asset to her grandchild worth £1,000.		✓	
Sarah sells an asset worth £20,000 to her best friend Cathy for £12,000. Sarah knows the asset is worth £20,000.		✓	

*A disposal is deemed to take place at market value when it is deliberately sold for consideration of less than market value.

Chapter 12

1 The correct answers are:

	True ✓	False ✓
A company with a nine-month period of account will calculate capital allowances for nine months and deduct them from adjusted trading profits.	✓	
A company with an 18-month period of account will calculate capital allowances for 18 months and deduct them from adjusted trading profits, and then prorate the answer between the appropriate accounting periods.		✓

	True ✓	False ✓
A company with an 18-month period of account will calculate capital allowances for the first 12 months, then capital allowances for the remaining 6 months, and deduct them from the relevant prorated trading profits allocated to each accounting period.	✓	

Capital allowances are calculated separately for each accounting period and then deducted from the prorated adjusted profits.

2 The correct answer is:

	✓
Added to trading income	
Added to net non-trading interest ie a NTL-R credit	
Deducted from trading income	✓
Deducted from net non-trading interest ie a NTL-R debit	

The loan is for trading purposes and is interest **paid**, not received, so it is included as an expense.

3 £ 385

Companies make donations gross, so the actual amount given to the charity is deducted from TTP.

4 The correct answer is:

	✓
1 June 2025 – 31 March 2026 and 1 April 2026 – 31 August 2026	
1 June 2025 – 31 May 2026 and 1 June 2026 – 31 August 2026	✓
1 June 2025 – 31 December 2025 and 1 January 2026 – 31 August 2026	
1 June 2025 – 31 August 2025 and 1 September 2025– 31 August 2026	

The first accounting period is always 12 months in length in a long period of account.

5

	Year ended 31.12.26 £	4 months ended 30.4.27 £
Trading profits (12:4)	240,000	80,000
NTL-R income (Investment) (accrued for each period)	1,200	400
Chargeable gain (allocate to period made)	0	20,000
Total profits	241,200	100,400

	Year ended 31.12.26 £	4 months ended 30.4.27 £
Qualifying charitable donation (allocate to period paid)	(15,000)	0
Taxable total profits	226,200	100,400

6 £ 38,750

The upper limit is £250,000 × 6/12 = £125,000, so P Ltd will pay corporation tax at the main rate (25%):

£155,000 × 25% =**£38,750**

7 £ 8,725

J Ltd and K Ltd are associated and therefore the upper and lower limits must be divided by 2.

J Ltd's upper limit = £250,000/2 = £125,000

Its lower limit = £50,000/2 = £25,000

	£
TTP × 25%	10,000
Less 3/200 × (£125,000 - £40,000)	(1,275)
Corporation tax payable	8,725

8 The correct answer is:

	✓
True	✓
False	

9

	£
Proceeds of sale	200,000
Less cost	(80,000)
Less enhancement expenditure	(10,000)
Chargeable gain	110,000

Chapter 13

1 The due filing date for an income tax return for 2026/27, assuming the taxpayer will submit the return online is: 31/01/28

2 The 2026/27 payments on account will be calculated as 50% of the income tax payable for 2025/26 and will be due on 31 January 2027 and 31 July 2027

3 £100 penalty for failure to deliver return on time.

Possible £10 per day penalty from 1 May 2028 until date of filing.

5% penalty on tax paid late. Interest on tax paid late.

4 The correct answer is:

	✓
31 January 2028	
31 March 2028	
6 April 2028	
28 January 2028	✓

A year after the actual filing date, because Susie filed the return before the due filing date (31 January 2027).

5 Jamie's 2026/27 payments on account will each be

£ 6,000 and will be due on (insert date as XX/XX/XX)

31/01/27

and

31/07/27

Jamie's balancing payment will be

£ 4,000 and will be due on (insert date as XX/XX/XX)

31/01/28 .

6 £ 0

No penalties for late payment are due on late payments on account.

7 The correct answer is:

	✓
30 September 2027	
31 October 2027	✓
31 December 2027	
31 January 2028	

Paper returns must usually be submitted by 31 October following the end of the tax year.

8 The correct answer is:

	✓
31 January 2028 and 31 July 2028	
31 January 2027 and 31 July 2027	✓
31 October 2027 and 31 January 2028	
31 July 2027 and 31 January 2028	

Payments on account are due on 31 January in the tax year and 31 July following the end of the tax year.

9 The correct answer is:

	✓
£5,100	
£3,400	
£1,020	✓
£2,380	

30% × PLR = **£1,020**

PLR = £17,000 × 20% = £3,400

1 1 June 2027

(12 months after the actual filing date)

2 £ 200

(The return is less than 3 months late)

3 The correct answer is:

	✓
14 July 2026	
1 October 2027	✓
31 December 2027	
1 January 2028	

Girton Ltd is not a large company for CT payment purposes, so all CT is due nine months and one day after the end of the accounting period.

4 The correct answer is:

	✓
14 July 2026	
14 April 2027	✓
1 October 2027	
31 December 2027	

Eaton Ltd is a large company and is required to pay corporation tax by instalments. The instalments are due in the seventh and tenth months of the accounting period and in the first and fourth months after the accounting period.

5 £ 60,000

1/4 × £240,000

Chapter 14

1 The correct answers are:

	True ✓	False ✓
A company must comply with fewer rules and regulations than a sole trader. **Explanation:** A sole trader must comply with fewer rules and regulations.		✓
A sole trader can extract profits from the business with no direct tax consequence.	✓	
Class 1 Employee's NIC is paid at 15% on any cash salary paid to an employee. **Explanation:** Employee's NIC is at 8%/2%. 15% is the rate for employer's NIC.		✓

	True ✓	False ✓
A company pays its tax in two payments on account (31 July and 31 January). **Explanation:** This is how a sole trader would pay their tax. A small company pays its tax 9 months and 1 day after the end of the accounting period.		✓

2 The correct answers are:

	True ✓	False ✓
There are fewer NICs due when profits are extracted by way of dividend rather than salary.	✓	
A dividend payment will reduce the company's corporation tax liability. **Explanation:** Dividends are not tax deductible for a company.		✓
When a company pays a salary, the salary and the employer's NIC thereon is tax deductible for the company.	✓	
Where profits are extracted as a dividend by a taxpayer who lives in England, the individual will pay income tax at 20%/40%/45%. **Explanation:** The tax rates on dividend income are 10.75%/35.75% and 39.35%.		✓
A basic rate taxpayer who lives in England will suffer a combined total of 28% tax on any salary they receive. **Explanation:** (20% income tax + 8% Class 1 NICs)	✓	
A higher rate taxpayer who lives in England will suffer a combined total of 52% tax on any salary they receive. **Explanation:** They will pay 40% income tax but only 2% NIC so a combined total of 42%.		✓

Reference material – Finance Act 2026 – for assessments from January 2027

Introduction

This appendix includes data that students may need to use during the Principles of Taxation assessment.

The material can be accessed during practice and live assessments by using the reference materials section at each task position. It is also made available as a separate document so students can familiarise themselves with the content before an assessment sitting.

Students are **not** able to take a printed version of this document into a live assessment sitting*.

This document may be changed to reflect periodical updates, so students must check they are using the most recent version while studying.

*Unless students need a printed version as part of reasonable adjustments for particular needs. This must be discussed with the training provider at least six weeks before the assessment date.

1 Income Tax rates and bands (England and Northern Ireland)

Tax rates	Tax bands	Non-savings income %	Savings income %	Dividend income %
Basic rate	£0–£37,700	20	20	10.75
Higher rate	£37,701–£125,140	40	40	35.75
Additional rate	£125,141 and over	45	45	39.35

Starting rate for savings income, 0% where it falls into first £5,000 of taxable income.

2 Non-savings Income Tax rates and bands (Scotland)

Tax rates	Tax bands	Non-savings income %
Starter rate	£0–£3,967	19
Basic rate	£3,968–£16,956	20
Intermediate rate	£16,957–£31,092	21
Higher rate	£31,093–£62,430	42
Advanced rate	£62,431–£125,140	45
Top rate	£125,141 and over	48

Savings and dividend income rates are as for England and Northern Ireland.

3 Non-savings Income Tax rates and bands (Wales)

Tax rates	Tax bands	Non-savings income %
Basic rate	£0–£37,700	20
Higher rate	£37,701–£125,140	40
Additional rate	£125,141 and over	45

Savings and dividend income rates are as England and Northern Ireland.

4 Allowances and reliefs

		£
Personal allowance		12,570*
Income limit for personal allowance*		100,000
Marriage allowance – transferable amount		1,260

		£
Savings allowance:	Basic rate taxpayer	1,000
	Higher rate taxpayer	500
	Additional rate taxpayer	0
Dividend allowance		500
Trading income allowance		1,000
Property income allowance		1,000
Rent a room relief		7,500

*The personal allowance is reduced by £1 for every £2 over the income limit.

5 Individual savings accounts (ISAs)

	£
Annual limit	20,000

6 High income child benefit charge

Adjusted net income (£)	Child benefit charge
<60,000	No charge
60,000–80,000	1% of amount received for each £200 above £60,000
>80,000	Full amount received

7 National Insurance contributions (NICs)

		%
Class 1 Employee	Earnings below £12,570	0
	Earnings between £12,570 and £50,270	8
	Earnings above £50,270	2
Class 1 Employer*	Earnings below £5,000	0
	Earnings above £5,000	15
Class 1A	Benefits	15
Class 4	Trading profits below £12,570	0
	Trading profits between £12,570 and £50,270	6
	Trading profits above £50,270	2

*An employment allowance of £10,500 may be available.

8 Restrictions on exempt benefits

Benefit	Restriction
Health screening	One per year
Incidental overnight expenses: within UK	£5 per night
Incidental overnight expenses: overseas	£10 per night
Medical check up	One per year
Mobile telephones	One per employee
Pay whilst attending a full-time course	£15,480 per academic year
Removal and relocation expenses	£8,000
Staff party or event	£150 per head
Staff suggestion scheme	£5,000
Trivial benefits	£50 (maximum £300 per tax year for directors)
Working from home	£6 per week/£26 per month

9 Car benefit percentage

CO_2 Emissions g/km	Electric range (miles)	%
Nil	NA	4
1 to 50	130 or more	4
1 to 50	70 to 129	7
1 to 50	40 to 69	10
1 to 50	30 to 39	14
1 to 50	Less than 30	16
51 to 54		17
55 to 59		18
60 to 64		19
65 to 69		20
70 to 74		21
75 or more		21% + 1% for every extra 5g/km above 75g/km (to a maximum of 37%)

10 Car fuel benefit

	£
Base figure	29,200

11 Van benefit charge

	£
Basic charge	4,170
Private fuel charge	798
Benefit for zero emission vans	NIL

12 Approved mileage allowance payments

Cars or vans: first 10,000 miles over 10,000 miles	55p per mile 25p per mile
Additional passengers in cars or vans	5p per mile per passenger
Motorcycles	24p per mile
Bicycles	20p per mile

13 Beneficial loans

Exemption limit	£10,000
HMRC official rate	3.75%

14 Trading profits

Customer gifts limit for allowable deduction	£50
Lease cost disallowance if leased car >50g/km CO_2 emissions	15%
Long lease threshold	50 years

15 Capital allowances

First year allowance: • Full expensing – companies only • First year allowance – all businesses (expenditure from 1 January 2026) • Cars with CO_2 emissions of 0g/km	100% 40% 100%
Main pool writing down allowance: • Plant and machinery • Cars with CO_2 emissions between 1 and 50 g/km - Rate until 31 March 2026 (companies) / 5 April 2026 (individuals) - Rate from 1 April 2026 (companies) / 6 April 2026 (individuals) - Hybrid rate for accounting periods spanning 1 April 2026 (companies) / 6 April 2026 (individuals)	18% 14%
Special rate pool: • Cars with CO_2 emissions above 50g/km	6%

Structures and buildings allowance	3%
Annual investment allowance	£1,000,000
Small pools allowance	£1,000

16 Capital gains tax

Annual exempt amount	£3,000
Basic rate	18%
Higher rate	24%

17 Corporation tax

Main rate of corporation tax	25%
Small profits rate of corporation tax	19%
Upper limit	£250,000*
Lower limit	£50,000*
Marginal small company relief	3/200 × (upper limit - TTP)

*reduced if:

- Accounting period <12 months
- Associated companies.

18 Payment and administration - companies

Filing deadline	• Filed on the later of 12 months after the end of the company's period of account or three months after the notice to deliver a tax return has been issued. • Amendments can be made within 12 months of the filing deadline.
Payment deadline	• Small companies (annual profits less than £1.5 million): nine months and one day after end of accounting period. • Large companies (annual profits greater than £1.5 million) must estimate the year's tax liability and pay 25% of the estimate on the 14th day of each of the 7th, 10th, 13th and 16th month from the start of the accounting period.
Penalties for late filing	• £100 immediate penalty for returns due before 1 April 2026 • £200 immediate penalty for returns due from 1 April 2026.. • After 3 months, a further £100 for returns due before 1 April 2026. • After 3 months, a further £200 for returns due from 1 April 2026. • After 6 months, 10% of unpaid tax. • After 12 months, a further 10% of unpaid tax.
Late payment	N/A
Notify chargeability	• Within 3 months of starting to trade.

Current year/carry back trading loss relief claim	• Within two years of the end of the loss-making period.
Enquiry	• Within 12 months of submission of return. • Penalty for failure to produce enquiry documents: £300 + £60 per day.
Record retention	• Six years after the end of the relevant accounting period. • Penalty for failure to keep proper records is up to £3,000.

19 Payment and administration - individuals

<table>
<tr><td>Making tax digital (MTD) for Income Tax Self-Assessment (ITSA)</td><td colspan="3">• Mandatory for sole traders and landlords with qualifying income over £50,000 in their 2024/25 tax return.
• Once in MTD, a taxpayer must remain in MTD until they have three consecutive years below the mandation threshold.</td></tr>
<tr><td rowspan="7">Filing deadlines</td><td colspan="2">MTD
• Quarterly updates:</td><td rowspan="7">Non-MTD
• 31 October following the end of the tax year if filing a paper return.
• 31 January following the end of the tax year if filing online.</td></tr>
<tr><td>Period</td><td>Deadline</td></tr>
<tr><td>6 April to 5 July / 1 April to 30 June</td><td>7 August</td></tr>
<tr><td>6 April to 5 October / 1 April to 30 September</td><td>7 November</td></tr>
<tr><td>6 April to 5 January / 1 April to 31 December</td><td>7 February</td></tr>
<tr><td>6 April to 5 April / 1 April to 31 March</td><td>7 May</td></tr>
<tr><td colspan="2">• Final Declaration - 31 January following the end of the tax year.</td></tr>
<tr><td>Payment deadline*</td><td colspan="3">• 31 January following the end of the tax year.
• If payments on account (POA) are due:
- First POA – 31 January during tax year
- Second POA – 31 July after tax year
- Balancing payment – 31 January after tax year.</td></tr>
</table>

<table>
<tr>
<td>Penalties for late filing</td>
<td><u>MTD</u>
• One point per late filing (no penalty points for late quarterly updates for the 2026/27 tax year)
• £200 penalty on reaching four points.
• A further £200 penalty each time a MTD for ITSA deadline is missed while the taxpayer has four points.
• Points expire two years after imposed providing the four-point threshold has not been reached.
• If the four-point threshold is reached, the points total is reset to zero if all MTD for ITSA deadlines are met for 12 months and all returns due in the past two years have been filed.</td>
<td><u>Non-MTD</u>
• £100 immediate penalty.
• After 3 months, £10 per day for up to 90 days.
• After 6 months, £300 or 5% of the tax due (whichever is greater).
• After 12 months:
- A further £300 or 5% of the tax due (whichever is greater) if not deliberate
- A further £300 or 70% of the tax due (whichever is greater) if deliberate and not concealed
- A further £300 or 100% of the tax due (whichever is greater) if deliberate and concealed.</td>
</tr>
<tr>
<td>Late payment</td>
<td><u>MTD</u>
• First penalty charge based on the number of days after the due date that payment is made:
<table>
<tr><td>0 to 15 days</td><td>No penalty</td></tr>
<tr><td>16 to 30 days</td><td>3% of tax owed at day 15, or no penalty if in first year of MTD</td></tr>
<tr><td>From day 31</td><td>3% of tax owed at day 15 plus 3% of the tax owed at day 30.
Plus, an annual rate of 10% per year on the outstanding amount, charged daily from day 31 until the tax is paid, or for up to two years.</td></tr>
</table>
• Interest will be charged from the date payment was due.</td>
<td><u>Non-MTD</u>
• 30 days late – 5 of tax outstanding at that date
• 6 months late – a further 5% of tax outstanding at that date
• 12 months late – a further 5% of tax outstanding at that date.</td>
</tr>
<tr>
<td>Notify chargeability*</td>
<td colspan="2">• 5 October following the end of the tax year for self-assessment.
• Failure to register for MTD for ITSA will result in late submission points rather than failure to notify penalties.</td>
</tr>
</table>

Current year/carry back trading loss relief claim	• First anniversary of 31 January following the tax year of the loss.
Amendment	• Within 12 months of the filing deadline.
Enquiry	• Within 12 months of submission of return. • Penalty for failure to produce enquiry document = £300 + £60 per day
Record retention	• Five years from 31 January filing deadline for trading and property income. • One year from filing deadline for other income. • Penalty for failure to keep proper records is up to £3,000

*Any Capital Gains Tax due on the disposal of residential property must be reported and paid within 60 days of completion.

20 Penalties for incorrect returns

Type of behaviour	Maximum	Unprompted (minimum)	Prompted (minimum)
Careless error	30%	0%	15%
Deliberate error but not concealed	70%	20%	35%
Deliberate error and concealed	100%	30%	50%

Glossary

Chapter 1: The UK tax system and ethical behaviour

Acts of Parliament: These are created via MPs debating in Parliament. There are a number of Acts that give the main rules for each of the UK taxes. These are updated each year by the annual **Finance Act**. Periodically they will be rewritten from scratch. This Course Book includes the provisions of the Finance Act 2026.

Case law: Decisions of the Tax Tribunal about the interpretation of tax statutes which serve as a further source of tax law.

General Anti-Abuse Rule (GAAR): A mechanism that allows tax authorities to counteract tax advantages arising from abusive tax arrangements that, while technically legal, are designed primarily to avoid tax and go against the spirit or intent of the law.

HM Revenue and Customs (HMRC): The UK Government department responsible for collecting, paying, administering and enforcing taxes.

Legislation: Laws created by the Government. These include Acts of Parliament and Statutory Instruments.

Money laundering: The process by which the proceeds of crime are converted into assets which appear to have a legitimate origin.

Statutory Instruments (SI): These are created by civil servants acting on behalf of the **Chancellor of the Exchequer**. They include the detailed rules for the operation of UK taxes. An SI will be laid before Parliament and becomes law if no objections are raised.

Tax agent: An accountant or firm of accountants that is authorised to act on behalf of a taxpayer in dealing with tax matters, including preparing tax returns, providing tax advice, and communicating with HMRC.

Tax avoidance: Interpreting legislation to reduce a tax liability in a way that it was not intended to be applied. This is not illegal but may involve finding loopholes in the law and is often considered unethical.

Tax digitalisation: The process by which tax authorities use digital technologies to collect, process, manage and monitor tax information electronically, replacing or reducing paper-based and manual tax systems.

Tax evasion: Illegal means by which taxpayers attempt to minimise their tax liability.

Tax planning: A legal and ethical means by which taxpayers can minimise their tax liability, using the law as it was intended to be used.

Tax year: The **tax year** runs from 6 April to the following 5 April. It is also known as the **fiscal year** or the **year of assessment**. Tax is calculated on the income earned, wealth transferred, and gains realised in the tax year.

Chapter 2: Calculation of income tax

Abatement of the personal allowance: The gradual reduction of an individual's UK personal allowance once their adjusted net income exceeds a specific threshold.

Additional rate band: Income in excess of £125,140 is taxed here.

Adjusted net income: Total income (before the deduction of the personal allowance), minus gross gift aid donations and gross personal pension contributions. This figure is used to determine whether the taxpayer's personal allowance is abated and whether they need to pay the high income child benefit charge.

Basic rate band: The first £37,700 of taxable income. The basic rate band may be extended by the gross amount of any Gift Aid donations and personal pension contributions paid by the taxpayer.

Construction Industry Scheme (CIS): A system where contractors deduct tax from payments made to subcontractors and pass it to HMRC. The deductions count as an advance payment towards the subcontractor's income tax and national insurance.

Dividend allowance: The amount of dividend income that an individual can receive in a tax year without paying income tax. Alternative term: Dividend nil rate band (DNRB).

Dividend income: Any dividends received that are subject to income tax.

Exempt income: Income that is not subject to UK income tax.

Gift aid donations: Donations to charity made under the Gift Aid scheme, which is a UK Government scheme that allows charities to claim back basic-rate income tax on donations made by UK taxpayers.

Gross gift aid donations: The total amount donated to a charity, including both the amount paid by the individual and the basic0rate tax relief added by the Government.

Gross personal pension contributions: Total contributions to a private (non-workplace) pension scheme, including both the amount paid by the individual and the basic-rate tax relief added by the Government.

High income child benefit charge: A UK tax charge that requires higher-earning individuals (or their partners) to pay back some or all of the child benefit that they receive, depending on their income level. Child benefit is a tax-free Government support paid to anyone responsible for a child.

Higher rate band: Taxable income from £37,701 to £125,140. The upper limit to the higher rate band may be extended by the gross amount of any Gift Aid donations and personal pension contributions paid by the taxpayer.

Income tax liability: The total amount of gross income tax due to HMRC, before accounting for any payments made.

Income tax payable: The amount of income tax that needs to be paid to HMRC after accounting for any tax already collected at source (eg PAYE)

Income tax: A UK tax charged on most types of income earned by individuals.

Marriage allowance: An allowance that lets a lower-earning spouse or civil partner transfer an amount of their personal allowance to their partner.

Net income: An individual's total income calculated prior to deducting the personal allowance.

Non-savings income: Any income subject to income tax that is not classified as savings income or dividend income. This includes employment, pension, trading and property income.

Pay As You Earn (PAYE): A UK system where employers deduct income tax and national insurance contributions from employees' wages and pay it directly to the government.

Personal allowance: The amount of income an individual can earn in a tax year without paying income tax.

Personal pension contributions: Contributions to a private (non-workplace) pension scheme.

Personal savings allowance: The amount of savings income that an individual can earn in a tax year without paying income tax..

Property business finance costs: Interest on mortgages, loans and overdrafts used to fund a property business, plus fees and other incidental costs for getting or repaying mortgages or loans.

Savings income: Any interest received that is subject to income tax.

Taxable income: Any income subject to income tax after deducting all allowances and reliefs.

Total/net income: The total amount of income from all taxable sources before deducting any allowances or reliefs.

Chapter 3: Property income

Accruals basis: An alternate method of calculating property income whereby accrued property income less accrued allowable expenses give the property income to be taxed.

Cash basis: The default method of calculation of property income for an individual. Under the cash basis the property income received less the property expenses paid are taxable. Rather than using the accruals basis.

Landlord: The person letting out the property.

Property allowance: The amount of property income that an individual can earn in a tax year without paying income tax.

Property income: All income derived from renting out land and/or buildings.

Rent a room scheme: A UK Government scheme that allows individuals to earn an amount of tax-free income from letting furnished accommodation in their own home.

Tenant: The person letting the property.

Chapter 4: Employment income

Allowable deductions (from employment income): Expenses that employees can deduct from their taxable employment income. They must be incurred wholly, exclusively, and necessarily in the performance of their duties.

Assessable benefits: Non-cash benefits provided to employees such as company cars or private medical insurance.

Employment income: This is the type of income received by someone who holds an office or employment. It is calculated using the detailed rules we will be considering in this chapter.

Exempt benefits: Employer-provided benefits that employees do not pay tax on because HMRC grants an exemption.

Net pay arrangements: Where an employer deducts an employee's occupational pension contributions from the employee's earnings before they deduct income tax.

Occupational pension contributions: Contributions to a workplace pension scheme.

Occupational pension scheme: is a scheme provided by an employer. Contributions are deducted directly from earnings. PAYE is then applied to just the remaining income. This is called a **net pay arrangement**.

Payroll deduction scheme: Set up by an employer to enable employees to make tax-deductible donations to charity.

Personal pension scheme: is a scheme organised by the taxpayer. Contributions are made net of basic rate tax (20%). As we saw in Chapter 2 - Calculation of Income Tax, additional relief is available for higher and additional rate taxpayers by **extending the basic and higher rate bands**.

Receipts basis: The standard method for taxing employment income, meaning earnings are taxed in the tax year that they are received, not when earned.

Temporary workplace: A workplace at which the employee expects to be for no more than 24 months.

Chapter 5: Trading income

Accruals Basis: An accounting method where income and expenses are recorded when they are earned or incurred, regardless of when the money is actually received or paid.

Adjustment of profits: The adjustment of the accounting profits to comply with tax legislation.

Badges of trade: A set of criteria used by HMRC to determine whether an activity constitutes trading.

Capital expenditure: Expenditure on the purchase or improvement of non-current assets.

Cash Basis: An accounting method where income and expenses are recorded only when they are actually received or paid.

Deductible expenditure: Expenses that can be deducted from a business's income when calculating taxable profit. If these expenses have been deducted in the accounting profit, no adjustment will be required. Alternative term: Allowable expenditure.

Expenditure wholly and exclusively for trade purposes: Expenditure that is incidental to the trade and that does not have a dual purpose.

Non-deductible expenditure: Expenses that cannot be deducted from a business's income when calculating taxable profit. If these expenses have been deducted in the accounting profit, they will need to be added back. Alternative term: Disallowable expensiture.

Revenue expenditure: All other expenditure incurred by a business that is not capital expenditure.

Trading allowance: A tax exemption that allows an individual to earn a specified amount of trading income per tax year without paying tax on it and, in many cases, without needing to register for Self Assessment.

Chapter 6: Capital allowances

40% first year allowances (FYAs): From 1 January 2026, a new 40% first year allowance (FYA) is available to all businesses.

- Available only on new and unused plant and machinery (not second hand)
- Not available on cars
- Not available on special rate pool expenditure (see later).

The 40% FYA will in practice only be utilised for expenditure not covered by the available AIA.

Annual investment allowance (AIA): A capital allowance that enables a business to deduct 100% of the cost of qualifying plant and machinery up to an annual limit from its taxable profits in the year the expenditure is incurred.

Balancing adjustment: Balancing adjustments ensure that over the life of the asset, the total tax relief given equals the actual cost to the business. Balancing adjustments will be required when:

(a) There is cessation of trade

(b) Assets are disposed of that are not in the main/general or special rate pool

(c) A disposal from the main/general or special rate pool result in a negative balance in the pool

Balancing allowance: Given when a positive balance remains at cessation or disposal of certain assets.

Balancing charge: Given when a negative balance remains at cessation or disposal of certain assets.

Capital allowances: An allowance that can be deducted when calculating a business's taxable profits, related to certain types of capital expenditure.

Capital expenditure: One-off expenditure that will bring benefits to the business over a number of years (eg purchase of machinery).

First year allowances (FYAs): A capital allowance that enables a business to claim an immediate deduction for the cost (or part of the cost) of qualifying plant and machinery in the year the expenditure is incurred.

Full expensing: A type of first year allowance that enables companies to deduct 100% of the cost of qualifying plant and machinery from their taxable profits in the year the expenditure is incurred.

Period of account: The period for which a business prepares its accounts.

Plant and machinery: Assets used by a business to carry out its trade. These are items that perform a function within the business rather than forming part of the building or structure.

Private use asset: Has restricted capital allowances but does not apply to companies.

Private use assets: A business asset that is used partly for business purposes and partly for personal (private) use.

Revenue expenditure: Regular ongoing expenditure that only brings benefit in the period in which the expenditure is made (eg payment of electricity bill).

Small pools allowance: A capital allowance rule that enables a business to write off the entire balance of a pool if the value falls below a specified threshold.

Structures and buildings: The physical premises or structural elements in which the business operates. These items do not qualify as plant and machinery.

Writing-down allowances (WDA): The annual tax deductions a business can claim on the unrelieved expenditure in its capital allowance pools for plant and machinery. The amount is calculated by applying the WDA percentage to the remaining tax written-down value.

Chapter 7: Trading profits - basis of assessment

Straddle periods: A period during which a taxpayer's accounting period overlaps two separate tax years.

Tax year basis: The basis of assessment is known as the tax year basis. Under the tax year basis, business profits are assessed and taxed in the tax year in which they arise. Therefore, for 2026/27, businesses will need to report their profits for the period 6 April 2026 to 5 April 2027.

Chapter 8: Partnerships

Appropriations of profit: How the profits of a partnership are shared amongst the partners.

Partnership: A group of self-employed people working together.

Chapter 9: Unincorporated trader losses

Carry back loss relief: Allows an individual to set a trading loss against total income in the tax year prior to the tax year of the loss (no need to make a current year claim first).

Carry forward loss relief: Allows an individual to set a trading loss against the first available profits from the same trade in the future.

Current year loss relief: Allows an individual to set a trading loss against total income in the tax year of the loss.

Trading losses: Losses incurred in the ordinary course of business that may be able to be offset against other income or profits, reducing the overall tax liability.

Chapter 10: National insurance contributions

Class 1A NICs: A UK tax incurred by employers on the provision of assessable benefits.

Class 4 National Insurance Contributions (NIC): A UK tax incurred by self-employed individuals on their trading profits.

Employee's National Insurance Contributions (NIC): A UK tax incurred by employees on employment income, deducted at source by their employer. Alternative term: Class 1 Primary NIC.

Employer's National Insurance Contributions (NIC): A UK tax incurred by employers as a result of employing an employee. Alternative term: Class 1 Secondary NIC.

Employment allowance: An amount that can be deducted from the employer's Class 1 Employer's liability.

Chapter 11: Chargeable gains

Allowable loss: When a chargeable asset is sold for less than its cost.

Annual exempt amount:

The amount of capital gains that an individual can make each tax year without paying Capital Gains Tax.

Capital gains tax: A UK tax incurred by individuals on gains made on the disposal of capital assets that have increased in value.

Chargeable asset: All assets other than exempt assets.

Chargeable disposal: The sale, gift or transfer of an asset that triggers a capital gain.

Chargeable gain: When a chargeable asset is sold for more than its cost.

Chargeable person: An individual, partners in a partnership, or a company that disposes of a chargeable asset.

Chattels: Tangible moveable property. For example, a painting or an antique.

Connected person: An individual is connected with the following persons for the purposes of capital gains tax:

(a) Their spouse or civil partner

(b) Their relatives*

(c) Relatives of their spouse or civil partner.

*Relatives are:

- Brothers or sisters
- Ancestors (eg parents, grandparents)
- Lineal descendants (eg children, grandchildren)
- Spouses and civil partners of any of the above relatives

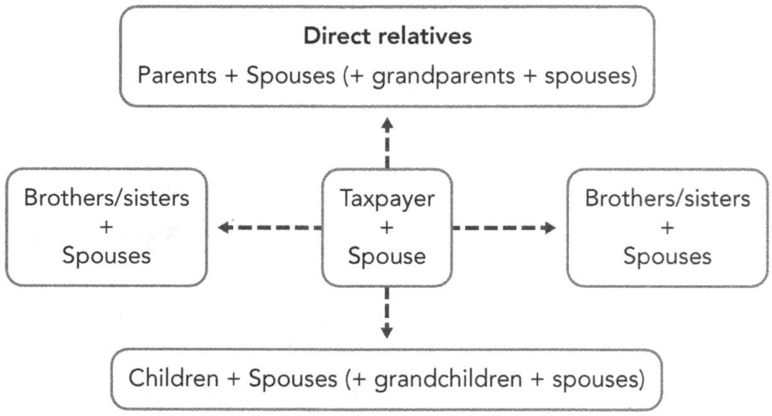

Enhancement expenditure: Capital expenditure that enhances the value of the asset and is reflected in the state or nature of the asset at the time of disposal.

Exempt assets: Assets that are not subject to UK capital gains tax.

Exempt disposal: A disposal on which no chargeable gain or allowable loss arises.

Market value: The price which an asset might reasonably be expected to sell for in the open market.

Part disposal: When part of an asset is disposed of rather than the whole asset.

Taxable gains: The chargeable gains of an individual for a tax year, after deducting allowable losses of the same tax year, the annual exempt amount and any unrelieved capital losses brought forward.

Wasting chattel: Chattels with apredictable life of 50 years or less, eg a racehorse or greyhound.

Chapter 12: Corporation tax

Accounting period: The period for which corporation tax is charged.

Carry back loss relief: Allows a company to set a trading loss against total profits (before deducting qualifying charitable donations) in the 12 months preceding the period of the loss (after it has made a claim against current year total profits first).

Carry forward loss relief: The trade loss is carried forward and can be offset with a claim against a future period's total profits.

Corporation tax: A UK tax incurred by companies on their taxable total profits.

Current year loss relief: Allows a company to set a trading loss against total profits before deducting qualifying charitable donations in the loss-making accounting period.

Financial year: Runs from 1 April to the following 31 March and is identified by the calendar year in which it begins.

Loan relationships: Loan relationship rules determine how companies are taxed on their interest paid and interest received. These rules look at whether the loans are trade-related or non-trade-related loans.

Period of account: The period for which a company prepares its accounts.

Period of account: The period for which the company prepares its accounts.

Qualifying charitable donations: Charitable gifts on which tax relief is given.

Taxable total profits (TTP): The total amount of profit on which a company must pay Corporation Tax, after all allowable deductions and reliefs have been applied.

Chapter 13: Administration

Disclosures - prompted and unprompted: When a taxpayer discloses an error to HMRC, those disclosures are classified into two categories:

(a) Unprompted disclosure: when a taxpayer tells HMRC about an error before they have any reason to believe HMRC has discovered or is about to discover the issue

(b) Prompted disclosure: when a taxpayer tells HMRC about an error after HMRC has initiated contact, such as writing to inform the taxpayer of a compliance check or investigation.

Enquiry window: The period during which HMRC is legally allowed to open an enquiry into a submitted tax return.

Errors: Errors are classified into three categories based on the behaviour of the taxpayer:

(a) Careless: an error caused by a failure to take reasonable care.

(b) Deliberate: an error where the taxpayer knowingly provides inaccurate information or withholds relevant information.

(c) Deliberate and concealed: a deliberate error (see above) where the taxpayer also takes steps to hide the inaccuracy from HMRC.

Filing due date: The date by which a return must be filed.

Filing due date: The date by which a tax return must be filed.

Interest: Charged on late payments on account and on late balancing payments.

Large companies: Companies with annual profits that exceed £1,500,000 for a 12-month accounting period.

Making Tax Digital for Income Tax: The requirement for sole traders and landlords to keep digital records, submit quarterly updates and file a year-end tax return with HMRC.

Payment on account: An amount paid on account of income tax.

Potential lost revenue (PLR): The tax that would have been lost if the error had gone undetected.

Chapter 14: Tax planning

After tax income: Is the income received by the individual after tax and national insurance contributions.

Business structure: How the business is set up. It can be an unincorporated business, such as a sole trader or partnership, or incorporated such as a company.

Extraction of profits: The ways owners take money out of their business, such as salary, benefits, dividends and drawings.

Tax saving: Is the difference between the tax payable with or without implementing the tax planning opportunity.

Index

Tell us what you think

Got comments or feedback on this book? Let us know.
Use your QR code reader:

Or, visit:
https://www.smartsurvey.co.uk/s/W30E6Y/

Need to get in touch with customer service?

www.bpp.com/request-support

Spotted an error?

https://learningmedia.bpp.com/pages/errata